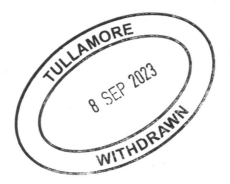

A HISTORY OF THE IRISH NAVAL SERVICE

LE *Emer* on patrol in heavy seas

AIDAN McIVOR

A HISTORY OF THE
IRISH NAVAL SERVICE

WITH A FOREWORD BY
CAPT. JOHN E. MOORE, RN

IRISH ACADEMIC PRESS

This book was typeset
in 11 on 13 Ehrhardt by
Koinonia, Bury
and first published in 1994 by
IRISH ACADEMIC PRESS
Kill Lane, Blackrock Co. Dublin, Ireland
and in North America by
IRISH ACADEMIC PRESS
c/o International Specialized Book Services,
5804 NE Hassalo Street, Portland, OR 97213.

A catalogue record for this title
is available from the British Library.

ISBN 0-7165-2523-2

Printed in Ireland by
BetaPrint

FOREWORD

Ever since the Boreal Seas rose sufficiently to form the islands of Ireland and Britain some 8000 years ago both have been dependant on water transport for their being. Their history has been formed by the sea from the days of the later Stone Age cultures to the present. Using various types of craft the original Celtic invaders landed from Britain some 2500 years ago; 500 years later the first Picts arrived from what is now Scotland. By the fourth century AD, Irish expeditions were landing in France and in 432 St Patrick arrived. As Ireland became the centre of learning for Western Europe, missionaries sailed forth to spread their message throughout not only the western seaboard but also Iceland.

It was by sea that the Vikings came in the eighth century, Henry II of England invaded four hundred years later, Cromwell's forces were unleashed on the unfortunate Irish and had it not been for sea transport ex-King James II and his French officers, the battle of the Boyne would never have been fought. More French attempts in the later 18th century showed the vulnerability of the long Irish coastline, but the defeat of the French at Bantry Bay in 1796 proved that the power of the British fleet was adequate for its defence against foreign invasion.

In this century there have been so many changes to the approach of the Irish to the sea that Aidan McIvor's book is both timely and necessary. Much has been written about the manifold problems of Ireland and many books deal with her extraordinary history. But this is a book in a different category. Based on a great deal of research, it is the tale of a maritime country which, since the Anglo-Irish Treaty of 1921, has consistently turned her back to the sea unless unusual events have caused a temporary change of heart.

Three of these events are dealt with in detail—the Irish Civil War of 1922-3 in which some two dozen small vessels played an important part; World War Two, when the importance of maritime affairs was brought home to the Irish, and the decision by the EEC in 1976 to introduce a 200-mile Exclusive Economic Zone about the waters of member countries.

After the Civil War, what had become the Coastal and Marine Service was disbanded on 31 March 1924. A poor country with over 1900 miles of coastline then had no means of protecting her shores or fisheries except for one elderly patrol vessel. World War Two brought a realisation that "something must be done". A group of small vessels was hastily put together including the extraordinary addition of six motor-torpedo boats, craft so ill-fitted for the patrol task that the decision to acquire them illustrates the depth of ignorance of the Dublin authorities and their indifference to professional advice.

Once the war was over and the Irish population had been supplied for six years thanks to convoys escorted by the Allies, a reaction similar to that of 1924 set in. Although, in March 1946, it was decided to set up the Marine Service as a permanent component of the Defence Force, three *Flower* class corvettes was clearly inadequate for the many tasks envisaged—a universal problem in all navies, large or small.

In 1961 the head of the Naval Service produced a memorandum stating his needs to carry out foreseen tasks—8 frigates, 6 coastal and 11 inshore minesweepers, 12 seaward defence boats. He might have spared himself the effort: none of these ships was forthcoming. Morale suffered and in 1965 the total active strength was 283 officers and men as against an establishment of 531. In 1971 the corvettes, long past their "sell-by-date", were replaced by three ex-RN coastal minesweepers. However, signs of new life were beginning to show. On 11 May 1972 the 960-ton patrol vessel *Deirdre* was handed over to the Naval Service, the first such ship built in Ireland at Cork. In 1976 the patrolling of 130,000 square miles of EEC waters presented huge problems. As this was an EEC requirement, between 1977 and 1980 Brussels paid for three new, improved *Deirdre* class vessels to be built. In 1979 the Air Corps received three aircraft for maritime patrol. Things were looking up, but not before time. In 1973 the IRA gunrunner *Claudia* had been intercepted by the Naval Service and her lethal cargo impounded; in 1984 a similar seizure of *Marita Ann* brought an even larger haul. Three months later the Naval Service commissioned *Eithne*, a patrol vessel of 1910 tons and, most importantly, equipped with a helicopter. With her fully modern facilities this is surely the way ahead for the Naval Service. The main requirements in those stormy waters are seaworthiness, range, long-range detection (radar and aircraft) and a reasonable speed. In every one of these categories *Eithne* comes out well. However, the closure of the Verolme yard at Cork prevented the construction of a follow-on ship and in 1988 two ex-RN patrol ships (then only four years old) of 700 tons were purchased. Although superior in speed (in reasonable weather conditions) to *Eithne*, they lack two essentials—long range and a helicopter.

The result of these programmes is that the Naval Service now operates seven ships of which two are of comparatively short-range. Even with the

Irish high rate of availability this is a small force to cover Ireland's area of oceanic and coastal responsibility. As the author says, "additional funding would have to be provided to finance the procurement of suitable inshore craft, the recruitment and training of personnel, and the possible establishment of a Naval Coastguard."

The EEC decision of 1976 caused the Irish government to pay some attention to the needs of the Naval Service and Brussels paved the way. But if the drug-runners, the gun-runners and those fishing illegally are to be hounded successfully, more ships and, particularly, more aircraft are needed. This is a joint matter for both Dublin and Brussels to resolve and the former should never again turn back from the sea.

All this is laid out and explained by the author in this fascinating, trenchant and informative book.

Capt. John E. Moore, RN

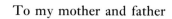

To my mother and father

CONTENTS

ILLUSTRATIONS

CREDITS

Commissioners of Irish Lights, Dublin 22; *Cork Examiner* 19, 25; Defence Forces Press Office 21, 23–4, 26–31, 33–35; Luke Cassidy Collection, Cobh, Co. Cork 5, 9, 11, 12, 16–18; Military Archives, Dublin frontispiece, 1-4, 10, 13-15, 20, 22, 32; Col. Anthony Morris 7; RTE, Dublin 6, 8

ACKNOWLEDGMENTS

This book could not have been written without the generous help given by the Irish Naval Service and the department of defence. In particular, I am indebted to the following individuals: Cmdr. John Kavanagh, FOCNS; Lt.-Col. Declan O'Carroll, Head of the IDF's Public Relations Section; Lt.-Cmdr. Shane Angerson, NS; Cdr. John Jordan, NS; Lt.-Cmdr. Daire Brunicardi, NS; Comdt. Peter Young and Capt. Victor Laing of Irish Military Archives; and Mr Gerry Gervin and Mr John Daly of the department of defence. In particular, I wish to acknowledge the invaluable assistance give by Mr John Daly and Lt.-Cdr. Anderson, NS who read the manuscript and thankfully corrected any factual errors that were contained within the text.

In the UK, I wish to acknowledge the assistance given by the Royal Navy's Fishery Protection Squadron at Rosyth, the Britannia Royal Naval College, Dartmouth, and the Scottish Fishery Protection Agency. The help given by the staff of the University of London's college libraries is also gratefully acknowledged, especially Ms Kate O'Brien of the Liddell Hart Military Archives Centre and Mr Kamal Mouale of King's College, London. In addition, generous help was given by the following libraries in Ireland and the UK: the British Library; the National Library of Ireland, Trinity College Library, Dublin; the Linen Hall Library, Belfast; Belfast Central Library; the National Newspaper Library, Colindale (London); the National Maritime Museum Library, Greenwich; and the Royal Naval College Library, Greenwich. I am particularly indebted to the advice given by Brigadier Peter Morton (Retd.) and Capt. John E. Moore, RN, who as with many notable RN officers is of Irish extraction.

From overseas, I wish to acknowledge the assistance give by over 35 navies and coastguard services, in particular those of Iceland, Norway, France, Germany, Australia, Canada, USA and Argentina. Finally, the assistance give by the following individuals is also gratefully acknowledged; Col. E. Doyle of the *Irish Times*, Professor Harold Kearsley, USN of the University of Southeastern Lousiana, Mr Luke Cassidy of Cobh, Co. Cork, Mrs Catherine Jennings of Carna, Co. Galway and Col. Anthony Morris of the Connemara and Clifden Heritage Group.

ABBREVIATIONS

AA	Anti-aircraft
ASW	Anti-submarine weapon
CMS	Coastal and Marine Service
DoD	department of defence
FCA	An Forsa Cosanta Aitiuil
GPS	Global Positioning System
HMS	His/Her Majesty's ship
HPV	helicopter patrol vessel
IAC	Irish Air Corps
IDF	Irish Defence Forces
INS	Irish Naval Service
LE	Long Éireannach (Irish ship)
ML	motor launch
MRCC	Marine Rescue Coordination Centre
MTB	motor torpedo boat
MV	motor (diesel) vessel
NS	Naval Service
OPV	offshore patrol vessel
PDF	Permanent Defence Force (of IDF)
RAF	Royal Air Force
RN	Royal Navy
RUC	Royal Ulster Constabulary
SAM	surface to air missile
SAR	search and rescue
SD	seaward defence
SFPA	Scottish Fisheries Protection Agency
SS	steam ship
SSM	ship to ship missile
TD	Teachta Dáil (Dáil Deputy, i.e. member of the Irish lower house of parliament)
USCG	United States Coast Guard
USS	United States Ship

Ranks and titles

Capt.	captain (equivalent army rank = colonel)
Cdr.	commander (equivalent army rank = lieutenant colonel)
Cmdr.	commodore (equivalent army rank = brigadier general)
Col.	colonel
Comdt.	commandant
CONS	Commanding Officer of the Naval Service (in use 1946–80)
FOCNS	Flag Officer Commanding Naval Service (in use from 1980)
Gen.	general
IC	(officer) in charge
Lt.	lieutenant (equivalent army rank = captain)
Lt.-Cdr.	lieutenant commander (equivalent army rank = major)
Lt.-Gen.	lieutenant-general
Maj.-Gen.	major-general
NCO	non-commissioned officer
OC	officer commanding
OCNBAD	Officer Commanding the Naval Base and Dockyard
PO	petty officer (eqivalent army rank = sergeant)
Sub-Lt.	sub-lieutenant (equivalent army rank = lieutenant)

INTRODUCTION

The story of the Irish navy is in some ways a parallel account of 20th-century Irish history. The island of Ireland is fundamentally a country of enormous naval importance. Lying astride the Western Approaches, Ireland dominates the maritime gateways to its densely populated and heavily industrialised neighbour Great Britain. In the 19th and early 20th centuries Britain possessed a vast maritime empire that spanned five continents. This huge domain was linked by trade and this in turn was protected by the "Empress of the Seas", the Royal Navy. When Ireland agitated for self-determination, the country's strategic importance to Britain could not be excluded from the negotiations; for he who controlled Ireland could throttle Britain. When independence was granted, the naval dimension made itself felt: Ireland was not permitted to have a navy. Naval defence was to be the responsibility of the Royal Navy, which was to possess three fortified anchorages in the new Irish Free State. Although an Irish navy was not allowed, a seaborne coast guard service was permitted. Such a service was quickly established and provided the new state with a creditable coastal navy. That this remarkable embryonic navy was allowed to disband only ten months after its creation, speaks volumes about the attitude of the new Irish State to its maritime circumstances.

In the inter-war period the Irish Free State, unlike the other resurrected nation states of post-Versailles Europe, took little interest in the country's maritime affairs. The Irish turned inward on a safe and familiar agricultural landscape. Ireland's harbours and ports were allowed to deteriorate; and her coastguard stations were sold off or left derelict. Such was the new State's aversion to the sea. While other small maritime countries endeavoured to build up and protect a deep-sea fishing industry, the Irish Free State employed one antiquated patrol boat armed only with a piece of boiler tubing to intimate foreign trawlers. Only when the valiant *Murichu* was nearly rammed and sunk in Bantry Bay by a contemptous trawler were measures taken to arm it with a real gun.

This very sad situation was made truly ironic by the Irish Free State's decision to attend two important naval disarmament conferences in

London. When Britain evacuated the Treaty ports in 1938, Ireland was now responsible for the defence of its own ports and territorial waters. This remarkable diplomatic achievement was in many ways motivated by a land-orientated political establishment in Dublin. The Royal Navy and British army had been removed from Irish soil, but no real effort was made to fill the gap left by the Royal Navy's South Irish flotilla. This was partly dictated by financial considerations and more discreetly by a unwillingness to duplicate the efforts of Royal Naval units based at Plymouth and Milfordhaven.

Defence was still land-orientated. When war came, this obsession with land defence became obvious when the Irish State's second attempt at creating a navy resulted in a force of only 300 regulars compared with over 50,000 in the regular wartime army—a remarkable situation for an island state with over 1900 miles of coastline. The *ad hoc* navy was a symbol of Ireland's determination to resist aggression. However, in reality, the success of Ireland's wartime neutrality was more a product of the country's fortunate geographic location, that is, away from German-controlled Europe, and de Valera's 'special consideration towards England'.

The post-war period confirmed the need for a small naval force. The era of the three corvettes had arrived. The officers who manned this force knew that it was grossly inadequate for the maritime defence of Ireland. However, ever since 1936 it had been recognised that Ireland's predicament was unsettling. The country was poor, sparsely populated and without any defence industries or means to repel seaborne attack. The Irish navy was therefore geared towards fishery protection duties. While Ireland in the 1950s endured economic stagnation and renewed emigration, plans for a properly equipped coastal navy were repeatedly shelved by the department of finance. Even when economic circumstances greatly improved in the following decade, the navy was starved of funds. The Army received Comet tanks, Panhard armoured cars; the Air Corps obtained Vampire jets and Alouette helicopters while the navy withered away. Extinction seemed inevitable in 1970, when the country's naval defence comprised one disarmed and worn out second-hand corvette.

Despite the decades of neglect by an agriculturally-orientated political establishment in Dublin, the Irish navy managed to function. However, it is not surprising that the highly efficient navy of the 1980s and 1990s is primarily a product of external funding, the EEC transformed Ireland and the Naval Service. After the introduction of the 200-mile exclusive economic zone (EEZ) in 1977, the Irish navy became responsible for policing over 130,000 square miles of the EEC's offshore waters. With this new and onerous responsibility came the real prospect of adequate funding. As a result within seven years the Irish Naval Service was transformed from being the Cinderella branch of Ireland's very modest national defence force into one of the most sophisticated and well-equipped EEZ patrol forces in Europe.

IRISH MARITIME TRADITIONS

The island of Ireland constitutes the westernmost outpost of the Atlantic fringe of the Eurasian landmass. Lying to the west of Great Britain, separated from Scotland by the North Channel and from Wales by the Irish Sea, it dominates the Western Approaches. Because of the deeply indented nature of Ireland's Atlantic coastline, no part of Ireland is more than 70 miles from the sea. These geographic circumstances afford Ireland with an array of opportunities to utilise and develop its maritime resources. Unlike Sweden, Denmark, Finland, Poland and the Baltic states, Ireland has unrestricted access to the Atlantic Ocean. To the east, Britain forms a physical buttress against any seaward attack. Yet regardless of these circumstances, Ireland does not rank with Norway, Britain and Greece as one of Europe's notable 20th-century maritime nations. In reality, Ireland's achievements in the field of maritime endeavour are sadly very few.

After Independence in 1921, Ireland, although forbidden to develop a navy, did not even establish a coastguard or a permanent coastal patrol service. In 1938 when the country became responsible for its own seaward defence, no serious attempt was made to establish a mercantile marine or a coastal navy. It was as if the Irish in the words of Commodore T. McKenna NS (CO, Irish Naval Service, 1956–73) "had turned their backs on the sea". This deep-seated lack of interest in maritime affairs has been attributed to the 700 years of English/British hegemony, as well as the fact that Ireland has traditionally had an agricultural economy. In contrast the Icelanders, Norwegians and Greeks inhabited lands which were not conducive to agricultural development. Therefore, they were obliged to look to the sea for their economic salvation. Until 1921, Ireland like 19th-century Poland was a subject nation and therefore did not officially exist. Even after Independence the benign influence of British maritime power was so great as to stifle any serious interest in establishing Irish maritime institutions. It was as if the 700 years of English domination had instilled in most Irish people a view that the sea was the preserve of Britannia.

Yet there is an Irish maritime tradition which spans fifteen centuries, although for a significant part of this period it was an émigré tradition in the service of foreign navies. Ireland's subjugation to the power of Britain meant that an indigenous naval and maritime tradition could not develop. The country was a colony and therefore denied the right to establish its own mercantile marine and navy. However, this did not inhibit Irishmen from deriving a livelihood from the sea. Poverty forced many to serve in the Royal Navy, although fortunately this was less so in the 20th century. While throughout the past 300 years, Irishmen have served in the navies of Imperial Russia, China, France, Spain, Portugal, the United States, the emergent Latin American republics and those of the British Commonwealth dominions. Many rose to prominence: for example, the navies of Argentina, Chile, Ecuador and the United States of America were all founded by Irishmen. Others distinguished themselves in battle and were decorated accordingly. In addition, Irishmen have made notable contributions to the design and development of ships and naval weapon systems.

THE CELTIC MISSIONARIES: IRELAND'S FIRST MARINERS

In the wake of the disintegration of the Roman Empire in the West, much of Europe regressed into banditry and ignorance. The cornerstones of Roman civilization—law, literacy and cities—faded away. In this period, one of the few parts of Europe where scholarship and a love of religious art prevailed was Ireland. The monasteries of the Celtic Church were beacons of learning in a Europe which was still largely pagan and violent. Irish monks were to make a significant contribution to European history by Christianising many of the barbarian kings who now ruled the territories of the former Roman Empire.

The first Irish missionary to venture out to sea was St Colmcille or Columba (AD 521-97). He crossed over to the west coast of Scotland on a currach or skin-covered boat and established a religious centre on the island of Iona. Other monks followed St Colmcille across the often treacherous waters which separate Ireland from western Scotland. Another intrepid monastic missionary from Ireland was St Aidan. In 634, at the invitation of King Oswald of Northumbria, he travelled to north-east England and established a religious house at Lindesfarne. It was St Aidan who was mainly responsible for Christianising this part of England. The first Irish missionary to travel to continental Europe was St Columbanus, who founded centres of religious and cultural learning at Annegary, Luxeuil and Bobbio, where he died in 615. Columbanus' colleague St Gall went on to establish the famous monastery of St Gallen in Switzerland. Another famous Irish monk of this era was Fursey who initially went to East Anglia and then travelled on to the continent where he established a monastery at Lagny. Fursey's brother, also a missionary, went on to establish the famous monastery of Nivelles in central France.

One of the most imaginative of these monks was Fergal, later to become archbishop of Salzburg. Fergal apparently attached credence to the views of the Roman writer Virgil, who in the second century AD argued for the existence of the antipodes, that is, people living on the other side of the world. St Boniface, a contemporary of Fergal, was a committed "flat earther". In the words of Fr Grosjean SJ, "it is not surprising that Fergal, an experienced sailor, should have visualised the earth as a sphere or a globe, this being in accordance with the well argued tenets of ancient Greek geographers."[1]

Irish monks also travelled beyond the Scottish Western Isles to the Orkney and Shetland Islands. From there they went onto the Faeroes and eventually to Iceland. When the Norsemen arrived in Iceland they discovered Irish monks resident on Westmannaeyar or Irishmen's Islands. How these monks managed to navigate through the North Sea and across the Atlantic is not certain. But their knowledge of Greek and Latin allowed them to come into contact with fellow thinkers and travellers who had read the ancient Greek treatises on astronomy, mathematics and geography. Irish monks also sailed south to north-west Spain and into the Mediterranean and Adriatic Sea areas—where to this day, there are over 120 Italian churches dedicated to Irish saints. All of these long distance voyages were carried out in wooden cargo boats. Although Irish monks settled in Iceland there is no evidence that they managed to reach Greenland or North America. However, this has not prevented some credence being attached to the legend of St Brendan, who, according to maritime historian, Tom Severin, managed to reach North America over a thousand years before Columbus.

Throughout the Middle Ages and post-medieval period, seaborne trade developed between Ireland and ports in Britain and continental Europe. In this period the naval importance of the island of Ireland became of increasing concern to England, the most notable examples being the failed attempt by Spain to subjugate England in 1588 by seaborne invasion and the English Civil War of 1642-6. In the latter conflict, Cromwell's parliamentary forces achieved success partly by denying the Royalists access to English ports. Cromwell's navy was then used with great effect to transport troops and supplies to Ireland. Irish resistance to this Cromwellian campaign took on a naval form when an Irish fleet was formed. Resistance was focused around the Confederation of Kilkenny which for the first time attempted to unify all of Ireland, Gaelic and Norman-Irish, in opposition to England. Although that Confederation was characterised by much in-fighting and division, it did establish an Irish Admiralty. Warships were purchased from France, but after 11 years resistance petered out in 1652. In the decades that followed, the number of Scottish and English settlements in Ireland increased. For many who aspired to a naval career, there were only two options—join the Royal Navy or enlist in a European navy.

THE WILD GEESE: THE IRISH IN THE SERVICE OF FOREIGN NAVIES

For over 400 hundred years Irish soldiers and sailors have fought in the armies and navies of many countries. Tens of thousands of Irishmen left their homeland to serve in designated Irish battalions, regiments and brigades in the armies of Britain, France, Spain and the United States. Others served on an individual basis in the armed forces of many more countries. The role of the Irish in the service of foreign navies is particularly significant, as Irishmen have served in nearly every major world navy.

Britain

The record of the Irish in the service of the Royal Navy is long, distinguished and somewhat ironic. Like the Polish regiments which served in the armies of the Russian Tsar, these men were serving in the navy of a country which for centuries had persecuted Ireland. Poverty forced most Irishmen to enlist, but others saw opportunities for adventure and possible advancement. The record of the Irish in the Royal Navy is too long to do justice to such a subject in a few brief paragraphs. However, it is worth noting that many of Britain's 20th-century naval war heroes were Irish or of Irish extraction. Admiral Beatty of Battle of Jutland fame was from Co. Waterford; Admiral Sir James Somerville, who sank the French fleet at Mers-el-Kebir in 1940, was from Co. Cork; and Admiral Cunningham, commander of the British Mediterranean fleet in World War II, was from Dublin.

One of the first VCs to be won in World War II was awarded to an Irishman named Fogarty-Fegen from Ballinlonty, Co. Tipperary. When in command of the auxiliary cruiser *Jervis Bay*, Fogarty-Fegen saved a merchant convoy from certain disaster when, as the convoy's sole escort, he engaged the pocket-battleship *Admiral Sheer* in an unequal duel. This engagement allowed the merchant vessels to scatter while the *Jervis Bay* held off the German battleship. Fogarty-Fegen was killed and his ship was sunk, but the convoy he was escorting was saved from destruction.

Another notable wartime VC winner was Leading Seaman James Joseph Magennis from Belfast. He was the only person from Northern Ireland to be awarded the Victoria Cross during the 1939-45 war. The action which merited such a high award occurred in July 1945, just before the war in the Pacific ended. Magennis and an English naval officer, Fraser, were sent into Singapore harbour to blow up the Japanese cruiser *Takao*. To reach the Japanese warship, they had to travel 64km in a midget submarine in oppressive tropical heat through numerous underwater defences and past sunken wrecks. When their midget submarine settled under the keel of the *Takao*, Magennis had to scrap away the barnacles in order that the limpet mines could be attached. This required great physical effort and courage as Japanese naval sentries were nearby on the quayside and on board the *Takao*. In the end, the mission was a total success: the *Takao* was sunk and Leading Seaman Magennis and Lt. Fraser managed to return to their "mothership" submarine without incident. Both men were decorated in person by King George VI at Buckingham Palace in November 1945.

Western Europe

From the Flight of the Earls (1607) onwards, Irish soldiers and sailors served under the flags of many European kings and emperors. Spain was one of the first beneficiaries of this outflow of Irish military talent. The commander of the Spanish Mediterranean fleet in the 1640s was Captain O'Donnell, Earl of Tyrconnell, a nephew of "Red" Hugh O'Donnell. Another famous Irish-Spanish naval officer was Felix O'Neill (1761-1809). He served for a period with the Regiment of Hibernia before enlisting in the Spanish navy; in 1809, he was made an admiral. Timoteo O'Scanlan, another famous Hiberno-Spanish naval officer of this period, became a senior administrative officer responsible for naval artillery and port defences. Irishmen also served in France. Indeed in the early part of the 18th century there were many Irish officers serving in the French navy.

Irishmen were to be found in the navies of other countries and states as well. There were Irish serving in the navy of the Papal States, as well as the Austrian Imperial navy. The latter was founded in 1719 in Trieste by an Irishman named George Forbes from Longford. This now-extinct navy was established thanks to the assistance offered to the Austrian emperor by King George I. He had arranged for British naval officers to be seconded to the Austrians. Another prominent Irishman in the service of Austria was Matthew Flanagan. In the late 18th century, he commanded the Danube flotilla, and later rose to the rank of admiral, remaining in the navy until his retirement in 1835. Irish mariners were also to be found in the service of Portugal and Imperial Russia. One of the most famous Irish-Portuguese officers was Gabriel Fallon, who after 35 years aboard Portuguese warships was appointed as director of the naval arsenal in Lisbon. Another famous Portuguese officer of Irish extraction was Diogo Keating, who left Portugal to help establish the Brazilian navy.

Russia

Imperial Russia, unlike France, Portugal and Spain had no historical or religious connection with Ireland. Yet this vast trans-continental empire on the edge of central-east Europe had Irish naval officers in its service. One of the most prominent Irish officers in the Imperial Russian navy was Henry Baillie from Co. Cavan. He joined the Russian navy in 1783 as a midshipman and by 1787 was in command of a galley in the Black Sea. He then progressed on to larger vessels and saw service in the Russo-Austrian wars. In 1797 he was given command of the frigate *Stchastlivyi*; it was with this ship that Baillie accompanied Admiral Ushakov's fleet into the Mediterranean. In the course of the joint campaign with Admiral Lord Nelson's forces, the Russians occupied the Ionian Islands and landed troops in southern Italy. The Italian landings were commanded by Baillie, who advanced overland on Naples with the Russian troops. In 1804, Henry Baillie, now a captain, was again active with Russian Black Sea fleet in conducting operations in the Adriatic and eastern Mediterranean.

Commodore Cronin was another notable Irish naval officer in the service of the Tsars. When in 1812 Napoleon invaded Russia, Cronin was the commander-in-chief of the Russian Baltic fleet. Under his expert guidance, the Russian fleet was successfully evacuated to the North Sea. Cronin, despite his intelligence and obvious abilities, had not been permitted to rise above the rank of master in the Royal navy. In Russia talent could rise regardless of national or social origin. Cronin's son later became an admiral in the Russian navy.

During the Crimean War (1851-4), a Russian officer of Irish extraction distinguished himself in a battle with the French and British navies in one of the most isolated regions of the north Pacific. The officer's name was Nikolai Moritsovich O'Rourke. He joined the Russian navy in 1853 and was attached to the frigate *Aurora*. This vessel was not sent to engage Anglo-French warships on the Black Sea but instead was dispatched to the Kamchatka peninsula on the edge of the north Asian landmass. In one of the most bizarre actions concerning the Crimean War, a joint French and British naval squadron chose to attack this desolate peninsula in the Russian Far East. The focus of their attack was the only port on the frozen and desolate Kamchatkan peninsula, Petropavlosk-Kamchatski. In the course of this action, the young O'Rourke was decorated for his efforts in repulsing the attack. A year later, the Anglo-French squadron returned and during this attack O'Rourke was decorated with the Order of St Stanislas. In 1856, he was allowed to leave Kamchatka. The Anglo-French action off Kamchatka was prompted by a genuine British fear that the Russian navy might attempt to invade Australia. To this day, Sydney's inner harbour is dominated by a man-made island fortress, Fort Dennison, which was built to ward off the Russian navy during the Crimean War.

United States of America

During the visit of President J.F. Kennedy to Ireland in 1963, the American head of state went to Wexford in south-east Ireland to unveil a memorial to a famous 18th-century Irish mariner—Commodore John Barry, the founder of the United States Navy. Born at Bally Sampson, Co. Wexford in 1745, Barry moved in 1760 to Philadelphia where eventually he became a successful sea captain and shipowner. When the American colonists rebelled against British rule in 1776, he offered his services to the rebels. In the same year, Barry, in command of the *Lexington*, captured HMS *Edward*, the first British warship to be seized in the War of Independence. Barry's reputation as a courageous and imaginative naval officer quickly spread. The British General Howe offered him $100,000, an enormous sum in the late 1770s, if he would desist from attacking his supply lines. In 1782, Barry captured nine richly laden merchant ships *en route* from Jamaica to England. He then sold the cargoes to the French, thereby providing the US Treasury with desperately needed finance. It was John Barry who took Lafayette back to France in 1781 and later on he commanded the US Mediterranean squadron which defended American merchant ships from the Barbary pirates. Prior to his death in 1803, John Barry commanded US warships in the West Indies.

During the American Civil War, Irishmen fought on both sides. The naval aspect of the war centred on the North's ultimately successful attempt to blockade the Confederacy into submission. When the Confederate States of America (CSA) was declared in 1861, it did not possess a navy; as the US fleet had remained loyal to President Lincoln. However, the CSA's dynamic naval secretary, Mallory, who himself was second-generation Irish, commissioned 23 iron-clad warships into service. Eighteen of these ships had Irishmen serving on board. In fact the commander-in-chief of the Confederate navy was another second-generation Irishman, Capt. Buchanan. During the Battle of Mobile Bay, Buchanan engaged 17 US warships while in command of his flagship, the iron-clad *Tennessee*. At the end of the battle, Buchanan who was captured in a wounded condition, was treated by a US naval surgeon who also was Irish. Of the 5000 officers and men in the Confederate navy, 845 are known to have been of Irish birth or origin. After the end of the civil war, Irishmen continued to serve in the United States Navy throughout the 19th and 20th centuries.

Latin America

In the wake of Napoleon's defeat in the Peninsula War, Spain and Portugal attempted to reassert control over their Latin American colonies. These territories had witnessed the weakness of their European masters and saw opportunities for lucrative trade with Britain, something which had been previously denied to them. As a result, a series of wars of liberation developed. During these conflicts several Irishmen made significant contributions to Latin American maritime history. One of these men was a Thomas Charles Wright. After distinguished service with the Royal Navy during the Napoleonic and Anglo-American wars, Wright offered his services to Simon Bolivar, the Liberator of South America. It was Wright who organised an embyronic navy for the newly created republic of Gran Granada. After this huge state disintegrated into the republics of present-day northern South America, Wright settled in Guayaquil and established the Ecuadorian navy. To this day, the Ecuadorian Naval Academy is named after this intrepid Irishman whose family came from Drogheda.

To the west, Argentina owes the foundation of its navy to an Irishman named William Brown. He arrived in Buenos Aires in 1810 and initially confined his energies to mercantile shipping. However, when the Spanish military governor of Buenos Aires, General Vigodet, unjustly arrested two of his cargo ships and imprisoned the crews, Brown sided with the Argentine rebels. In view of his maritime experience, he was given command of what naval forces were at the disposal of the patriots. At Martin Garcia in 1814, the newly-appointed Admiral Brown of the Argentine navy was victorious during his first major engagement. Later on he defeated the Spanish navy at the Battle of Montevideo. The Argentine navy's founding father later went on to serve in naval engagements against neighbouring Brazil. To this day, the Argentine Naval Academy is named after William Brown. The Chilean navy also owes its foundation to Irishmen. When in 1817 the country revolted against Spanish rule, its first president, Bernardo O'Higgins, established a navy. The man who was given the responsibility for overseeing the development of this navy was an Irishman named Captain George O'Brien. During a successful engagement in which Spanish warships were captured, Capt. O'Brien was killed while in command of the frigate *Lautaro*. Since then the Chilean navy have repeatedly honoured the memory of this Irishman by naming warships after Capt. O'Brien. Later on in the 19th century, two of Chile's most distinguished naval figures, Admirals Patricio Lynch and Carlos Condell, were the offspring of Irish settlers in Chile. Both men rendered great service to Chile during the Pacific wars with neighbouring Peru.

The Far East

China, India, Japan and Thailand have all benefited in the past from the services of Irish mariners. The Chinese Imperial navy contained several Irishmen who distinguished themselves in China's wars with Japan and inland rebels. A man named Mellows from Co. Waterford, who had originally served as a gunner in the Sino-Japanese War of 1894, later became the commander of one of the Taku naval ports. It was Robert Hart, originally from Ulster, who set up the Anglo-Chinese river flotilla which helped contain banditry along China's main rivers. Many of the men who crewed these small gunboats were Irish, for example, Hugh Burgoyne VC, who commanded the gunboat *Patlin*. Another intrepid Irish mariner who sought success in overseas service was Michael Deasy from West Cork. He joined the Royal Navy "but became dissatisfied with a service where talent and experience are held subordinate to wealth and accident of birth". Frustrated by a lack of opportunity in the Royal Navy he later obtained a commission in the Royal Siamese Navy before becoming harbourmaster of Bombay. Irishmen were among some of the first Royal Naval instructors to be sent to train the Japanese Imperial navy in the 1880s. While the Royal Indian Navy was also staffed with many men who were Irish or of Irish extraction.[2]

GUN-RUNNING, AN IRISH MARITIME TRADITION

Ireland's struggle for independence has always had a distinctive maritime dimension. Many of those who rose up against British rule were armed with weapons which were smuggled into Ireland by gun-runners. Others fought in the hope that assistance would come in the form of anti-British seaborne invaders. Indeed in 1796 a French invasion fleet of 41 ships with 15,000 troops on board assembled in Bantry Bay but stormy weather dispersed the invaders. Two years later, a small French force under General Humbert managed to effect a successful landing in Co. Mayo, but this force was repulsed and defeated within two weeks. During the 1867 Fenian rising, Irish-born veterans of the American Civil War sailed to Ireland on board *Erin's Hope*. However, their attempt to smuggle weapons ashore did not succeed. When in the years 1912 to 1914, the British parliament seemed willing to consider a form of Irish Home Rule, a north-south conflict seemed inevitable. The Ulster unionists, especially those of Scottish descent who were concentrated in the north-east of the island, were prepared to resist by force if necessary the perceived hegemony of an all-Ireland parliament. The threat of resistance came in the form of the Ulster Volunteer Force, a para-military group which in

April 1914 received a large shipment German arms. These had been smuggled in by ship. Some months later, Irish nationalists, who wanted an all-Ireland state, smuggled ashore German arms.

The voyage of the Asgard

The ongoing political crisis surrounding Home Rule prompted Irish nationalists to seek out a possible supply of arms. Early in 1914, an Anglo-Irish journalist, Darrel Figgis, was sent to Europe to buy weapons. In the course of his visit he procured 1500 German-made Mauser rifles and 49,000 rounds of ammunition from the firm of Moritz Magnus in Hamburg. The rifles were second-hand relics from the 1870 Franco-Prussian War. However, regardless of their age, these weapons were desperately needed because in April 1914, the Ulster unionists had succeeded in smuggling in 25,000 firearms and three million rounds of ammunition. These arms had also been bought in Germany and shipped to the port of Larne on board the cargo vessel, *Clyde Valley*.[3] The Larne gun-running operation was carried out with military precision, and it was a clear indication of the violent resistance that could be expected should an Irish parliament in Dublin attempt to exercise its authority over the north-east of the island.

The weapons and munitions which were purchased by Irish nationalists were to be smuggled into Ireland on board three yachts—the *Asgard*, the *Kelpie* and the *Chotah*. It was arranged that a German tug would transport the arms from Hamburg to a point off the Belgian coast near the Ruytigen lightship. The rendezvous was to take place on 12 July, and the crates of rifles and boxes of ammunition were to be transferred at sea from the German tug, *Gladiator*, to the Irish yachts. It was a daring plan and its timing was perilously close to the outbreak of the First World War.

The *Asgard* was a 28-ton yacht which had been given to Mary Alden Osgood on the occasion of her marriage to Erskine Childers in 1904. Childers, although English by birth, was an ardent supporter of Irish independence and, incidentally, a highly respected mariner (his book *The Riddle of the Sands*, published in 1902, is still a yachtsman's bible). On 1 July, the *Asgard* set out on the first stage of her journey from Conway in north Wales. On board were Mary and Erskine Childers, the Hon. Mary Spring-Rice (an Anglo-Irish aristocrat and committed republican), Gordon Shephard (another English sympathiser) and two fishermen from Co. Donegal. These intrepid gun-runners had to run the gauntlet of British naval patrols. The *Asgard* sailed south along the Welsh coast and up through the English Channel to Cowes, where they had arranged to meet up with the *Kelpie*.

The Hon. Mary Rice-Spring kept an account of the journey:

I was half-appalled at the daringness of it—half delighted at the idea of the coup if it really came off. But there seemed many a slip—Howth so near Dublin—trams—telephones—soldiers—coastguards—and cruisers. How we discussed all these possibilities as we sat round after supper that evening and many evenings to come.[4]

After the two yachts met up, the *Kelpie* (part of whose arms cargo had been transferred off the Welsh coast to the *Chotah*) departed for the rendezvous with the German tug *Gladiator* in the North Sea. Several days later the *Asgard* put out to sea and sailed past four British warships at anchor off Folkestone. On Sunday 12 July, the *Asgard* met up the *Gladiator*. Immediately, work began on transferring the remaining part of the *Gladiator*'s cargo to the *Asgard*; the *Kelpie* had already collected 600 rifles and 20,000 rounds of ammunition. The rifles were wrapped in straw and a good deal of the packing had to be torn away in order that the weapons could be stored more easily. The crew of the *Asgard* worked through the night until the rifles and boxes of ammunition filled the saloon, cabin, passenger-ways and companion-ways. In all 900 rifles and 29,000 rounds of ammunition (due to overloading 4,000 rounds of ammunition had to be thrown overboard) were taken on board. This was a remarkable feat for a 28-ton yacht which also had to accommodate a crew of six. On the return voyage to Ireland, the heavily laden *Asgard* found itself in the midst of a British fleet off Devonport. On another day, a British warship fired a warning shot as they passed close by. Terror filled the crew as they expected the *Asgard* to be boarded by Royal Marines, but they were allowed to proceed without further incident.[5]

On 26 July, nearly four weeks after they had embarked on their epic voyage, the *Asgard* arrived off Howth on the north side of Dublin. A motor boat was to have met the gun-runners, but it did not turn up. However, this did not deter Erskine Childers from bringing his cargo into Howth. At the quayside 1000 Irish Volunteers had assembled to help off-load the cargo. Two of those who had marched from Dublin were Arthur Griffith, founder of Sinn Féin, and Eamon de Valera. Griffith would later negotiate the Anglo-Irish treaty with Lloyd George, while de Valera would come to dominate Irish political life for nearly half a century.

Four coastguards observed the landing, but there was little they could do except launch distress rockets. Within several hours the arms and ammunition had been carefully stored at pre-selected arms dumps. An attempt by police and British troops garrisoned in Dublin to intercept the weapons was unsuccessful. However, the day was not without bloodshed, as a unit of the King's Own Scottish Borderers opened fire on a hostile crowd in central Dublin. They killed three and wounded 32 other civilians. The *Kelpie*'s cargo of rifles and ammunition arrived a week later off the Wicklow coast and was landed without incident. These weapons allowed the Irish Volunteers to stage an anti-British rising on Easter Monday 1916.

The voyage of the Aud

When the First World War broke out in August 1914, the decision to introduce Irish Home Rule was postponed until the end of hostilities. Many of the Ulster Volunteers who had threatened to resist by all means legislation passed by parliament now demonstrated their conditional loyalty to the British Crown by enlisting in the British army. To the understandable consternation of many Irish nationalists, over 100,000 Irishmen volunteered for service in the same British army. In this period, a hard core of nationalists wanted to act on John Mitchel's famous maxim: "England's danger is Ireland's opportunity." An anti-British uprising in Ireland would be of great benefit to Germany, as it would oblige Britain to divert tens of thousands of troops from the Western Front for occupation duties in Ireland. To enable such a rising to take place, large quantities of weapons and munitions were required. Sir Roger Casement, a former British diplomat of Anglo-Irish extraction and now an ardent Irish republican, persuaded the German government of the merit of a German-sponsored rebellion. This appreciation of the utility of an anti-British uprising in Ireland was also shared by the German military attache in Washington DC, Fritz von Papen.

On St Patrick's Day, 17 March 1916, a conference was held at the German naval headquarters at which it was agreed to send a consignment of arms to Ireland. The cargo was to consist of:

- 20,000 rifles with 4,000,000 rounds of ammunition
- 10 machine-guns with 1,000,000 rounds of ammunition
- 400 kilograms of high explosives.[6]

The weapons were to be shipped to Tralee Bay in south-west Ireland on board a "Norwegian" tramp steamer, where it would be met by an Irish pilot boat. The vessel chosen to navigate its way through the British naval blockade of Germany as well as the picket ships patrolling off north Scotland and Ireland was a former British cargo vessel, SS *Castro* of Hull. It had been captured by a German destroyer in 1914 and was renamed the *Libau*. For this operation the *Libau* was again renamed as the *Aud*. Great pains were taken to conceal the purpose of the *Aud*'s real mission from any British naval search party. A secret hold was constructed and the vessel's exterior was painted in accordance with requirements of vessels from neutral Norway. The interior was fitted out with Norwegian newspapers, magazines and tinned food with Norwegian labels. The *Aud*'s sick bay was fitted out with dressings of Norwegian manufacture, as were the vessel's electric torches and tools. The crew were supposed to be Norwegian merchant seamen, although in reality they were all from the German Imperial navy. Their commander was a German naval reservist, Lieutenant Karl Spindler.

Spindler's orders were to leave Germany on 8 April and arrive at Tralee between 20 and 23 April, where he would be met by an Irish pilot boat. In addition, Spindler was ordered to rendezvous with a German submarine U-19 one mile north-west of Inistookert Island in Tralee Bay. The submarine was to transfer three passengers to the *Aud*. They were Sir Roger Casement, Captain Monteith and Sergeant Bailey. On 9 April the *Aud* left the Baltic port of Lubeck and steamed north-west towards the Kattegat. After negotiating the mine defences and patrol boats of neutral Denmark, the *Aud* proceeded into the open North Sea. Heavy fog protected the vessel from being closely scrutinised by patrolling British naval pickets. However, 75 miles east of the Shetland Islands, the *Aud* was nearly spotted by a British cruiser. This prompted Lt. Spindler to move north into Arctic waters in order then to swing south towards Ireland via the Faeroes-Iceland Gap. Even in these desolate waters, the Royal Navy maintained a force of 12 large merchant-cruisers to patrol "the outpost line". To reach Tralee Bay for its rendezvous with U-19 and the Irish pilot boat, the arms ship steamed at full speed through heavy fog. Then suddenly, while the *Aud* was cloaked in thick fog, it nearly collided with a British auxiliary cruiser. To the astonishment of Spindler, the British naval picket did not stop and search the supposedly innocent Norwegian cargo ship. The *Aud* had broken through the outpost line and into the North Atlantic. Spindler and his men proceeded in a sou'-south-east course towards Rockall Island north-west of Co. Donegal. *En route* they struggled with gale force winds and stormy seas. After passing Rockall Bank, an area of shallow water renowned as a shipping hazard, the *Aud* was spotted by two British cruisers. Fortunately for Spindler, the Royal Navy did not query his presence in the area. During their journey far off the Scottish west coast, the *Aud* was repeatedy spotted by British naval patrols but was never challenged.

On 20 April, the *Aud* reached the coast of south-west Ireland, where Spindler and his men changed into German naval uniform. However, when they arrived at the pre-arranged rendezvous, that is, one mile north-west of Inistookert Island in Tralee Bay, there was no one there to meet them. There was no sign of an Irish pilot boat and the only human activity which Spindler observed was a British sentry patrolling Fenit pier. An understandably nervous Spindler decided to wait in the bay. The following morning at 5 a.m., a British patrol boat, *Shatter II*, came alongside the *Aud* and enquired as to its presence. What followed was a mixture of comic farce and military daring. While the British gunboat was approaching the *Aud*, Spindler and his crew frantically changed back into Norwegian uniform. To the astonishment of Spindler, only one person boarded the *Aud*, namely the commander of the *Shatter II*. This British naval officer then proceeded to search the vessel. However, after glancing at the jumbled pile of pitprops in the upper hold, he quickly terminated the search. The sight of the pitprops·had convinced him that Spindler's explanation of being forced to shelter after encountering stormy weather was correct. The British officer then gave the *Aud*'s shipping papers a cursory glance before announcing that everything appeared in order. After this gratifying announcement, Spindler played the part of a kindly Norwegian skipper by entertaining the young British officer. In return the Royal Naval officer gave the "Norwegian" captain a bundle of English newspapers. From these Spindler quickly discovered that the Irish rising was now doomed, since many suspected Irish nationalists had been arrested in the Tralee area by the British military. Spindler could not have known of these developments as the *Aud* was not equipped with a radio. Furthermore, Spindler's hospitality in the form of free flowing alcohol had allowed the British officer to become quite talkative. The young naval officer told the "Norwegian" skipper that the Royal Navy now knew that German arms were to be brought ashore in the Tralee area and that "a warm reception was being prepared for them".

Thanks to this vital information coming as it did from an unusual source, Spindler made immediate preparations to extricate the *Aud* from Tralee Bay as quickly as possible. When the vessel was ready to depart, Spindler saw a British patrol boat approaching at speed. He immediately took his ship out of Tralee Bay and into the open sea. *En route*, he passed the *Shatter II*, whose friendly but gullible commanding officer signalled "Bon voyage" to Lt. Spindler and his crew. Spindler thanked the young Royal Naval officer with the flag signal for "Thank you". Once at sea, the *Aud*, still in the guise of a Norwegian cargo ship, steamed southwards away from British naval pickets. At 6 p.m. Spindler sighted a British fast auxiliary cruiser on the horizon, which seemed to signify that his luck had finally run out. Within an hour the cruiser, HMS *Bluebell*, was steaming alongside and signalled to the *Aud* that she should proceed to Queenstown (Cobh). Escape was now impossible as other warships were visible in the distance. Off Galley Head, the *Aud* was encircled by British destroyers. Spindler, realising that the epic voyage was nearly at an end, was going to cheat the Royal Navy of acquiring the *Aud* and its cargo. At the entrance to Cork harbour, he "spun the wheel hard a-starboard, swinging the *Aud* right across the channel and signalled stop". Pre-arranged demolition charges set against the ship's keel were detonated within a few minutes. The German naval ensign was run-up and the *Aud*'s crew now in German naval uniform took to the ship's lifeboats.

It was a moment of profound humiliation for the Royal Navy. Lt. Spindler had not only eluded interception by the Royal Navy's picket ships strung out across the North Sea and North Atlantic, but he had escaped the clutches of the Royal Navy in Tralee Bay thanks to the gullibility of an RN officer. Finally, not only had he denied the Royal Navy the prize of recapturing a former British merchant ship with its cargo of German arms, but his act of sabotage blocked the mid-channel of an important convoy assembly port and naval base.

Spindler and his crew were picked up by British ships and taken to Spike Island. After three days, Spindler and his men were sent to Chatham for interrogation and then to POW camps in England. After the armistice, he was released and deported to Holland (in 1931 Karl Spindler and the surviving members of his crew were presented with a specially engraved *Aud* medal by the Executive Committee for Freedom in America). The young naval officer in command of the *Shatter II* was less fortunate. He was court-martialled for gross dereliction of duty, deprived of his commission and given a stiff term of imprisonment. The German submarine U-19 did arrive off the coast of Kerry—but before the *Aud* could rendezvous with it. Sir Roger Casement was arrested shortly after being rowed ashore by German submariners. The police officer from the Royal Irish Constabulary who detained and searched Casement found a Berlin tram ticket in his possession for which he could offer no reasonable explanation. Casement was later executed for high treason at Pentonville Prison in London. His remains were repatriated to Ireland with full ceremonial in 1965. Casement aerodrome, headquarters of the Irish Air Corps, is named after him.

When Ireland was granted Dominion status in 1921, one of the important conditions attached to the Anglo-Irish agreement was that the maritime defence of the island was to be responsibility of the Royal Navy. Furthermore, the north-eastern part of the island was to remain under British jurisdiction. In the words of Dr Hal Kearsley, "in the military sense, Ireland guards Britain's back door and despite Ireland's assurances, the British would rather hold the key than put it into Irish hands."[7] The British have never underestimated the maritime significance of Ireland. When Britain granted self-determination to the 2.8 million people of Southern Ireland, it was not to be at the expense of the maritime security of Great Britain's 41 million inhabitants or its links with the 436 million peoples of the British Empire and Commonwealth.

Regardless of these rather unpleasant geo-strategic realities, in the inter-war period, no serious effort was made by successive Irish governments to establish a coastguard service, a mercantile marine, a deep-sea fishing industry or a coast defence force. Even after the Royal Navy evacuated the Treaty ports (see pp. 61-4), little serious interest was attached to developing a maritime defence force. In reality, such a scheme would have been prohibitively expensive and unnecessary, as Ireland's offshore waters were guarded by the Royal Navy. This implicit reliance on Britain to defend Ireland from external seaborne attack has inhibited any attempt by Ireland to develop a maritime-orientated defence policy. In contrast the experience of other small maritime countries has been quite different.

THE EXPERIENCE OF OTHER COUNTRIES

Europe

Iceland in contrast to Ireland is not geographically adjacent to its former colonial master. In addition, the relationship between the Danes and the Icelanders was not as long and antagonistic as that between the Irish and the British. Indeed, in 1918 Iceland was granted considerable autonomy by the Danish government, a process which permitted the Icelanders to develop their own fishery protection service. When in 1944, the Danish government in exile acceded to the demand for independence, the Icelanders by virtue of the country's physical isolation from Denmark, were obliged to build up their own mercantile marine and a highly efficient coastguard service. In Iceland, the sea is seen as the main source of the country's livelihood and the coastguard is a symbol of nationhood. After all, this highly respected institution has "fought" and won three "Cod" Wars with the Royal Navy. Iceland's decision not to establish an army or an air force has allowed the government to concentrate all available resources on building up a seaborne coastguard service. In contrast, Ireland's experiences are the inverse of those of Iceland.

In Ireland, defence is a land affair. While other island or maritime countries possess navies which are often one-third the size of their regular armies, the Irish have historically concentrated meagre resources on land and not maritime-orientated defence. This was for understandable reasons, for example, the prohibitive costs involved in financing naval defence, the absence of a perceived external threat and most importantly the unofficial protective cover provided by the Royal Navy. In Ireland the Army is seen as a symbol of political sovereignty attained. Unlike the Naval Service, the Army can trace its origins to the insurrectionists of 1916; many Army barracks in Ireland are, in fact, named after IRA activists from this period. Nearly every county and large town has an army training centre, while there are only four very small naval reservist centres in the whole country. The naval reserve currently consists of only 432 officers and men, while the army reserve can muster 16,000 men and women.

It is ironic that while Ireland, an island with over 1900 miles of coastline, possesses such a modest navy, other nations without any coastlines still see the need for maintaining naval forces. Until 1968, Hungary, a landlocked central European state possessed a navy, that is, until the Danube flotilla was transferred to the army. During the Second World War, the country's wartime ruler was an admiral. Prior to entering the political arena, Admiral Horthy was a senior officer in the former Austro-Hungarian Imperial navy—a force which operated from ports on the Adriatic coast. Today, the Hungarian armed forces still maintain a maritime brigade comprising 400 officers and men. They patrol 420km of the River Danube with a fleet of six river minesweepers, 45 river patrol craft and one transport barge. Similarly, Switzerland, although a landlocked country, operates a force of six 11-metre long Reliance-type patrol craft and 11 Aquarius class 5.2-ton patrol boats. These are stationed on Lakes Geneva, Constance and Maggiore. In addition to these 17 patrol craft, a marine company is based at each of these locations.

Latin America

The political importance attached to possessing a navy is no more evident than in Bolivia. This landlocked high Andean state continues to retain a navy even though Bolivia lost its coastline to Chile during the Pacific War of 1879-84. Today, the *Armada Boliviana* is confined to patrolling Lake Titicaca and navigable inland rivers. Regardless of its geographic circumstances, Bolivia is sub-divided into five naval districts, each with one flotilla of patrol craft. The 5000 officers and men of this landlocked navy are commanded by a vice-admiral. These men operate a formidable fleet of 26 patrol craft, three transport/survey vessels and one hospital ship. In addition, Bolivia has an independent marine corps, in which most of its marines belong to the Almirante Grau Battalion. The Bolivian navy even has a maritime aviation branch (land-based, of course) comprising eight Helibras helicopters and one Cessna 402-C maritime patrol aircraft.[8]

The existence of such a large inland navy is not viewed with derision in Bolivia, but on the contrary is seen as proof of the country's determination to regain the lost Pacific ports of Antofagasta, Cobija, Tocopilla and Mejillones. In a country where all official maps only show the pre-1879 Bolivian frontier, no government would dare contemplate disbanding the navy. To do so would be seen as abandoning the national goal of regaining the lost Pacific territories. Bolivia's enduring desire to regain these ports is not unique. Other countries have long existing territorial grievances as well, for example, Poland over the cities of Vilnius and Lvov, Japan over the Kurile Islands and Finland over Karelia.

Bolivia's southern neighbour, Paraguay, is another country which regardless of its geographic circumstances has developed a significant navy. This inland state is only connected with the open sea by way of the River Paraguay, which flows south along the Argentinian-Brazilian border. Yet even though Paraguay is a virtually landlocked country, it possesses a formidable riverine and sea-going navy. This 3680 man navy (including 500 marines) comprises 18 patrol ships/craft, seven support vessels, two transport ships, two landing craft and seven naval aircraft.[9] These forces operate from four naval bases on the River Paraguay. In comparison, Ireland's approach to naval and maritime affairs must seem incomprehensible to the officers and men of these navies. The Bolivians dream of once again being able to operate from a seaport, while the Paraguan navy is confined to river patrol duties or sea-going voyages which obilge it to transit Argentinian/Brazilian territory.

IRISH MARITIME ENDEAVOUR

Polar explorers and submarine inventors

Irish maritime endeavour was not confined to serving in overseas navies. Irishmen have been found in the forefront of polar exploration as well. In 1845, the Royal Navy sent two former coastal bombardment ships, HMS *Erebus* and HMS *Terror*, into the Canadian Arctic to discover the North-West Passage, that is, the route from Hudson Bay to the Bering Strait. The expedition was led by a veteran of Trafalgar, Sir John Franklin. His second-in-command was an Irishman Captain Francis Crozier from Banbridge, Co. Down. The expedition was a complete disaster as both ships became trapped in the ice flows. All of the expedition members perished, even though some did resort to cannibalism. The Royal Navy made frantic efforts to search for Franklin and his men: a total of 39 expeditions were sent into the Canadian Arctic to look for survivors but to no avail. One of those active in the search was Sir Robert McClure from Wexford. In 1850 this Irishman, who was born next door to Wexford's famous White's Hotel, was the first person to discover the North-West Passage. In recognition of his courage and skill as a mariner, the French and British geographical societies awarded him their gold medals.

Probably the most famous polar explorer from Ireland was Ernest Shackleton. He led four Antarctic expeditions and in 1909 reached within 160km of the South Pole. During his third expedition to the Antarctic,

Shackleton's ship became ice-bound for over nine months. After this period of confinement their ship, the *Endurance*, began to sink. This obliged them to drift for five months on the ice before they reached landfall on the desolate Elephant Island. In order to avoid certain starvation and death, Shackleton decided to seek out relief by sailing in one of *Endurance*'s lifeboats from Antarctica to the island of South Georgia. During this epic voyage, Shackleton was accompanied by *Endurance*'s second officer, Tom Crean, who was also Irish. Shackleton reached South Georgia and thanks to his efforts the lives of his fellow explorers on Elephant Island were saved. Shackleton died in 1922 during another Antarctic expedition.

The role of the submarine in modern naval warfare is without parallel. During the First World War, the early U-boats nearly starved Britain into defeat. During the Second World War, it was the threat posed by the U-boat which caused Churchill the greatest concern. In the Far East, it was the US Navy's submarine-imposed blockade that forced Japan to submit. The atomic bombs certainly had a terrifying psychological effect, but it was the US Navy's submariners who starved Japan's war industries of vital fuels and raw materials.

One person who was in the forefront of submarine development was an Irishman named John P. Holland. Born in Liscannor, Co. Clare, in 1841, he emigrated to the USA in 1873 and settled in Boston. In the 1880s and 1890s, Holland struggled without official financial backing to develop a submersible torpedo boat. In 1893, Holland submitted his plans to the US Navy, but because of interference from naval engineers his vessel, the *Plunger*, was not a success. Five years later, the US Secretary for the navy, Theodore Roosevelt, gave Holland's ideas a sympathic hearing. As a result, on 11 April 1900, USS *Holland* was commissioned into service as the United States Navy's first submarine. The *Holland*-class experimental submarine was 53 feet in length and had a displacement of 74 tons. It was armed with three torpedoes which could only be fired from its single tube. It cost $150,000 to build.[10] This little craft ushered in a new and terrifying age of naval warfare. Small underwater craft such as the USS *Holland* had the capability to sink battleships and blockade ports.

It is quite clear that the Irish contribution to international maritime history has been disproportionately large for such a small European nation. Irishmen established the navies of three Latin American republics and of the United States, a navy which would come to dominate the world's oceans. Irishmen's involvement in maritime affairs has also extended to polar exploration, submarine development and mercantile shipping.

EARLY BEGINNINGS, 1921-39

Ireland's geographic proximity to Britain has dominated British defence planning since the days of the Spanish Armada. The Roman Empire may have decided not to occupy the Emerald Isle, but England could not afford to withdraw from it in case a powerful maritime enemy should elect to use the island as an invasion platform. For the British, this fearful scenario was resurrected during the Napoleonic Wars, when French armies seemed intent on attacking Britain through Ireland. In fact several unsuccessful landings were attempted by the French. This threat prompted the British government to fortify the important natural deep-water harbours and to garrison Ireland with thousands of regular troops. The geo-strategic importance of Ireland was firmly inbedded in the minds of successive British governments.

During the First World War, Ireland's ports and sheltered deep water harbours were of enormous assistance to the British and American navies in their campaign against the German U-boat. Not only were trans-Atlantic convoys successfully assembled in Irish ports and escorted across the ocean, but anti-submarine and minesweeping operations were conducted from Irish ports. The Royal Navy operated 13 E, D, and H class submarines off the west coast of Ireland. These vessels hunted U-Boats and sunk them with surface gun fire.[1] Most significantly the Royal Navy had 557 armed yachts, trawlers, whalers, drifters and motor launches in Irish waters.[2] Nine airships operating from two different air stations were also on duty. In October 1914 the 1st and 4th Battle Squadrons and the 2nd Destroyer Flotilla of the British Grand Fleet were moved from the fleet's main base at Scapa Flow in the Orkney Islands to the safety of Lough Swilly in Co. Donegal. Later on, the battleships *Emperor of India* and *Barham* of the 4th Battle Squadron would be moved to Berehaven in south-west Ireland.[3]

During the First World War the following naval forces were based in Ireland:

Queenstown Force: 1   light cruiser
              37   destroyers

	4	torpedo boats
	11	sloops
	9	minesweepers
	1	decoy ship
North Coast of Ireland:	27	destroyers
	12	sloops
	1	decoy ship
West Coast of Ireland:	3	American battleships (based at Berehaven)
	13	submarines (based at Berehaven)
Naval Aviation:	24	seaplanes at Bantry Bay
	18	seaplanes at Wexford
	24	seaplanes at Queenstown (Cobh)
	24	seaplanes at Lough Foyle

There were also kite balloon stations at Berehaven and Lough Swilly.[4]

The First World War highlighted Britain's achilles' heel, namely that a densely populated industrial island state is completely dependent on a free flow of seaborne mercantile traffic if it is to keep its population adequately fed and its industries supplied with fuel and raw materials. If an enemy power had succeeded in severing these mercantile lifelines, then Great Britain could have been starved into submission. Britain was not, but the experience of submarine warfare left an indelible mark on the British. In the wake of the Allied victory over the Central Powers, Britain was confronted with a crisis in Ireland. The First World War had allowed previously subject nations such as the Czechs, Poles, Finns and Baltic peoples to strive for national self-determination; now Britain was faced with a similar demand from the Irish. In 1914, Britain agreed to the concept of Irish Home Rule, but this threatened to provoke an armed rebellion from Ireland's unionists. Most of these were concentrated in the north-east, within the ancient province of Ulster. Their opposition to Irish independence was prompted by a fear of being subsumed into a State where they might suffer the same fate as other ethno-religious minority groups in the newly created republics of post-war Central/Eastern Europe. The onset of the World War intervened to prevent further conflict in Ireland; but in 1916, an armed rebellion by Irish nationalists was put down with considerable force. By 1919, the nationalist Sinn Féin party had won a landslide victory (except in the north-east of Ireland) and now demanded an all-Ireland republic: armed conflict with Britain ensued. In 1921, anxious for a settlement of this matter, Britain's coalition government, led by one of the victors of Versailles, Lloyd George, sat down with an Irish delegation to negotiate a settlement. The end product was the 1921 Anglo-Irish Treaty.

During the course of their negotiations, the British government made it clear that although they would concede Dominion status to Ireland, they would not coerce the newly created statelet of Northern Ireland into an all-Ireland republic or relinquish the strategically important naval bases. To press home the significance of these ports, Lloyd George invited the Royal Navy's most distinguished officer, Admiral Beatty, to impress upon Michael Collins their importance to Britain. According to Winston Churchill, during the course of these discussions with Admiral Beatty, Collins commented "Of course you must have the ports—they are necessary for your life."[5] Collins knew that in the recent world war Britain had lost over 11 million tons of merchant and naval shipping. Unlike many of his contemporaries, Collins was no doctrinaire nationalist but a courageous pragmatist who had a clear grasp of the strategic value of these naval facilities to Britain. He seemed to appreciate that the British could not and would not concede on the issue of naval facilities in Ireland.

Britain's rights to naval bases in post-Independence Ireland were guaranteed under Articles 6 and 7 of the Anglo-Irish Treaty. The details of these articles are as follows:

ARTICLE 6 Until an arrangement has been made between the British and Irish Governments whereby the Irish Free State undertakes her own coastal defence, the defence of Great Britain and Ireland shall be undertaken by His Majesty's Imperial Forces, but this shall not prevent the construction or maintenance by the Government of the Irish Free State of such vessels as are necessary for the protection of the revenue or the fisheries.

ARTICLE 7 The Government of the Irish Free State shall afford to HM Imperial Forces—in time of peace, harbours and other facilities as indicated or such facilities as may be from time to time agreed. In time of war—such harbour and other facilities as the British Government may require.

The specific facilities were listed in an Annex as:

1. Dockyard port at Berehaven—the Admiralty property was retained and harbour defences remained in the charge of British care and maintenance parties.

2. Queenstown (renamed Cobh)—harbour defences remained in British care and maintenance and certain buoys were retained for use by HM ships.

3. Belfast Lough and Lough Swilly—harbour defences to remain in British care and maintenance.

4. Oil fuel storage at Haulbowline and Rathmullan (Lough Swilly, Co. Donegal) to be offered for sale to commercial concerns under a guarantee that they maintain a certain minimum stock of fuel for Admiralty requirements.

5. Aviation—facilities in the neighbourhood of the named ports for coastal and air defence.

THE IRISH CIVIL WAR

In the wake of the signing of the Anglo-Irish Treaty British military forces began to evacuate Southern Ireland. In the process they handed over their fortified barracks and military posts to whoever was available to unburden them of these premises. During the course of the British withdrawal, a 700-ton cargo vessel, the *Upnor*, which was under charter to the British government, was seized by what would later become known as Irregular elements of the IRA. The *Upnor* was transporting arms and ammunition from Haulbowline Island to Portsmouth when, on 29 March 1922, she was seized (the consignment consisted of 1500 rifles, 55 Lewis machine-guns, six Maxim machine-guns, three Vickers machine-guns, 1000 revolvers, 1000 pistols, 3000 grenades and over half a million rounds ammunition). The cargo vessel did not have a naval escort or armed naval personnel on board when it became a victim of marine piracy. Personnel from Cork's No. 1 Brigade of the IRA had commandeered a tug, the *Warrior*, and forced the cargo vessel to turn about and make for Ballycotton Bay. It was a well-organised operation as lorries were waiting at the quayside in Ballycotton to carry the arms away. The seizure of the *Upnor* took place three days after 200 IRA officers at an Army Convention had repudiated the new Irish parliament. Nearly three months earlier this parliament had voted to accept the Anglo-Irish Treaty. In April, another but smaller consignment of arms was smuggled in to Ring Pier, near Dungarvan, Co. Waterford. These weapons had come from Bremen, Germany[6] (a consignment arranged by an IRA activist from Derry, Charlie McGuinness; in November 1921, he arranged for a smaller consignment of arms to be smuggled into Co. Waterford from Hamburg). In view of the fact that Britain had agreed to disengage from most of Ireland, the arrival of such large quantities of arms into the hands of non-government forces did not bode well for the future.

By June 1922 the British military were only present in the Dublin area and in the harbours granted to them under articles 6 and 7 of the Treaty. The Provisional government in Dublin held a tenuous hold on its new state and its legitimacy was being constantly challenged by the IRA. This unsatisfactory situation came to a head when on 28 June the armed Irregulars occupying the architectural splendour of the Four Courts in central Dublin were presented with an ultimatum to surrender. Their refusal obliged the newly constituted National Army to eject them by force. This event is commonly cited as the date on which the Irish Civil War started.

The Four Courts' garrison of 150 Irregulars succumbed within two days to the superior firepower of the Free State army's British-supplied artillery. However, the Provisional government had to assert its sovereignty over the whole of the 26 counties of Ireland that constituted the Free State. In the course of this struggle, the Army Council and local military commanders recognised that Ireland's maritime circumstances acted greatly in their favour. The fact that the country was an island argued in favour of the combatant who had access to shipping. Not only could inland strongholds be circumvented by the rapid movement of troops and war material by ship to government-controlled seaports, but captured Irregulars could be safely moved by ship back to secure prison accommodation in Dublin.

The Irish Civil War was not characterised by pitched battles fought between field armies; rather it was quite similar to the previous Anglo-Irish War. However, in this campaign the anti-Treatyite guerrilla fighters faced an Irish army which had the support of an increasing percentage of the population, especially among prosperous farmers and the middle classes who yearned for an end to the anarchy. Most importantly, the Provisional government had the support of the Roman Catholic Church. In this campaign the Army Council exhibited a great deal more tactical and strategic resource and guile than the British in the Anglo-Irish war. In addition, the Provisional government introduced draconian measures to suppress the rebellion, for example, summary execution of suspects without right or recourse to a trial. Seventy-seven Irregulars were executed (twice the number shot by the British), one of whom was Erskine Childers, the man who masterminded the Howth gun-running and who later attended the Anglo-Irish peace talks in London.

The Provisional government's military goal was unambiguous, namely the suppression of armed rebellion by the republicans against the new Irish State. To achieve this aim the 4000 strong National Army was quickly expanded to a strength of 60,000. Ten thousand British rifles were handed over to what Winston Churchill called "trustworthy Free State troops".[7] Britain also supplied the Free State army with artillery and armoured cars. Recruitment was not difficult as the onset of the post-war economic slump had created very high levels of unemployment. Nearly one thousand volunteers a day were recruited, many of whom had former service in the British Army. It was primarily an infantry-orientated army, although separate support arms and services were established.

The role of military aviation

Two months after the Royal Air Force evacuated Baldonnel aerodrome, in February 1922, it was re-occupied by Free State troops. At the time, the only military aircraft in Irish service was a Martinsyde A MK II, which had been purchased prior to the signing of the Anglo-Irish Treaty. Its purchase had been prompted by the need to provide Michael Collins with an effective means of escape from London should the Anglo-Irish talks fail. The Free State's new air force was entitled the Irish Air Service, and it was to be an integral part of the National Army. Initially the Air Service only had two pilots. These were former RAF pilots who had seen service in World War One. However, by the end of the year, the two aviators, C.F. Russell and M.J. McSweeney, were to be joined by a further 12 pilots. All of them had much needed flying and wartime experience with the Royal Flying Corps and the RAF. In July, the Air Service took delivery of three ex-RAF Bristol fighters and by December another five Bristols fighters were handed over by Britain. Before the end of the civil war, Britain had supplied the Free State government with six DH9 bombers, six Avro 504Ks and three more Martinsyde F4s.[8]

These aircraft operated not only from Baldonnel, but from airstrips in Waterford, Kilkenny. Limerick, Fermoy, and Tralee. The first recorded use of military aircraft in the civil war was an air sortie against rebels in Dundalk in August 1922. The Air Service also undertook coastal patrols: the whole coastal area from Waterford to Kenmare Bay was constantly patrolled by Air Service aircraft. The day before the seaborne landings at Cork, Col. C.F. Russell flew over the city to reconnoitre the positions of anti-government forces. The use of military aircraft allowed the Dublin government to patrol the coasts of "rebel Cork", as well as to maintain contact with isolated garrisons, regardless of disrupted inland communications.[9] The anti-Treatyites did not have any military aircraft in service.

The role of military shipping

Initially the military balance was perilous as the Irregulars held sway over most of the west and south of Ireland. Even in Dublin, they had not been decisively defeated, rather they had gone to ground. The Free State's two main port cities, Limerick and Cork, were under the control of the Irregulars, and the River Shannon was beyond the Dublin government's control. It was General Michael Brennan, the Free State military commander in the Limerick area, who correctly summed up the situation: "the Shannon was a barricade and whoever held Limerick held the South and the West."[10] Gen. Brennan firmly believed and with much justification that the outcome of the Irish Civil War turned on Limerick. The Irregulars, although numerically stronger and in possession of most of the

Free State territory, did not move on Dublin. They surrendered the initiative to the National Army's forces and embarked on a systematic plan of destruction of all communications and anything that might be of assistance to the Free State army. In the course of this campaign of destruction, which in the words of the Conference of Roman Catholic Bishops "wrecked Ireland from end to end", the country's transport infrastructure was devastated: 236 bridges were damaged; 468 railway locomotives, carriages and other rolling stock were destoyed.[11] The great railway viaduct over the Blackwater at Mallow linking Cork with the north was blown up. The reign of anarchy, which left factories and creameries destroyed and period mansion houses with their priceless art treasures burnt out, obliged the Provisional government to restore order as quickly as possible. In order to avoid a zone of isolation being created beyond the effective jurisdiction of Dublin, military formations were to be moved by sea thus avoiding a long and possibly costly overland advance.

Seaborne operations west of the Shannon

On 21 July 1922 Waterford was occupied by Free State forces advancing overland. Limerick fell on 27 July after being shelled. The Irregulars burned their abandoned barracks and fled. The 600 Irregulars who were captured were eventually sent to secure prison accommodation in Dublin. Gen. Brennan, mindful of the importance of the Shannon, positioned six river patrol boats at the entrance to the estuary in order to ensure greater security for the port. Some of the river patrol boats were manned by Gaelic-speaking Aran Islanders. Further north in Co. Donegal, Free State troops under Commandant General Sweeney had cleared the Irregulars out Ballyshannon and Bundoran on 29 June. Early in July the Inishowen peninsula bordering the British Treaty port of Lough Swilly was quickly secured in a skilful pincer movement. During these operations the small British garrison at Fort Dunree and a Royal Navy destroyer which happened to be steaming up Lough Swilly at the time did not intervene. With the fall of Glenveagh Castle on 27 July, Ireland's most northerly county had been pacified. In Lough Swilly a government-chartered steamer performed a dual role early on in the conflict, namely, the transportation of an outward cargo of military supplies and a return consignment of 40 recently captured prisoners. These anti-Treatyites (many of whom were from neighbouring Derry) were shipped back to Kilmainham military prison in Dublin.

By mid-July the city of Galway was under government control, although the influence of the Free State army was limited in the surrounding countryside. However, the effective strength of the Irregulars in the west of Ireland was soon to be neutralised by the landing of troops at Westport, Co. Mayo. After the success of this landing, the important western towns of Castlebar and Ballina came under Free State control. In Sligo, government forces still suffered from harassment even though the town garrison had been reinforced on 21 July. The military commander Colonel Commandant McCabe, used a small coaster, the *Tartar*, to escort the local ferryboat which plied between Sligo and Rosses Point in Co. Donegal. In the course of this seaborne escort duty the Free State troops on board the *Tartar* were fired on from the Irregular positions on the shoreline. In one engagement a 20-minute gun battle took place between the *Tartar* and Irregulars on board old hookers and curraghs (small fishing craft) from Co. Donegal. The *Tartar* must have had the upper hand during such encounters as not only was she equipped with a Lewis gun, but the vessel's superstructure was protected by a patchwork of iron shutters. This form of protective armour made the *Tartar* ressemble one of General Grant's ironclad gunboats from the American Civil War. The *Tartar* was also employed as a supply ship for isolated garrisons along the coast of Co. Mayo, such as Ballina.[12]

The Cork landings

The fall of Limerick to the Free State army allowed General Dalton to persuade the National Army Staff to agree to a series of bold seaborne landings instead of a laborious campaign through the countryside. On the evening of Monday 31 July, 450 officers and men of the Dublin Guards boarded the steam packet *Lady Wicklow* at South Wall in the Port of Dublin. These soldiers, together with an armoured car and an 18-pounder field gun, were bound for Fenit in the south-west of Ireland. According to Niall Harrington, one of the young soldiers on board the temporary troopship, "the misery was total and is an abiding memory with me. To step on to a companionway to a lower deck, was to slither on vomit into an abyss of them having their first taste of what the sea has to offer and what it expects in return."[13] The young Harrington played a significant role in the operation, as he was the only person on board who had an intimate knowledge of Fenit harbour and the environs of Tralee. Fenit was only a village, but its pier extended 600 yards out to sea and ships of up to 5000 tons could off-load their cargo alongside the pier and into railway wagons; it was a busy port, as ships called in from Britain, Europe and even the Americas. Niall Harrington (1901–81) later became the OC of the Marine Service; he retired from the Irish Army in 1959 as deputy to the Director of G2 (Intelligence) Branch of GHQ.

The anti-government garrison in Fenit consisted of only 20 men armed with rifles, grenades and a single machine-gun. However, they had mined the pier. When the *Lady Wicklow* came into view, all troops were ordered below decks. The pilot, a man named Fitzgerald, was ordered at gunpoint to bring the ship into port. The Irregulars were not too perturbed by the

1 The *ad hoc* troopship *Lady Wicklow*

sight of a civilian vessel, as Fenit was a commercial port. When the vessel came alongside, Free State troops suddenly stormed onto the pier and occupied the village. Some of the Irregulars put up resistance, but machine-gunners on the *Lady Wicklow* discharged such a volume of suppressive fire that resistance was quickly overwhelmed. An attempt to blow up the pier was foiled, when the detonating cable leading to the pier was quickly severed by a villager, sympathic to the Free State cause. Tralee with its good harbour was captured after only encountering limited resistance. According to the official communique from Army General Headquarters (GHQ) on 4 August in the course of the Fenit landing only "three of the troops were slightly wounded".[14] However, in characteristic form the retreating Irregulars destroyed the old military barracks. The following day at 3.00 a.m. 300 Free State soldiers belonging to Gen. Brennan's command were ferried across the Shannon in three small fishing vessels. They landed at Tarbert in Co. Kerry and thus secured both sides of the Shannon Estuary. In a separate operation 140 Free State soldiers under General Hogan sailed on board the vessel *Corona* and 100 other Free State troops sailed in smaller boats; their objective was the capture of Ballylongford and Listowel. As Hogan's small force moved southwards, Daly's troops advanced east towards Castleisland and Farranfore.

The most spectacular and strategically important seaborne landings took place on 7 August 1922, only four days after the fall of Tralee. As Gen. Dalton had correctly argued, a landward advance was totally impractical because of the level of disrupted communications. Therefore, a seaborne landing afforded the Free State authorities the opportunity of shattering any attempt by the Irregulars of establishing a rival Irish state with its temporary capital in Cork. Two Irish steam packets (cross-channel ferries) were commandeered and used as *ad hoc* troopships. They were the *Arvonia* of the London and North Western Railway Company, and the *Lady Wicklow* of the British and Irish Steam Packet Co. The two ships left Dublin on 6 August and while en route to Cork were challenged by a Royal Navy patrol. Gen. Dalton who was on board the *Arvonia* informed the British naval picket of his destination and the nature of his operation. The British naval officer on board the picket ship advised Gen. Dalton of the need for a deep sea pilot if he was to take the troopships into Cork harbour.[15] (During the Civil War consideration was given by the British government to using the Royal Navy to help the Free State Army. However, it was decided that such an action was unnecessary and would only embarrass the Provisional government in Dublin. The Royal Navy remained aloof during the conflict, although its presence dominated Ireland's coastal waters.)

The entrance to Cork harbour was not undefended, as the Irregulars had mined the upper reaches to Cork. They had also commandeered two

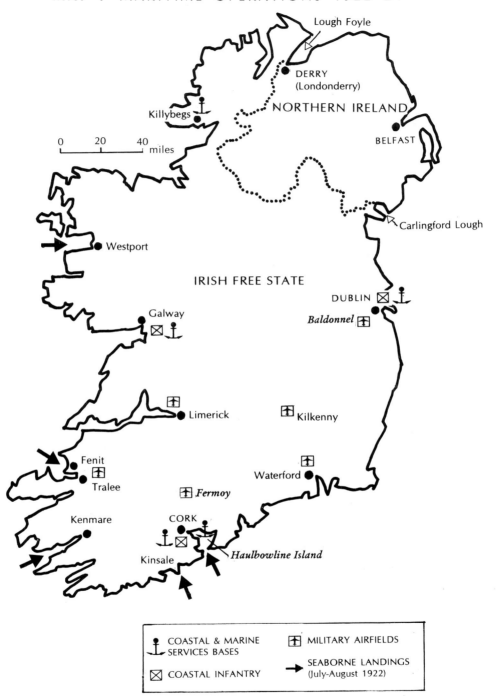

MAP 1 MARITIME OPERATIONS 1922–24

Lough Foyle

DERRY
(Londonderry)

NORTHERN IRELAND

Killybegs

BELFAST

0   20   40
miles

Carlingford Lough

Westport

IRISH FREE STATE

DUBLIN

Baldonnel

Galway

Limerick

Kilkenny

Fenit

Waterford

Tralee

Fermoy

Kenmare

CORK

Kinsale

Haulbowline Island

COASTAL & MARINE
SERVICES BASES

MILITARY AIRFIELDS

COASTAL INFANTRY

SEABORNE LANDINGS
(July-August 1922)

"hoppers" from the Cork Harbour Commissioners and mounted Lewis guns and armed soldiers on them. These small vessels were moored on either side of the channel and were styled "Republican Dreadnoughts". A makeshift boom was erected at a point between Passage West and Blackrock Castle, three miles inland from the reserve territory of the Royal Naval facility at Haulbowline. When the *Lady Wicklow* and the *Arvonia* rounded Limekiln Point, two miles down the channel, they were spotted by the Irregulars. One of the commandeered hoppers, the *Owenacurra*, which was three times bigger than its sister vessel, was placed in mid-channel and scuttled. The deep-sea pilot who had originally advised Gen. Dalton not to bring his vessels into Cork, helped the master of the *Arvonia* to safely navigate past the partly submerged *Owenacurra*. The Free State forces landed at three separate locations—Youghal, Passage West and Union Hall in Cork city. At Union Hall the Irregulars who had partly destroyed the pier fired on the incoming Free State troops as they came ashore in small boats.[16] Once ashore the Irregulars abandoned their firing positions in the old coastguard station and fled. At Passage West, troops and military supplies including armoured cars and artillery were unloaded. Gen. Dalton's audacious landing had cost the lives of only seven of his soldiers. The Irregulars lost six dead. Fifty prisoners were seized, the remainder fled after leaving a trail of destruction in their wake. The Royal Naval Hospital and the Admiralty House from where the World War One convoy strategies had been planned, were burnt down. The Victoria (now Collins) barracks was also burnt out. Much of the commercial district suffered greatly as well.

Although the landing was a success the British Admiralty continued to advise commercial traffic to be wary of sailing into Cork harbour because of the prevalence of Irregular snipers. One vessel which was obviously unaware of the fighting was the cargo ship SS *City of Dortmund* from Antwerp. As the vessel entered Cork harbour on the same day as the landings had occurred it was swept by machine gun and rifle fire. The remarkable, courageous captain managed to navigate his vessel through the sniper fire and past the scuttled wreck of the *Owenacurra*. Unfortunately for the *City of Dortmund*'s captain the anarchic situation in Cork obliged him to take his cargo to Dublin for customs clearance.[17]

The Kenmare and Kinsale landings

Less than five days after Gen. Dalton's forces had successfully secured Cork, another ambitious seaborne operation was initiated. At 9.00 p.m. on 11 August the *Margret*, a 600-ton coaster, cast off from Limerick's South Quay with a military force under the command of Gen. MacManus. In order to ensure maximum secrecy for the operation the Free State troops aboard the *Margret* did not arrive at the quayside until a short time before the vessel was to depart. The *Margret* sailed down the Shannon for 12 miles until it reached the prearranged rendezvous point with its sister ship at Ballylongford. The vessel in question, the *Mermaid*, a former river pleasure craft, was taken in tow by the *Margret* and sailed out into the open sea and both vessels made their way past the Skellig Islands. The rough seas and the inclement weather made conditions for those aboard the *Mermaid* unpleasant. Eventually the objective of their sea journey became visible—Kenmare Bay. One of the senior officers aboard the *Margret*, Commandant O'Connor, was a native of this locality. He and a small reconnaissance party were put ashore at Coogmar harbour, a small bay on the northern end of the Kenmare river. They spotted 30 Irregulars encamped at a former coastguard station three miles east of where they had landed. To ensure surprise, the entire force disembarked without incident at Coogmar harbour and advanced inland towards the coastguard station. Startled by the sudden and unexpected arrival of Free State soldiers, the Irregulars set fire to the coastguard station and fled Kenmare.[18]

Two weeks later on 25 August, the historic port of Kinsale was captured when 150 Free State troops under Commandants Bryne and Hale landed in open boats and chased out the Irregulars. Predictably the Irregulars left a trail of devastation in the form of burnt-out police and coastguard stations, and the 17th-century military barracks at Charles Fort.

By the end of August 1922 the military situation had altered considerably for the Provisional government. Thanks to several audacious sea-borne landings and the continued use of various forms of shipping, the Irish Free State army had significantly reduced the ability of the Irregulars to challenge the new government in Dublin. All the main coastal towns and port cities were in government hands; the Irregular strongholds in the south-west were hemmed in by Free State garrisons on the coast. The Civil War continued until a unilateral ceasefire was declared by the rebels on 23 March 1923. Even after this some sporadic resistance continued and the threat of further violence prevailed—a factor which contributed to the decision to form a coastal patrol service.

COASTAL AND MARINE SERVICES

In May 1923 the Irish Civil War was coming to end. However, the risk of continued violence and insurrection prompted the Irish government to establish a coastal patrol service. The role of the Coastal and Marine Service (CMS) was to interdict gun-runners and provide the State with a fishery protection service. Although the 1921 Treaty had denied the Irish

Free State the rights of Admiralty, the country was allowed to possess a force of coastal vessels for the protection of revenue and fisheries. The commander of Ireland's new seaborne coastguard type service was an army officer, Major General Joseph Vize. Two army colonels acted as quartermaster and adjutant, and an experienced master mariner, Eamonn O'Connor, was appointed as Superintendent of sea-going operations. The headquarters of the CMS was located at Portobello barracks in Rathmines, Dublin. The Service comprised three branches—a coastal patrol service, a marine investigation department and coastal infantry units. The latter were army personnel, but they worked exclusively with the coastal patrol vessels of the CMS. The new coastal service had four bases—the recently evacuated Royal Naval facility at Haulbowline Island in Cork harbour, Dun Laoghaire (Kingstown), Galway and Killybegs in Co. Donegal.

Personnel for the new Service came mainly from the merchant marine. A total of 124 marine officers, 13 cadets and 219 ratings were recruited.[19] Most of these recruits were ex-Merchant navy. One of the sea captains was 70 years old.[20] The Army provided 15 officers—one major general, one commandant-general, one vice-brigadier, two colonels, two commandants, two captains, four lieutenants and two second lieutenants. The marine officers were not given formal naval ranks. There were six senior marine officers—two superintendents and four shore captains. These were assisted by 118 deck and engineering officers who all held merchant navy ranks and qualifications. Formal naval training was limited to some foot drill, gunnery and musketry practice. The level of training conducted at the Service's new depot and base on Haulbowline Island was very limited.

According to Eamonn O'Connor, the Service's senior marine superintendent, "the uniform for officers was a blue double-breasted jacket with half inch gold bands with a laurel leaf cap peak. Captains of patrol vessels had three bands, their chief officers two bands, and second officers, one band. The petty officers and ratings wore double-breasted reefers, pants, and jersey."[21] The cap badge for all ranks was the same as for all Free State army personnel, namely the letters FF (Fianna Fáil) mounted on a small ring, bearing the words "Oglaigh na hÉireann". This was mounted on a representation of a sunburst. The conventional use of an anchor in naval cap badges was not employed.

Coastal Infantry and Marine Investigation Department

In essence the Coastal and Marine Service was a temporary seaborne coastguard service. In its new internal security role, the CMS worked in conjunction with a new army formation—the Coastal Infantry. According to Eamonn O'Connor, "around the coast there was a string of signal stations manned by Coastal Infantry. A system of signals arranged and

2 SS *Dainty*

coded was in use and by means of these flag signals, all patrolling vessels could pick up information which governed their movement at sea."[22] Coastal Infantry was a short-lived formation as it was disbanded on 1 September 1923. The official communique of 23 October 1923 simply stated "that the duties previously carried out by these troops will be carried out by infantry battalions on the coast."[23] The Marine Investigation Department suffered a similar fate on 1 December 1923 when this branch of the CMS was disbanded. The 200 officers and men of the Marine Investigation Department had been responsible for monitoring the coast from Narrow Water in Carlingford Lough (on the Northern Ireland/Irish Free State border) round by the east, south and west coasts to Moville in the North on Lough Foyle (on the new frontier with Northern Ireland). Demobilisation of these *ad hoc* coastal forces was inevitable if one bears in mind that the Civil War had already ended and armed resistance to the new state had petered out. The devastated Irish economy could not shoulder the burden of a large army; consequently, phased reductions had to be implemented.

The Irish Free State's embryonic coastal navy possessed an impressive fleet of armed trawlers, river patrol craft, harbour auxiliaries and an armed deep sea tug (ex-Royal Navy). The CMS's fleet consisted of:

- one deep sea tug/patrol sloop
- one patrol vessel
- six Mersey-class trawlers
- six Canadian Castle-class trawlers
- two drifters: *Inisherer* and *John S. Somers*
- five chartered river patrol boats
- three 80-foot long motor launches (wooden): ML 1, ML 3, ML 4
- two steam launches (wooden): "190" and "199".[24]

The CMS's largest vessel was a 469-ton ocean-going tug, SS *Dainty*. She had formerly belonged to the British Admiralty and was handed over to the Irish Free State at Haulbowline. All of the patrol vessels were each armed with a single 12-pounder gun, while the smaller craft were mounted with light machine-guns on their foredecks. The *Dainty* in addition to being the designated leader of Coastal Patrol, was specially fitted out for salvage and towing duties. In fact in September 1923, the *Dainty* had just come out of dry dock at Haulbowline after a thorough overhauling. The *Murichu*, was formerly HM armed yacht *Helga II*, while one of the fast patrol launches, ML 1, was reputedly a former sub-chaser in the US Navy. Two of the river patrol boats were stationed on the Shannon, while one each was located at Waterford and on the River Lee; a fifth unit was kept in reserve. The armed trawlers were purchased from

3 CMS gunners man the *Dainty*'s 12-pounder gun

the Admiralty through Ross Street Foundry, Inverness. Officially the role of these armed trawlers was "controlling the coast and dispatching troops by water to the different parts of the coast". The trawlers were purchased from Britain in February 1923 and cost £87,000.[25] According to Eamonn O'Connor, "most of the trawlers had a crew of a captain and two officers with five deck petty officers, three engineroom petty officers, six deck ratings and six engineroom ratings".[26]

The Coastal and Marine Service's fleet of armed trawlers and river patrol craft was ideally suited to the needs of a poor and sparsely populated island state in the wake of a bitter civil war. The armed trawlers were a creditable deterrent against insurgent gun-runners and foreign fishing vessels. However, the need for urgent economies obliged the Irish government to disband the Coastal and Marine Service on 31 March 1924. All the Service's officers were either demobilised or transferred to the Army. The CMS's first and only OC, Major-Gen. J. Vize, was appointed deputy quartermaster general on 1 April 1924. The coastal patrol vessel *Murichu* was returned to the department of agriculture and fisheries; all the other vessels of the CMS were handed over to the Office of Public Works (OPW) to be either sold or scrapped at a later date.

In the words of Cmdr. T. McKenna: "So it would appear that the first Irish navy lasted only ten months and 27 days from 4 May 1923 to 31 March 1924."[27]

THE INTER-WAR PERIOD, 1924-38

With the disbandment of the Coastal and Marine Service, the Irish Free State had lost any physical means of effectively policing its coastal waters. The *Murichu*, the only government-owned armed ship, was fully preoccupied with the herculean task of protecting the Irish Free State's inshore fisheries. The disbandment of the Marine Investigation Department and the Army's coastal infantry formations had left the new state without an effective replacement for the comprehensive 109-station coastguard service which, prior to 1922, had been provided by HM Coastguard. An all-volunteer Coast Life Saving Service was set up by the department of industry and commerce in order to fulfill the new State's international obligation of providing a means of rescue for those driven ashore. However, sea rescues had to be performed by the Royal National Lifeboat Institution.

In 1926 the Ports and Harbours Tribunal was commissioned to report and recommend on administration and facilities in Irish ports. Published in 1930, the report was headed "Public Apathy in Port Affairs". Paragraph 4 of the report states: "We have however to record our regret at the apparent lack of interest in matters relating to the ports. The public generally do not, we fear, appreciate the importance of our harbours as a vital part of the country's economic structure and are prone to forget that the external trade of the Saorstát [Free State] is, with the exception of trade with Northern Ireland, entirely water borne and that inefficient harbour administration inevitably reacts on the trade, handicaps exporters and raises the cost of commodities imported."

Furthermore, the report highlighted the absence of any hydrographic survey machinery in the Irish Free State which would be capable of surveying the ports and their approaches and preparing up-to-date charts. The report went on to state that "the matter is one of great importance and the present neglect cannot be allowed to continue without risk of serious mishap and ultimate disadvantage to our trade. As an example of what is happening we were informed that ship owners have refused Charters for the Saorstát ports as a result of inaccurate information as to the depths of water given in the only available but obsolete charts." The report followed on by stating "we recommend that the State should take steps to have this important work kept up to date. It is a duty that which might well be assigned to a coast defence force, should one be ultimately established."

The coast defence force was not established, and the State's only sea-going vessel had been disarmed three years earlier in 1927. According to Commodore McKenna: "in 1935 the Irish Free State's only fishery protection vessel, the *Murichu*, was having so much difficulty in trying to arrest offending trawlers because they refused to believe that the boiler tube on the forward gun mounting was an actual gun." [28] In the same year, the *Murichu* was nearly sunk when a foreign trawler tried to ram her in Bantry Bay. Similarly, the *Murichu*'s attempts to police Irish fishery limits off the coast of Co. Donegal were viewed with contempt by trawlers from Britain.[29] Eventually the British Admiralty was petitioned for permission to mount a gun on the fishery cruiser. Permission was granted, but on the condition that solid shot should only be used; no high explosive (HE) shells were permitted to be carried.[30]

The *Murichu* was the only Irish vessel permitted to fly the flag of the Free State. All other vessels were subject to the 1894 Merchant Shipping Act which obliged all British and Commonwealth ships to fly the Red Ensign (commonly called the Red Duster). Any deviation from this would result in a fine. Section 73 of the 1894 Act prescribed that the fine should not exceed £500. Regardless of these British-imposed restrictions, the Irish nation in the words of Commodore McKenna "had turned our backs on the sea and on the sovereign territorial waters which lay seaward of the beach."[31]

To understand why there was this widespread indifference to maritime affairs within Irish society, one must appreciate both the economic

4 The *Murichu*

circumstances of the Irish Free State in the inter-war period and the historical legacy left by Britain. The Irish Free State may have achieved Canadian-style Dominion status but the country's geographic proximity to the industrial and economic monolith of Great Britain worked against any serious attempt to argue for separate maritime services. The Irish Free State was a sparsely populated (2.9 million) and poor country with an agricultural economy. Its island neighbour Great Britain possessed the largest mercantile marine in the world and the Royal Navy was rightfully acclaimed as the "Empress of the Seas". Therefore, in a country which had been dominated by England since the Middle Ages, and where the farming lobby had enormous influence, it was hardly surprising that there was little debate on establishing a navy. Also, one must appreciate that the Royal Navy was the naval protector of all Commonwealth Dominions. Therefore, the Irish Free State's reluctance to spend money on naval defence was echoed by other Dominions.

The Union of South Africa had a very long coastline bordering both the Indian and South Atlantic Oceans, yet the South African navy in 1924 was tiny. The defence of the strategically-important port cities of Durban, Port Elizabeth and Cape Town (Simonstown naval base) was in reality the responsibility of the Royal Navy. South Africa's sea-going fleet of two 325-ton minesweeping trawlers, one 800-ton survey ship (armed with a single 3 pdr) and three unarmed small auxiliary craft was unlikely to deter a possible act of aggression by a major naval power. Likewise, the vast Dominion of Canada possessed a relatively small navy—comprising of two submarines, four minesweeping trawlers, two destroyers and one light cruiser—to defend both its Pacific and Atlantic coastlines. However, Canada's Department of Marine and Fisheries did operate a fleet of 25 patrol vessels of varying size (one of these was named *Aranmore*, after the small island off Co. Donegal). These vessels had an onerous task as they were responsible for policing Arctic, Pacific and Atlantic waters in addition to their duties on the Great Lakes. In marked contrast to the relative small size of Canada's navy and fishery protection force, the offshore island Dominion of Newfoundland (which remained independent of Canada until 1949) possessed a significant coastal fleet. Under the control of the Newfoundland Ministry of Finance and Customs, the fleet comprised one 1250-ton sloop and 16 patrol vessels (ranging from 248 to 1055 tons).

Other sparsely populated maritime countries which did not benefit from the Royal Navy's protective presence did build up their own mercantile marine and coastal naval forces. The newly independent states of Estonia and Finland made enormous strides in these areas. In 1924 the 2100 officers and men of the Estonian navy manned two 1800-ton destroyers (ex-Imperial Russian navy), six gunboats and one torpedo boat. The Finnish navy operated three 3000-ton coast defence ships, two destroyers, two minelayers, six submarines and 30 coastal motor boats. An impressive achievement for a country of only 3.7 million people and which had been ravaged by civil war.[32]

In the Irish Free State no such strides were made because offshore naval defence was not the responsibility of the Irish government but of the Royal Navy's South Irish Flotilla. Under the terms of the 1921 Anglo-Irish Treaty, the Irish Free State was permitted "the construction or maintenance of such vessels as are necessary for the protection of the Revenue or the Fisheries". Unlike Newfoundland's fleet of 17 sea-going patrol vessels, the Irish Free State operated one 1908 vintage 325-ton inshore fishery cruiser. In 1932 some thought was given to form a "coastal defence force" that would provide for fishery protection, hydrographic survey and patrol duties. However, the proposal came to nothing primarily because of a shortage of funds. Another contributing factor was the advice given by fishery officers that no coastal motor boat (CMB) could operate off the south and west coasts of Ireland in winter. This advice was obviously ignored when in 1939 the Irish government placed an initial order for two motor torpedo boats from Thornycrofts in England. According to Commodore McKenna, who was an MTB O/C during World War Two, these boats were completely unsuited to the needs of an Irish maritime defence force.[33]

The 1936 appraisal of Irish defence needs

In May 1936, the G2 (Intelligence) Branch of the Irish Army produced a remarkable paper entitled "Fundamental Factors Affecting Saorstát Defence Problem". The paper was marked "secret", as its contents would have been quite unsettling to the general Irish populace. The paper stated that the fundamental factors affecting Irish defence were:

Geography and Ireland's strategic position

The Irish Free State's lack of potential for defence capacity, i.e. the absence of an Irish defence industry.

The general defence status of smaller states

Prevailing lack of knowledge as to Ireland's strategic and defence position.

According to G2 Branch, "just as Great Britain is a barrier to sea communications with Western Europe, so Ireland is a barrier 300 miles long to sea communications with Great Britain. Therefore, a hostile power in alliance with France and in control of Irish ports could threaten the survival of Great Britain." The paper went on to make the observation, which no doubt was in Lloyd George's mind in 1921, that "in the same way as Britain (in 1936) controlled access by water to Germany, the Baltic and the Low Countries, Ireland could similarly throttle Britain"— the act of maritime strangulation being carried out not by the Irish, but by a foreign naval power at war with Britain.

Such fearful scenarios were also in the minds of naval and defence planners in Britain. The Versailles Treaty had created a power vacuum in central Europe. What remained of the German navy after the scuttling of the Imperial fleet at Scapa Flow in 1919, was stripped of all of its submarines. Most of its medium and large cruisers and battleships were also scrapped. By 1920, the German navy was only suitable for coast defence. Similarly, the German army had been reduced to a force of 100,000 men comprising seven divisons. The German air force was disbanded and the country was forbidden to possess or manufacture offensive weapons, such as tanks. Great Britain was therefore faced with a Europe that was dominated by the might of the French army, in alliance with the equally large Polish army in the east. In this period the Royal Navy made contingency plans for war with France and even with the United States.[34]

According to Admiral Mahan, "communications dominate war—they are the single most important element in strategy. Of the world's sea communications, 75 per cent are located in the North Atlantic."[35] How prophetic these words were to be during the height of the Battle of the

Atlantic. Admiral Mahan went on to state that "in wars between maritime powers, strategic measures in the second category—those of an economic character assume a predominant importance, that is to say, the function of the fleet are exercised in attack and defence of seaborne trade." Ireland's role in such a conflict would be crucial. According to Major-General Bird, author of *The Direction of War*, it would be catastrophe if Ireland were to come under the control of a maritime power hostile to Great Britain.

The G2 officers were not only mindful of the threat posed to the Irish Free State by Britain's enemies, but by the problem of alerting Irish people to this potential threat. According to the paper, "because the external defence of Ireland has been in the practically unchallenged control of Great Britain for a long period, we [Irish] are sovereignty conscious but not security conscious." The G2 officers went on to state that "Irish people and even Free State public officials are largely ignorant of the the problems raised in this paper."

In the late 1920s, the Irish army acquired 4000 German-style "coalscuttle" steel helmets. The Versailles Treaty had made it impossible for the Irish Free State to acquire these helmets from Germany. Therefore, they were purchased via a Belgian firm.

The paper went on to outline the condition of the Irish Free State Army in 1936:

Effective strength (including reserves)	20,000 men
Available small arms	a) 21,354 modern rifles b) 15,666 older rifles c) 537 light automatics of an obsolete type d) 273 machine-guns Ten days' supply of rifle ammunition, five days' supply of ammunition for machine-guns and light automatics.
Artillery	36 pieces of artillery. Only a few days' supply of artillery ammunition.
Armoured vehicles	16 armoured fighting vehicles. Only two were rated as being in serviceable condition. The remainder were worn out and could not stand up to more than a few days' service.
Military aircraft:	Six in serviceable condition.

The G2 officers concluded that "these are the relative strengths of the land and air forces; the situation could hardly be more serious from our standpoint." All weapons, munitions and spare parts had to be imported. Unlike Estonia, Finland, Poland, Romania, Hungary and Switzerland, Ireland did not attempt to develop an arms industry in the inter-war period. Even bullets and explosives had to be imported.

In order for a strategically important island state such as Ireland to remain neutral, the G2 Branch recommended that "we should have to maintain naval forces on the scale of Holland, Norway, Sweden, Portugal or Belgium." The G2 officers discreetly noted that "Great Britain would probably be quite glad that we should take over these coastal defence activities, even on a considerable scale." Furthermore, Great Britain would probably expect that the Irish Free State should undertake the aerial activities necessary for coastal defence. The question of Irish involvement in coast defence had been raised in 1927, but the British refused to discuss the handing over of the Treaty ports and their defences on the grounds that they were integral to Imperial defence. The G2 report concluded that "the Irish Free State is not capable with her own resources of effectively defending herself against any Great Power."

Throughout the inter-war period the maritime defence of Ireland was the responsibility of the Royal Navy. Although, the presence of British military personnel in the Treaty ports was irritating, it seems that most Irish people were quite happy with this arrangement. If British aircraft carriers, battleships and cruisers were prepared to defend Ireland at no extra cost to the Irish people, then there seemed no reason why the country should undergo the expense of establishing a viable coastal navy. Even after the formal handover of the Treaty ports, this unspoken arrangement continued; the Royal Navy protected Ireland from seaborne attack.

Public indifference to Ireland's maritime circumstances was well known, but the Irish government did take an interest in international maritime affairs. In 1930 the Irish Free State attended the Imperial Defence Conference in London. Six years later the Irish Free State, a country without a navy, a mercantile marine or a coastguard service, chose to attend the Second Naval Conference in London. At this important naval disarmament meeting, the representatives of the British Empire and Commonwealth met with their counterparts from Italy, Japan, USA and France. When the general agreement was signed by the attending delegates, the Irish Free State and the Union of South of Africa refused to ratify the agreement.[36] Their reason being that since they were not naval powers, the agreements did not concern them. One wonders why they decided to attend these important meetings at all.

In 1937 the Irish Free State became Éire a *de facto* republic within the

British Commonwealth. The progressive attempts to dismantle the 1921 Treaty would have significant defence implications. Seventeen years after achieving Dominion status, the Irish State was about to regain control of the Treaty ports, an act which would oblige the new Irish authorities to be responsible for the defence of its own ports and territorial waters. The creation of an Irish navy was not far off.

THE HANDOVER OF THE TREATY PORTS

The 1921 Anglo-Irish Treaty, which granted Southern Ireland dominion status, also allowed Britain (under articles 6 & 7) the right to retain control of three strategically important deep water harbours and their port defences—Queenstown, Berehaven and Lough Swilly. During World War One these anchorages had assumed great importance in the naval war. Lough Swilly and Berehaven (Bantry Bay) were assembly points for convoys to the United States, as well as being bases for anti-submarine and minesweeping operations. In addition, in 1914 a large part of Britain's Grand Fleet vacated its vulnerable home base at Scapa Flow in the Orkney Islands for the safety of Lough Swilly. The vital importance of these protected anchorages to British imperial trade and maritime defence was not ignored during the Anglo-Irish negotiations in 1921—hence the inclusion of articles 6 and 7 in the Treaty.

In the inter-war period these anchorages were infrequent ports of call for vessels of the Royal Navy's South Irish Flotilla. The coastal forts were manned, but only on a care and maintenance basis. In the wake of the 1932 electoral victory of the nationalist Fianna Fáil party, the new Irish Taoiseach (Premier), Eamon de Valera, sought to disentangle the Irish Free State from its obligations to the British Empire and Commonwealth. An "economic war" with Britain developed over land annuities and trade tariffs. On 1 July 1937 a new constitution was approved and came into force on 29 December 1937. The tricolour became the national flag and Gaelic was declared to be the official language. The head of state was to be a President; there was no official mention of the British King. However, the External Relations Act introduced in 1936 did provide a role for the King in the appointment of diplomatic personnel.

However, the new constitution did not alter Britain's control over the three vital anchorages. In the eyes of Irish nationalists the presence of British warships sheltering under the protection of British manned batteries was very irritating and proof of the qualified nature of Irish political sovereignty. Éire's experience was not unique: the Soviet Union occupied the Finnish naval fortress of Porkkala until 1956. Portugal refused to relinquish the tiny port enclave of Goa in India until its explusion in 1961; and to this day, the United States still retains control of Guantanamo Bay military base in Cuba.

In view of the uncertain international situation, both the Irish and British governments were anxious to resolve their outstanding problems on trade and defence relations (in 1938, the United States ambassador to Britain, Joseph P. Kennedy, father of President J.F. Kennedy, urged the Chamberlain government to settle the matter of the Treaty ports). The talks which decided the outcome of these matters took place in London in early 1938. An agreement, signed on 25 April, stated that the transfer of the Treaty ports was to be completed not later than 31 December 1938. These negotiations took place in the same year that saw two other small European countries, Austria and Czechoslovakia, lose their independence to Nazi Germany. The Irish leader, Eamon de Valera, was anxious to assume sovereignty over these vital ports and their defences, before another European war would erupt and inadvertently drag Ireland into the conflagration. The return of the Treaty ports was vital if Éire wished to remain neutral in any future war. De Valera knew that in time of war, Ireland was obliged under article 7 of the Treaty to "afford such harbours and other facilities as the British Government may require". Under such conditions Ireland's policy of military neutrality would be worthless. No foreign power could have any serious regard for Irish neutrality if the Royal Navy continued to use these protected anchorages. Article 7 was deliberately created to serve the security interests of Great Britain. Therefore, it is astonishing that a British government should so willingly surrender it during such a period of international uncertainty.

In 1936 the British War Office was advised that it would cost £276,000 to upgrade the Treaty port defences, especially as the heavy guns lacked hardened shelters and adequate anti-aircraft defences.[37] Although provision for military aviation had been written into article 7 of the 1921 treaty, the forts and anchorages lacked any form of protection against aerial attack. The Royal Air Force and Fleet Air Arm were not present in Éire, and none of the forts were equipped with any medium or heavy calibre anti-aircraft guns. The forts were completely reliant on a small number of light machine-guns for their defence against low-flying dive-bombers. Without the provision of air cover and a significant upgrading of port defences, the Irish Treaty ports were now less attractive as a strategic asset than had been anticipated back in 1921.

The War Office was also advised that the isolated garrisons could not prevail against a hostile Irish population and that it would require a division of troops to defend these geographically isolated ports. Memories of the Anglo-Irish war were still vivid—the tenacity of the Old IRA and the Royal Navy's forced evacuation by sea and under fire of isolated coastguard stations. (During the Anglo-Irish war, coastguards from Belrig coastguard station had to be evacuated under fire by a Royal Navy trawler. During the course of an attack on Fenit coastguard station, a RN gunboat, HMS *Urchin* had to use its four-inch gun to scare off attackers.)

These arguments were valid, but experience in the coming four years would also illustrate the value of fortified strong points. On 1 September 1939 the first shots of then Second World War were fired at a coast defence fort when the pre-Dreadnought German battleship *Schleswig Holstein* bombarded the Polish fort of Westerplatte. Westerplatte, which guarded the port of Gdynia, withstood incessant aerial and seaborne bombardment for ten days before the garrison surrendered. On the nearby Hel peninsula, Polish sailors and soldiers held out until 1 October—the last Polish formation to surrender in that short but disastrous autumn campaign. Throughout this war there are other examples of the ability of well-constructed fortresses to withstand attack for a significant period of time—the Soviet border fort of Brest-Litovsk in June 1941, Corregidor in the Philippines, and Sevastapol (both in 1942). However, Singapore's fall in February 1942 would illustrate the vulnerability of a fortified seaport whose guns faced seaward, yet lacked adequate land defences and air cover.

In view of the costs involved, it was felt that British Imperial interests would be better served if the handover was amicable. The negotiations resulted in Éire agreeing to pay £10,000,000 as a final lump sum settlement of the land question. To the astonishment of a former First Lord of the Admiralty, Winston Churchill, the British Prime Minister, Neville Chamberlain, had unconditionally handed over the "sentinel towers which guard the Western Approaches". Churchill's deep concerns were not alleviated by de Valera's assurances that no Irish government would allow its territory to be used by a foreign power for the purposes of attacking Britain. In Churchill's words, "A more feckless act can hardly be imagined—and at such a time. Many a ship and many a life would soon be lost as a result of this improvident example of appeasement." He went on to comment that the Treaty ports were vitally important because "they were the refuelling bases from which our destroyer flotillas ranged westward into the Atlantic to hunt U-boats and protect incoming convoys as they reached the throat of the narrow seas. To abandon these ports would mean that our flotillas have to start in the north from Lambash and in the south from Pembroke or Falmouth." In essence this meant that convoy escorts now had to add an extra 400 miles (there and back) to their patrols. Churchill correctly predicted that every major power would recognise Irish neutrality. "Once the ports had been handed over, the legal hold over them had gone. The British could only return as conquerors."[38]

The Irish delegation were astonished that Neville Chamberlain's government had agreed to hand over the ports. Sean T. O'Kelly (later President of Ireland) expressed his country's sense of euphoric triumph when he said: "In the past six years we have whipped John Bull everytime."[39] Even the London *Times* commented that "further releases (handovers) might have been obtained by handing over Gibraltar to Spain and Malta to Italy. Neither touched the actual existence of our country as directly as the handing over of the ports".[40] The timing of the handover of Berehaven and Lough Swilly was indeed ironic, because these ports were handed over during the height of the Munich Crisis. Berehaven was formally evacuated on 29 September, two days after the Royal Navy had been placed on "War Alert". Lough Swilly was quietly evacuated four days later. Thousands of British merchant seamen and Royal Naval personnel were to die as a result of this monumental blunder.

For the Irish it was a great diplomatic triumph. The Admiralty's concern about defending the ports was unrealistic. The Royal Navy dominated Ireland's coastal and offshore waters; the Irish army could not pose any threat to these garrisons, which anyway were capable of being re-supplied by sea. In 1936, the regular Irish army had only 7000 troops, 36 pieces of light artillery, two serviceable armoured cars and six serviceable bi-planes. A reinforced brigade could have held off the entire Irish army. Had the Royal Navy remained in the Treaty ports between 1939 and 1941, it is unlikely that the *Luftwaffe* would have respected Irish neutrality. Therefore, it is not surprising that when the British asked for the ports back in the following year, they received a negative response. Ireland's refusal to hand back the ports was the main reason why Nazi Germany agreed to respect Irish neutrality.

COAST DEFENCE ARTILLERY

The 1938 Anglo-Irish accord had significant defence implications for Éire. Britain's evacuation of the ports had given substance to any serious attempt to stay out of a future European war. However, Éire was now responsible for the defence of her own ports and long coastline; an onerous task for a country without a navy or a coastguard. The Irish army was numerically small and ill equipped; the Air Corps possessed only a very limited number of mostly obsolete aircraft.

The defence of the former Treaty ports was now the responsiblity of six newly-formed coast defence batteries. Two were deployed in Lough Swilly, three in Cork and one in Berehaven. Live firing exercises were conducted, but until the arrival of the first motor torpedo boats in 1940, the forts lacked any seaward defence craft, without which port defence was undermined. In addition, the forts were very vulnerable to air attack, as the nearest military aerodrome with fighter aircraft was 150 miles away at Baldonnel, outside Dublin. The Treaty port defences were as follows.

Cork

Three forts defended the approaches to Cork harbour—Camden, Carlisle and Templebreedy. Their defensive armaments were formidable.

Camden, on the western edge of the two headlands, was equipped with one 9.2-inch gun (255mm), one 6-inch gun (152mm), two 18-pounder guns and Vickers and Lewis machine guns. Carlisle on the opposite shore had two 6-inch guns. Both Forts Camden and Carlisle controlled double torpedo tubes on a permanent setting that could send their projectiles across across the gorge at 90 degrees.[41]

To the south-west lay Fort Templebreedy. Although smaller than Camden, it possessed the heavier armament: two 9.2-inch counter-bombardment guns (a 15-man gun crew was required to operate these 1895 vintage guns. Their primary role was to deter attacks from battle-ships. In 1954 the guns were cut up and sold for scrap). These guns could hurl a 380-lb high explosive, armour piercing or shrapnel warhead over seven miles out to sea. The 6-inch guns on the other forts had a maximum range of 18,750 yards (warhead weight 100 lb approximately).[42] Ammuni-

MAP 2
CORK HARBOUR'S DEFENCES IN 1938

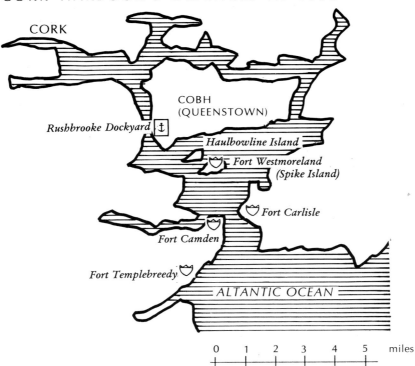

tion for the coastal guns was supplied by underground narrow guage railways which ran through tunnels (Fort Camden's were one and a half miles long).

At the centre of Cork harbour lay Spike Island, a landmass where ships sheltered in the harbour not only from inclement weather conditions but from offshore submarines and surface vessels engaged in espionage. For Irish nationalists, the island was synonymous with British oppression, as it was a holding centre for Irish prisoners destined for deportation to penal colonies in Australia. Spike Island was home to Fort Westmoreland (later renamed Fort Mitchel), which had a defensive armoury of two six-inch guns and one 9.2-inch gun (in reserve). After the British evacuation of the ports, the headquarters of the Irish Coast Defence Artillery was located on Spike Island.

The forts were self-contained military townships with barracks, married quarters, mess, canteen, shops, sports facilities and garrison chapels. Those guarding Cork harbour had accommodation for 2377 officers and men. Fort Templebreedy held six weeks' supply of water sufficient for 200 men. The other three forts held three and a half months' supply of water sufficient for 995 men.[43]

Fort Westmoreland (Spike Island) and the other forts guarding Cork harbour were formally handed over to the Irish Army on 11 July 1938 (the 17th anniversary of the truce in the Anglo-Irish War). Spike Island remained in army hands until 1980 when it was formally handed over to the Naval Service as a training centre. In 1985 the department of justice acquired the island as a temporary prison for young offenders. Today Fort Mitchel Prison still functions as a detention centre. Fort Camden is now a museum and Fort Templebreedy is the headquarters and training centre for An Slua Muiri (Second Line Naval Reserve) in Cork.

Berehaven

Bantry Bay, at the south-west corner of Ireland, is 22 miles long. In the Bay lie several islands, the largest of which is Bere Island, some six miles in length, and between the island and the mainland is a stretch of water known as Berehaven. This is five miles long and on average three-quarters of a mile wide. When the British evacuated Bere Island on 29 September 1938, the coast artillery defences which protected the safe anchorage, had been considerably reduced from their First World War levels. During the winter of 1927-8 almost the entire armament at Berehaven was withdrawn. A plan to upgrade the island's defences never materialised. Although Berehaven (unlike Portsmouth) was beyond the range of French land-based bombers, the programme of expansion was not undertaken because it would have required the approval of the Irish government, and this was not thought to be forthcoming. In 1938 only two batteries were in operation—Lonehort Battery with two 6-inch (152mm) guns and two searchlights; and Ardaragh Battery with two 12-pounder QF guns and four searchlights.

The Irish renamed the area Fort Berehaven. The island was an important port control centre during World War II and its defences were fully manned during this period. Today, Fort Berehaven is still used as a military training camp and Irish Naval Service vessels are frequent visitors to Berehaven.

Lough Swilly

The Swilly forts were the last to be handed over to the Irish authorities (3 October 1938). They protected the entrance to the 25-mile long Lough Swilly which extends from Dunaff Head to the mouth of the River Swilly, near Letterkenny. The entrance to the Lough is four miles wide (6.4km) between Dunaff and Fanad Heads, but some six miles up the Lough between Knockalla and Dunree Head it narrows to just over one mile. Deep water extends up the Lough for 18 miles, so that there is a large anchorage off Buncrana (during the First World War, the Royal Navy established an important shore station at Buncrana, HMS *Hecla*. After America's entry into the war in 1917, Lough Swilly was extensively used by the US Navy). In his book, *The Grand Fleet*, Admiral Jellicoe, wrote of the importance of Lough Swilly: "For the first time since the declaration of war the fleet occupied a secure base." The defences of this natural deep water harbour which had given the Royal Navy's Grand Fleet secure shelter in 1914 were impressive. According to the 1937 Committee on Imperial Defence, Lough Swilly's forts were equipped with two 9.2-inch BL counter-bombardment guns (Fort Lenan), two 6-inch BL guns (Fort Dunree), four 4.7-inch (120mm) QF guns and four machine guns. Both forts had accommodation for a total of 556 officers and men (Lenan's complement was 147).

The actual handover of the Donegal forts was a very low-key affair; no politicians or public figures travelled to north Donegal for the occasion. At Dunree the soldiers of the two countries were drawn up within a few yards of each other—the British under the command of Major G.E. Laing MM, Capt. Dykes and Lt. West, and the Éire party under Lieutenant Donagh, of the 5th Coast Defence Battery. As the British flag was hauled down from the main flagstaff by Sergeant King, the Irish soldiers presented arms. Immediately afterwards Sergeant McLoughlin of the Irish army ran up the tricolour, and the British soldiers present came to the present-arms (Sergeants King and McLoughlin of the British and Irish armies, respectively, were brothers-in-law). The ceremony was over in about three minutes. The British soldiers then marched away giving the "Eyes Right" salute as they passed the Irish soldiers. The British sentry handed the key of the gate to the Irish sentry. The British soldiers then travelled by bus to Derry, being cheered farewell along the route to the border by local villagers.

During the Emergency (World War II) these forts were fully manned, although Fort Lenan's role was reduced in 1943. In fact, during the early part of the war, anti-aircraft gunners at Fort Dunree actually fired on a British aircraft flying over Lough Swilly. Such occurrences were not uncommon during the Emergency. In all cases the intention was not to shoot the aircraft down, but to let the pilot know that he was over neutral Irish territory. For the British pilot overflying Lough Swilly it was ironic that the warning shots were coming from former British army machine-guns which had been handed over with the fort less than two years before. Fort Lenan was formally closed in 1946 and in 1954 the 9.2-inch guns were sold for scrap. In 1952 the regular army vacated Fort Dunree and it became a training centre for local FCA personnel and coast defence gunners from the Southern Command. The last live firing of its 6-inch guns took place in 1964. In response to the outbreak of communual violence in Northern Ireland in August 1969, the fort was briefly re-occupied by regular troops. The Irish army formally withdrew in 1990. In July 1986 a dedicated Coast Defence Artillery Museum was opened by President Hillery.

3

THE EMERGENCY, 1939-45

When Britain declared war on Germany on 3 September 1939, Ireland*
opted to remain neutral. By doing so, the Irish government sought to
demonstrate the sovereignty and independence of the Irish state. Ireland's
ability to pursue such a policy was greatly assisted by two significant
factors: Britain's unconditional handover of the Treaty ports in 1938 and
Northern Ireland's provision of secure air and naval bases, which were to
prove so vital to Britain in the forthcoming Battle of the Atlantic.

Neutrality had obvious advantages for a small offshore European
country like Ireland. The successful implementation of such a policy was
an affirmation of the country's independence in the arena of international
relations. Neutrality would safeguard Ireland's towns and port cities from
the horrors of aerial attack, to which she was ill equipped to withstand.
Finally, neutrality was a policy which would unify the population of
Ireland, preventing old civil war hatreds from re-emerging. All political
parties in the Irish parliament supported it, especially as the concept of
neutrality became inextricably associated with that of national sovereignty
and independence.

Although glaringly unique among Commonwealth member states
(South Africa did waver initially), Ireland's policy was very much in tune
with the rest of the international community. Ireland shared her neutral
stance with such varied countries as the United States, Turkey (former
World World I ally of Germany), Spain, Italy, Belgium and the traditional
neutrals Sweden, Switzerland, Denmark and Holland. Of 20 European
countries which adopted a policy of neutrality in 1939, only five would be
able or willing to maintain it by 1945.

The Second World War not only imposed enormous economic burdens
on neutral Ireland, but it alerted the Irish people to the importance of

* During the period 1937-49, it was customary to refer to the 26-county state as Éire—this
being the Irish for Ireland. During the war, the word 'Éire' marked the sides of Irish
merchant ships and coastal headlands, thereby alerting belligerent aircraft and warships of
Ireland's neutrality. For the purposes of this book, I will use the English translation of this
word, Ireland.

possessing an independent mercantile and naval capability. The significance of the sea in the new conflict was vividly demonstrated on the first day of the war when the Cunard passenger liner SS *Athenia* was torpedoed *en route* to Canada and sunk by a German submarine (U-30) 200 miles off the west coast of Ireland: 132 lives were lost; the survivors were taken to Galway. Over two weeks later on, 18 September, the 22,500 ton British aircraft carrier HMS *Courageous* was sunk by a German submarine (U-29) off Ireland's south-west coast with a loss of 518 sailors.[1] These two events in the first weeks of the war illustrated that, although a phoney war was being fought on the Western Front, the naval war was being conducted with unrestrained ferocity. This was a campaign, which, in part, was fought off Ireland's coastline, and its course and consequences had the potential to threaten the country's existence as a neutral and independent state. It was for these reasons that Ireland was obliged to make arrangements for her own maritime defence.

MARITIME DEFENCE MEASURES

On 3 September 1939 Ireland's defence forces comprised a 7494-strong regular army supported by 5066 reservists and 7233 volunteers. The army was an infantry orientated force and would remain so throughout the war—although it would greatly expand to a maximum wartime strength of 56,000 regulars. In 1939 it possessed only a thin sprinkling of 21 armoured cars, 13 of which were of World War I vintage, armed with a single .303 Vickers machine gun. There were no tanks except for two Swedish-built Landswerk L60 light tanks which were used for instructional purposes at the cavalry school. Anti-aircraft artillery consisted of four 76mm guns delivered in 1928, four 40mm Mark 1 Bofors guns delivered in June 1939 and eight searchlights. There were no anti-tank guns.

The Air Corps possessed 16 serviceable aircraft for operational use—six Avro Anson short-range maritime patrol planes, five Lysander army co-operation aircraft, two Walrus seaplanes and three Gladiator fighter aircraft. In 1942 the Gloster Gladiator, although a bi-plane, was to prove a most effective machine in the aerial defence of Malta. The naval branch of Ireland's defence forces was non-existent even though the country was now responsible for the defence of its ports and territorial waters. These waters lay astride the Western Approaches, the maritime gateway to Britain's busy mercantile and naval ports.

The words of Cmdr. T. McKenna (commanding officer of the Naval Service, 1956-73) sum up Ireland's predicament: "We were on our own with nothing but a 1908 vintage fishery protector armed with a three-pounder and solid shot, to look after 5127 miles of the then territorial sea on a perimeter of 783 miles and a coastline of 1970 miles."

Ireland's maritime defence was to take five forms: a small seaborne branch (the Marine Service); a coastal monitoring force strung out along Ireland's long coastline (the Coastwatching Service); a naval security force comprised of volunteers based in the country's main sea and fishing ports (Maritime Inscription); a port control and examination service, which controlled the movement of merchant shipping to and from Irish ports; and the coast artillery batteries which guarded the entrances to five of Ireland's main ports and deep water anchorages. In addition, maritime defence was also assisted by air corps coastal patrol aircraft and by army ordnance personnel who bolstered Ireland's port defences by laying minefields at appropriate locations.

Marine and Coastwatching Service

Sixteen years after the disbandment of the Coastal and Marine Service and the army's coastal infantry battalions, a Coastwatching Service was established on 29 August 1939 (two days before war broke out). The new service was a belated recognition of Ireland's status as an island. The decision to establish such a service was actually taken in January 1939, and in May two motor torpedo boats were ordered from Thornycrofts in England. Recruits for the new service were to be drawn from members of the Army's territorial volunteers who lived in coastal areas. In March 1939 a central depot was established at Portobello barracks in Dublin. However, recruitment did not begin until the end of August.

By 1 September 34 men had been recruited and eight look-out posts (LOPs) had been established at various points along the coast between Cahore Point in Co. Wexford and Dursey Head, Co. Kerry (the first coastwatchers were accommodated under canvas, but hardened shelters and blockhouses were soon constructed). Coastwatching sub–depots were set up in four of the Army's command areas (Western, Eastern, Southern and Curragh) and the coast was divided into nine districts. These were sub-divided into "look-out-areas" in the form of observation posts sited at approximately ten miles apart; eventually 88 LOPs were to be erected and manned along Ireland's long coast. According to Cmdr. T. McKenna:

> The 3rd September 1939 will always stand out in Irish maritime history not as the day on which the Second World War was declared—the bloodiest, most vicious and most global war in history— but as the day the realisation dawned in Ireland that the country was surrounded by water and that the sea was of vital importance to her. Neutrality was declared with just nothing whatever to defend to it within the internationally vital area of territorial sea.

With the formation of the Marine Service on 6 September, it was decided to amalgamate both services under the title "Marine and Coastwatching Service". Recruitment for the new service was undertaken in earnest. Most of the new recruits came from the merchant service, harbour authorities and fishing industry. An ex-Royal Navy chief petty officer torpedo coxswain was recruited by arrangement with the British Admiralty. At this stage in the Service's early history all recruits wore army uniforms and held army ranks. The first commanding officer of the Service was an army officer, Colonel A.T. Lawlor. The enactment of the Defence Forces (Temporary Provisions) (No. 2) Act 1940 on 7 June 1940 provided for marine ranks and ratings. However, conventional naval uniforms would not become available until April 1941. Basic military training, including weapons instruction was provided by army NCOs who had transferred over for this purpose. The old Royal Naval Repair and Victualling Yard and Naval Hospital on Haulbowline Island in Cork harbour was inspected and pronounced suitable as a base and depot for the new Service. Haulbowline was taken over by the Marine and Coastwatching Service on 7 July 1940.

The wartime establishment of the Marine and Coastwatching Service was announced on 7 December 1939 and its duties were intended to comply with the 1907 Hague Convention's 13th Schedule—rights and duties of neutral powers in naval war. These covered:

- control of the use of territorial waters and ports by belligerent warships
- control of the use of territorial waters and ports by merchant shipping
- minelaying, minesweeping and the notification and destruction of mines
- protection of the country's fishing limits
- escort duties
- protection of navigational aids; and sea rescue work.[2]

Acquiring vessels for the Marine Service

The marine branch of the new service acquired its first craft from the Air Corps—a seaplane tender, a target boat and a skimmer (long remembered in the Marine Service as the "flying flea"). The high speed seaplane tender was employed by Dublin Port Control during 1939-40 before being transferred to Cork harbour as a seaplane direction launch. Cork harbour was designated as an emergency landing site for seaplanes. The armour-plated target boat was redesignated as a river patrol launch and transferred from Dublin to Lough Derg on the Shannon, where it remained until 1945. The tiny (it was only 13 feet long) skimmer remained in Dublin.

The *Murichu*, Ireland's only armed sea-going patrol ship, was still under the control of the department of agriculture and fisheries.

In May 1939, seven months after the last Treaty port had been evacuated, consideration was obviously given to acquiring a seaborne element to port defence, as two motor torpedo boats (MTBs) were ordered from the shipbuilders John I. Thornycroft & Co., Southampton. According to the naval commentator, Capt. John E. Moore RN, "the choice of Thornycroft MTBs for seaward defence craft was a lunatic decision". Capt. Moore went on to comment that from personal experience of sailing around Ireland, "even when the sea is slight one encounters long periods of heavy swell at any time of the year—anathema to any MTB".[3] Indeed in the 1930s, when there was some official discussion on the subject of setting up a coast defence force, the advice of serving fishery officers was clear. No coastal motor gunboat (CMB) could live off the south and west coasts of Ireland in winter. Ironically, one of those fishery officers, Thomas McKenna, would later take delivery of one of these craft—now re-titled MTB. In his own words: "in later years we proved the correctness of our advice the hard way, that is, by having to hang on by my back teeth off the same coast in winter for two years as OC of one of the said MTBs."[4]

Despite the advice given by professional marine officers, an order for four additional MTBs followed. The first of these craft (M1 and M2) arrived in Ireland in March and July 1940 respectively—the former having been held up by bad weather. The cost of establishing the new navy was given during a debate on defence in the Irish parliament on 5 March 1940. The estimates given were £172,422 for capital purchases of fighting vessels, £58,000 for maintenance and £48,950 for stores and equipment. An additional £1640 was allocated for the re-opening of Haulbowline dockyard.[5]

MTB M3 was formally handed over to the Marine and Coastwatching Service on 25 July 1940 at the Thornycroft boatyard in Hampton, Surrey. On the following day it was commissioned by Lt. J. Flynn. The homeward voyage of M3 was certainly eventful. While off the Isle of Wight, the small MTB, which was under a Royal Navy protective escort, was bombed and nearly sunk by a German plane. When M3 reached the safety of the outer reaches of Cork harbour, she was fired on by one of the coastal batteries.

Eventually, on 1 August M3 reached the safety of the Service's new base, at Haulbowline Island. The first two MTBs, M1 and M2, had originally been intended for use by the Estonian and Latvian navies, but the Soviet Union's annexation of these countries in 1940 allowed Ireland to acquire these unused naval craft.[6] The fact that the MTBs were intended for use in the relatively calm waters of the Baltic meant that their employability off the Irish coastline, especially in winter, would be limited. The remaining MTBs (M4, M5, M6) were not handed over until 2/23 December 1942 and 24 February 1943 respectively. The delay in acquiring these boats was due to Thornycroft's understandable difficulty in obtaining SLM gearboxes for the MTBs; these had to come from Switzerland, which was marooned in Nazi-occupied Europe.[7]

The MTBs were the Marine Service's most potent seaborne craft. Although small, they were fast (40 knots), agile and theoretically could sink any size of warship with their 18-inch torpedoes. These boats were formed into a small strike force which was supposed to protect Cork harbour from seaborne invaders. In fact they were the only real naval craft which the Marine Service possessed. The defensive armament of the Irish MTBs was modest—four depth charges (M2 and M3 had two depth charges) and one .303 Hotchkiss machine gun. The Irish army did install a 20mm Madsen cannon on M4, M5 and M6. MTBs were ideal sea-going counterparts to the coastal batteries which guarded the Service's main base, Cork; as a war fighting craft, they were to prove their worth throughout World War Two. One of the most notable examples of their potential to inflict massive damage occured on 28 April 1944 at Slapton Sands near Dartmouth, England when German E-Boats (MTBs) on a routine patrol from their home port of Cherbourg attacked a US Navy convoy in training for the Normandy Landings (Exercise Tiger). In the course of the naval assault, two tank landing ships were torpedoed and sunk with a loss of 639 American lives. Although agile and hard hitting, the Irish MTBs were expensive to run as they consumed over 200 gallons of high octane aviation fuel per hour.

Prior to the arrival of the MTBs, the Marine and Coastwatching Services's first sea-going vessels were two former inshore fishery protection vessels—*Murichu* and the *Fort Rannoch*. The *Fort Rannoch* was a steam trawler (built in 1936) on charter in 1939 to the department of agriculture and fisheries from the Aberdeen Steam Trawling Co. The vessel was taken over on 10 October 1939 and purchased outright. It was commissioned as a public armed ship on 15 January 1940. Its armament comprised a single 12-pounder gun. The venerable *Murichu* (formerly HMY *Helga*, built in 1908) was already a veteran of the three previous conflicts: the First World War, when it sank a German submarine off the "Chickens" (Isle of Man) in 1918; the 1916 Rising, when it shelled central Dublin with devastating inaccuracy; and the Irish Civil War. The *Murichu* was taken over from the department of agriculture and fisheries on 12 December 1939 and commissioned as a public armed ship on the same date as the *Fort Rannoch*. Its sole armament was a 3-pounder gun, which was capable of firing only solid shot. However, this was later upgraded to a single 12-pounder gun.

5 MTB M1 on patrol in sheltered waters

6 Marine Service ratings on board a MTB man a 20mm Madsen AA gun

At the beginning of the war the Irish government attempted to buy two trawlers for minesweeping and armed patrol duties, but the Admiralty subsequently refused their consent. Without the Admiralty's consent no British trawling or shipping company could sell their vessels to overseas customers: the British war effort had priority. On 8 October 1940 the department of defence acquired an *ad hoc* minelayer from a local shipowner, S. Palmer of Ringaskiddy. The 162-ton vessel SS *Shark* was commissioned as a public armed ship on the same date. Of iron construction (she was built in 1891), the *Shark* was designated as a mine planter. Her role was to carry and lay mines. She was unarmed. In December the Marine Service's final sea-going acquisition of the war was procured and pressed into service as a training vessel. The 134-ton three-masted schooner *Isaalt* (built in 1909) was employed for the sole purpose of seamanship training. However, regardless of the considerable sum of money which was spent on converting her into a training vessel, she was not regarded as a success.[8] The *Isaalt* was fitted out only for day trips, as she did not have any suitable accommodation. Therefore, she was obliged to confine her training duties in waters adjacent to Cork harbour. She was unarmed and was never formally commissioned into service.

On 3 March 1941 an ex-Royal Naval Officer, Lieutenant Commander S. O'Muiris, was appointed as commanding officer of the Marine and Coastwatching Service. Lt.-Cdr. O'Muiris (Morris) was a former career officer in the Royal Navy; originally from Co. Mayo, he had seen action at the Battle of Jutland in 1916. His elder brother Charles, a fellow RN officer, was killed at Jutland. By 1920 Lt. Cdr. Morris, RN, than aged 31, was second-in-command of the light cruiser HMS *Castor*. In this same year, *Castor* was tasked with transporting Irish political prisoners to internment camps in England. It was this distasteful duty that prompted Morris to sacrifice a very promising career in the Royal Navy and resign in protest over British policy in Ireland.

In the inter-war period, Morris (now renamed O'Muiris) wrote every year, in Gaelic, to the Government, saying how important it was for Ireland to have its own sea defences. He never got a reply.

The Service was developing into two distinct arms—a sea-going marine branch and a coastguard (the Coastwatchers). This divergence in roles and duties was recognised and on 17 July 1942 the Service was divided into two independent branches—the Marine Service and the Coastwatching Service. By 1943, with the arrival of the last MTB, M6, the Marine Service's fleet of ten sea-going vessels was complete—six MTBs, two inshore patrol vessels, one antiquated minelayer and one sail training auxiliary. In addition the Marine Service also operated over 15 assorted small craft, tugs and work boats which were used by the Port Control Service and Maritime Inscription. One of the Marine Service's most

7 James Morris (in British Naval uniform, left; and Irish Naval uniform) changed his
   name to the Irish, Seamus O'Muiris, and became Commander and Director in 1941
   of the Irish Marine Service.

unusual acquisitions was a landing craft (presumably Allied) which had
been salvaged off the Aran Islands in 1941. The landing craft was repaired
and pressed into service as a transporter in Cork harbour. Its cargo was
not to be naval assault troops but inoffensive cattle *en route* to Spike Island
from the mainland. Eighteen ships' lifeboats were also salvaged and these
were used for seamanship training by the Maritime Inscription.[9]

Port Control and Examination Service

Although the port of Dublin had been declared "closed" on 3 September
1939 and Air Corps harbour launches were commandeered for the
purpose of enforcing this closure, it was not until the declaration of a state
of emergency on 7 June 1940 that measures were taken to control the
movement of merchant shipping to and from all ports in Ireland. On 1
July 1940 under Emergency Order No. 31, Competent Port Authorities
were established and a Port Control and Examination Service was set up
as an auxiliary to the Marine and Coastwatching Service.[10]

   This Service operated from 13 ports—Dublin, Dun Laoghaire, Waterford, Dundalk, Drogheda, Galway, Sligo, Rosslare, Lough Swilly, Cork,
Limerick, Fenit and Bantry. In most cases local harbour masters were
appointed as the Competent Port Authority and were given a temporary

commission in the Marine Service—although in the former Treaty ports of Bantry, Lough Swilly and Cork, local army commanders were appointed as CPAs. They were very powerful as they were answerable only to the minister of defence. They had complete legal control over all ships' crews, shipowners, shipping agents and dock workers. The CPA controlled the Port Control and Examination Service and those who served in the Marine Service.

One former chief petty officer in Dublin Port Control was the Hon. Patrick Campbell. In 1943 he gave a visiting journalist an outline of the Service's role:

> It's our job, as the Port Control Service, to board incoming vessels and give them a clearance signal into port. This looks like a fascinating profession from O'Connell Bridge, but it cools down as you get into it. We used to get some good ships at first, white Norwegian tankers, greasy Egyptian tramps, Greeks from Rosario and the River Plate but now we enjoy a few visiting colliers and our own Irishmen home from overseas.[11]

Once the merchant vessel had been searched and given permission to enter port, the ships' defensive guns and radios were made inoperable until they left port. During the vessel's stay armed Maritime Inscription ratings were placed on board and stood guard over the ship.

All of Ireland's main ports had designated port examination launches which ferried armed search parties out to awaiting merchant ships. Dublin had two examination craft: the *Tony* and the *Noray*, the latter being a former Dublin Port Authority tug. Cork's Port Control Service, with its headquarters at Fort Camden, had four examination boats—*Shiela*, *Colleen* and Examination Boats No. 1 and 3. The last two were wrecked at sea, with the loss of four lives on No. 3. On that occasion, on the night of 12 December 1942, the inspection boat, which was having to cope with a force eight gale, was caught up in the propellors of the SS *Irish Poplar* (ex *Vassilos Destounis*). Only one man managed to swim ashore to Spike Island to raise the alarm; it was the Marine Service's worst disaster of the Emergency. Limerick's Port Control boat was a yacht, the *Sylvia*, which carried out inspections under the protection of the examination battery at Ardmore Point. Waterford had two examination launches—the ML *Colleen* (ex *Wuzzer*), and *Inishowen*. Finally, Lough Swilly in north Donegal which was a welcome safe anchorage for many battered stragglers from the North Atlantic convoys, had one examination launch, the *Eileen*. The Competent Port Authority (an army officer) was based at Fort Dunree, where the medium and heavy coastal guns provided protective cover for the Port Control Service (PCS).

The Port Control and Examination was disbanded on 1 June 1945. The majority of its personnel were demobilised immediately, while the remainder were transferred to Haulbowline. The examination boats and equipment which belonged to the PCS were disposed of and all officers holding commissions as CPAs were retired.

Maritime Inscription

The naval equivalent of the army's Local Defence Force was the Maritime Inscription. It was founded on 20 September 1940, and was attached to the commanding officer of the Marine and Coastwatching Service. Its curious title was adopted from Jean Baptise Colbert, minister of marine in 17th-century France, who while in the service of King Louis XIV had set up a localised maritime volunteer reserve (L'inscription maritime).

The Maritime Inscription was different from most conventional naval reserves. It was a localised organisation, each part relating to a given port or coastal area and administered, operated and staffed locally. Volunteers were attached to shore companies, each of 100 men, of which there were 12 by June 1942. An additional two companies were raised in 1943, raising the Maritime Inscription's manpower strength to 1400. It was raised from fishermen, yachtsmen, harbour and coastal populations. The Maritime Inscription was wholly organised by coastwatching sub-depots and trained by the Port Control Service. They had complete coastal coverage from

8 Seamen of the Maritime Inscription (Ireland's second-line Naval Reserve) provide a guard of honour. It will be noted that they are wearing summer rig and drill order.

Dundalk, south about, to Sligo. Ironically, there were no Maritime Inscription units in Co. Donegal, an area of the country which bordered the Allied convoy assembly point of Lough Foyle in neighbouring Northern Ireland.[12]

Although manpower was always below establishment, many of these naval reservists registered whatever boats they possessed with their local Competent Port Authority for possible use in the national interest. These were used for the purposes of harbour patrols and in assisting the Port Control and Examination Service. In addition, a peculiar practice was introduced of calling new recruits out on permanent service and then immediately granting them indefinite home leave, on the understanding that they would be available to be recalled to regular service as and when required. Another unusual feature of the Maritime Inscription was the fact that it had to acquire its officer cadre from within its own ranks. All volunteers entered the Maritime Inscription as a seaman recruit and potential officers worked their way up the ranks until they were earmarked for commissioned rank. In 1942 14 volunteers were commissioned as ensigns.[13]

The Maritime Inscription's main role was to ensure the security of the port and coastal area assigned to them. This was done by mounting shore and quayside foot patrols, as well as harbour and bay patrols aboard small craft. In Dublin, these duties were carried out in conjunction with the Army's 26th Battalion (the Port Security Battalion). In addition, Maritime Inscription ratings stood guard on visiting merchant ships and assisted the Port Control Service as and when required. When carrying out these tasks, they were armed only with 1914 pattern bolt action Lee-Enfield rifles and army issue revolvers.

Easter Sunday 1941 is a significant date in Irish naval history because on this date, the 25th anniversary of the 1916 Rising, the first Irish naval uniforms went on public display when detachments from the Marine and Coastwatching Service's sea-going and shoreside branches paraded through Dublin. In 1943 millions of cinema-goers worldwide did catch a glimpse of the new Irish naval uniform. In that year Ealing Film Studios in England made a drama documentary film entitled *San Demetrio, London*. It was based on the true story in 1940 of the British fuel tanker *San Demetrio* which was abandoned by its crew in mid-Atlantic after a German night attack. Two days later they reboarded the smouldering but intact vessel from their lifeboats and sailed it without charts and compass to the west coast of Ireland. In the movie the vigilant Irish naval rating is the first person to spot the battered vessel as it limps into port. After its arrival in Ireland the *San Demetrio* was escorted by the Royal Navy to Clydeside with its much needed and undamaged cargo of 11,500 tons of petrol.

With the disbandment of the Port Control and Coastwatching Services in 1945, the numerical strength of the Maritime Inscription rapidly contracted. This process of decline was accelerated by the closure of the Coastwatching Service's sub-depots. It therefore became impossible to control and train isolated units. On 10 June 1947 the Maritime Inscription was reorgansied as An Slua Muiri with a new establishment of nine companies. In February 1949 this was modified when it was decided to organise An Slua Muiri on a five company basis centred around four port areas—Dublin, Cork, Limerick and Waterford.

Coast defence artillery

The most potent deterrent facing a would be invader were the formidable coastal batteries which protected the country's main ports and deep water anchorages. As outlined in the previous chapter, the former Treaty ports of Berehaven, Lough Swilly and Queenstown (Cobh) were defended by heavy guns (9.2- and 6-inch). After the handover, some of the batteries had their physical defences improved thanks to the efforts of army engineers, for example, Fort Davis (Carlisle) had its 6-inch guns protected by concrete shelters. Spike Island was protected by two 40mm Bofors guns and two 3.7-inch anti-aircraft guns.

In addition to the old Treaty ports, coastal batteries were also established at the entrance to the Shannon Estuary, and the port of Waterford. Waterford's defences comprised two 12-pounder guns positioned at Fort Duncannon; the Shannon's defences comprised two 6-inch guns located at Ardmore Point. This gun section, entitled Fort Shannon, protected the entrance to the port of Limerick and the military aviation sites at Rineanna (Ansons and Lysanders) and Foynes (Walrus seaplanes). Dublin was protected by artillery batteries located at North Bull and Sandycove. The neighbouring port of Dun Laoghaire was protected by two 12-pounder guns.

Minefields and blockships

In 1941 a minefield section was established and observation (controlled) mines were laid at the entrances to Waterford and Cork harbours and at various locations around Cobh—at Belmount off Cobh, alongside the deepwater quay at Cobh, and above the Rushbrooke Dockyard. It was a "by guess and by God" affair, as nobody had any experience of mine warfare. Initially these mines were of Irish manufacture. The casts were made by Thompsons of Carlow, the gelignite charges were supplied by ordnance corps, and the electrics were provided by the Marine Service. However, in 1943/44 the British Admiralty agreed to supply some ground observation mines,[14] which replaced the home-made mines. The destruction of rogue mines which had broken off from their moorings was one of the duties of the Marine Service: 183 mines are officially recorded as having been destroyed at sea by Marine Service rifle fire, while 751 were destroyed ashore by the Ordnance Corps.[15]

At the end of the Emergency, the minefields were blown up, that is, where it could be done in safety. If immediate destruction was not possible, the mines were lifted and destroyed elsewhere. In addition, in the period 1945-7, over 6000 Allied sea mines were swept by two Royal Naval minesweeping flotillas operating out of Cobh. Concrete observation posts which were located on private land were demolished and removed. If they were on government-owned land, they were simply abandoned where they stood.

In addition to minefields, coastal batteries, and Marine Service MTBs, the entrance to Cork harbour was defended by two blockships. The bucket dredgers SS *Owenacurra* and *Owenabuee* were under charter from Cork Harbour Commissioners from 1940 to 1944 for the sole purpose of obstructing the entrance to Cork harbour to any invader. They were held at Passage West and kept under steam at critical moments ready for immediate and violent disposal at their pre-arranged sinking positions. The object being to block the main navigable channel in the event of invasion. In addition, all essential shoreside facilities were to be destroyed. The invader was to be denied any operational ports in Ireland.[16]

Maritime aviation

Ireland's maritime defence was not solely the responsibility of the various naval and coastwatching units established between 1939 and 1942; the Irish Air Corps, although very small, also possessed a maritime defence capability. During World War II the Air Corps operated from four aerodromes and one seaplane station—Baldonnel, Gormanston, Fermoy, Rineanna (present-day Shannon airport) and Foynes. At Foynes, Walrus seaplanes operated as maritime patrol and search and rescue aircraft. From Rineanna, a flight of four Avro Ansons mounted long coastal patrols as far north as Malin Head in north Donegal to Wexford—a physically arduous duty for both the aircrews and their machines. The Anson, nicknamed "Faithful Annie", was a durable aircraft, but it had its limitations. Its maximum bomb load was extremely limited (360 lbs), and its defensive armament comprised two (single).303 machine guns.

On 24 January 1941 the Air Corps took possession of a much more advanced maritime surveillance aircraft, namely a Lockeed Hudson twin engined medium bomber. The aircraft in question (Reg. P5123) was from the RAF's 233 Squadron, when it crash landed in Ireland. The Hudson was one of 163 belligerent aircraft to crash land in Ireland during World War II. The damaged machine was repaired and pressed into Air Corps service after having been formally purchased from Britain. This Hudson

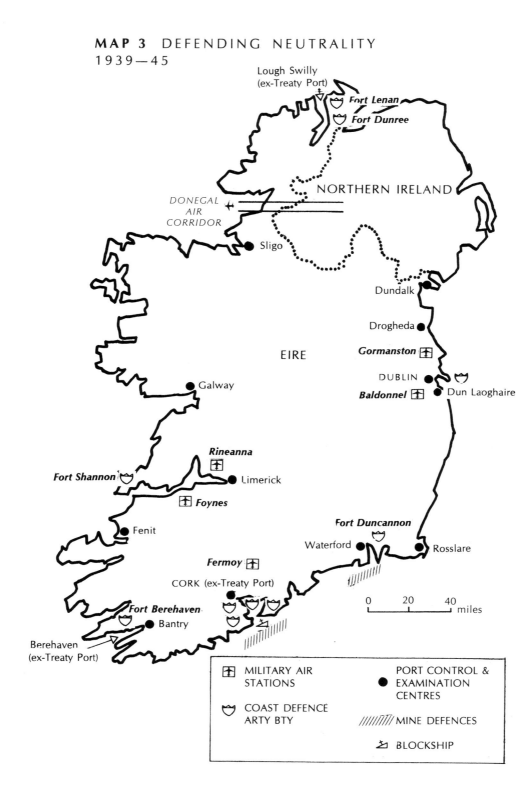

MAP 3 DEFENDING NEUTRALITY 1939—45

Lough Swilly
(ex-Treaty Port)

Fort Lenan

Fort Dunree

NORTHERN IRELAND

*DONEGAL
AIR
CORRIDOR*

Sligo

Dundalk

Drogheda

EIRE

Gormanston

DUBLIN

Baldonnel

Dun Laoghaire

Galway

Rineanna

Fort Shannon

Limerick

Foynes

Fenit

Fort Duncannon

Waterford

Rosslare

Fermoy

CORK (ex-Treaty Port)

0   20   40 miles

Fort Berehaven

Bantry

Berehaven
(ex-Treaty Port)

	MILITARY AIR STATIONS	●	PORT CONTROL & EXAMINATION CENTRES
	COAST DEFENCE ARTY BTY	///////	MINE DEFENCES
			BLOCKSHIP

bomber was attached to the Air Corps' Medium Bombing and Reconnaissance Squadron (Air Corps Reg. 91). It was in this machine that Ireland's prime minister, Eamon de Valera, untook an aerial tour of Ireland's coast and border defences in 1942.

With the outbreak of war in September 1939, it became nearly impossible for the Irish Air Corps to obtain aircraft. A pre-war order for an additional nine Ansons and seven Gladiators was not fulfilled. Understandably Britain was now at war and could not afford to export modern military aircraft to a country which was not allied to it. In lieu of obtaining modern warplanes through conventional channels, crash landings were to provide the Air Corps with its most modern combat aircraft. Between September 1940 and August 1941, three RAF Hawker Hurriance fighters and one RAF Fairy Battle light bomber which had crash landed in Ireland, were repaired and eventually pressed into service.

However, Britain did supply Ireland with 30 unarmed trainer and utility aircraft in the period 1940-3. In addition, between 1943 and 1945, the British authorities agreed to transfer 17 ex-RAF Hurricane fighter aircraft to the Air Corps.[17]

MARITIME NEUTRALITY

After Germany had assumed direct and indirect control over continental Europe, the British Isles (including Ireland) were totally dependent on the merchant convoys for their survival. When war broke out in September 1939, nearly two years after Ireland had declared itself a *de facto* republic, the country, although an island, still did not have a merchant marine. On 29 September 1939 William Norton TD (member of the Irish parliament) proposed: "At this stage before ships reach a premium, before the worst effects of the war at sea are discernible, it might well be desirable for the Government to consider the possiblity of inaugurating something in the nature of a state mercantile marine."[18] His suggestion was rejected. The *Irish Independent*'s editorial comment summed up the government's attitude: "that while neutral ships were available, to charter was better than to send ships with their flag (the Irish tricolour) into dangerous waters with all the dangers to our neutrality."

In 1939 only five per cent of imports came in aboard Irish flagged vessels. The gross tonnage on the Irish register in September 1939 was 41,105 tonnes, a completely unrealistic figure inflated by an Antarctic whaling fleet using an Irish address for whale quota reasons. Even this figure is very small in relation to the mercantile tonnage registered in other small European countries. The little Baltic state of Estonia, which, like Ireland, had secured independence after World War I, had 145 vessels

Table 1: Minor European Navies in 1939

	Albania*	Denmark	Estonia	Finland	Ireland	Latvia	Norway
Coast defence ships (small battleships)	0	2	0	2	0	0	4
Destroyers	0	0	0	0	0	0	6
Submarines	0	12	2	5	0	2	9
Minelayers	0	4	4	8	0	0	4
Minesweepers	0	3	1	18	0	2	2
Gunboats	2	8	6	8	1	1	5
Motor torpedo boats	0	17	1	7	0	0	29
Motor gun boats	4	0	0	14	0	0	0
Auxiliaries (incl. icebreakers & depot/repair ships)	0	4	10	10	0	4	2
Populations (millions)	1	3.7	1.1	3.8	3	2	2.9

Source: *Jane's Fighting Ships*, 1939

* On 7 April 1939, Italy invaded Albania and forcibly incorporated the country within the Italian Empire. As a result the small Albanian navy ceased to exist. A similar but much worse fate awaited the Baltic republics in 1940.

on its national mercantile register and a total tonnage of 126,427 tonnes. A remarkable figure for a country half the size of Ireland and with a population of only 1.1 million people (even smaller than that of Northern Ireland). Latvia had 190,247 tonnes on its register; Denmark with a population of 3.6 million had a merchant fleet of 702 vessels (1,101,047 tonnes); and Norway with just 3 million inhabitants (the population of Ireland) had the fourth largest merchant navy in the world with 1970 vessels on its register, 4,079,133 tonnes of Norwegian mercantile shipping.

These countries were not significantly wealthier than Ireland, (Norway had still to discover North Sea oil), yet they all managed to maintain effective naval defence forces. Estonia, which should have received Ireland's first MTB before the country was brutally annexed by the USSR, possessed an impressive coastal navy (see Table 1). In fact four destroyers were on order before the country was annexed. Neighbouring Latvia also possessed a strong coastal force. However, in contrast to these two Baltic states, Lithuania's navy was tiny. It comprised a single World

War I vintage minesweeper (ex-German). Finally, Iceland although subject to Danish rule and with a population of only 117,000 was able to maintain a fishery protection force of three armed ocean-going trawlers.

Ireland's virtual self-sufficiency in food did not insulate it from the world economy, as vital petroleum products, medicines, machine parts and fertiliser, so vital for an agricultural economy, had to be imported. The increased ferocity of U-boat attacks on British shipping reduced the tonnage available for Ireland's needs. In addition, Ireland's dependence on the British merchant navy would put the country at the mercy of Churchill, whose hostility to Irish neutrality was well known. In response to the crisis, it was belatedly decided to act upon William Norton's prophetic advice and establish a State Mercantile Marine, which was entitled Irish Shipping Ltd. It was set up in 1941. In all 15 vessels were either purchased or chartered. Two, the *Irish Oak* (ex *West Neris*) and *Irish Pine* (ex *West Haematite*) were sunk by U-boats in the North Atlantic, the latter with total loss of her entire crew. Irish merchant vessels were unarmed, unlike their British counterparts. They had to rely on enormous neutral markings, the letters "EIRE" which were marked on the sides of Irish ships to protect them from an unintentional attack. Aerial attacks by Allied or German maritime patrol aircraft added to the danger of sailing alone. One air attack took place because the Allied pilot confused the ship's Irish tricolour with that of Vichy France.

In April 1942, after 12 years of closure, Rushbrooke Dockyard in Co. Cork was reopened and employed for the purposes of maintaining both vessels of Irish Shipping Ltd and the Marine Service. In all, 136 Irish merchant seamen died at sea during World War II. In the course of their very dangerous voyages, they saved over 511 lives of stricken seamen, Allied, Axis and Neutral.[19]

DETERRING POSSIBLE INVASION

In September 1939 Ireland was almost defenceless. Seaward defences were non-existent; the Air Corps possessed only three serviceable fighter aircraft for the defence of the whole country; and the Irish army, although well trained and lead, was too small and lightly armed to offer effective resistance to a determined invader. However, in 1939 invasion seemed unlikely especially as the ground and aerial war in Europe had all but ended with Poland's capitulation. Even before the collapse of organised resistance in Poland, the department of finance advised the government that the present crisis did not constitute a war situation. The department argued against maintaining more than 18,000 men in the regular defence forces. This figure was later reduced to 15,000 and in November 1939 the department of finance requested that the defence forces be returned to their peacetime establishments. (When the Netherlands was invaded on 10 May 1940, Ireland had only 13,335 men in her permanent defence forces.)

On 5 April 1940 Denmark was overwhelmed by a German invasion force of two and half divisions; sporadic resistance lasted no more than 12 hours. Only one Danish aircraft managed to take off before being promptly shot down by the Luftwaffe. The Germans suffered only 20 casualties in what was to become known as the "whipped cream campaign". In April neutral Norway succumbed to a German invasion force of six divisions. Oslo airport was captured by airborne troops, a threat that would haunt Irish defence planners in months to come. During the Norwegian campaign, one of the British warships sunk in the fighting was the destroyer HMS *Acasta*. She went down with the loss of all hands except one crewman. The *Acasta* was the last British warship to leave Cork harbour on 11 July 1938, when it repatriated the Royal Artillery gunners on Spike Island back to England. By the end of June 1940 Germany controlled the coastline of continental Europe from North Cape in Norway to the Spanish Pyrennes.

In July 1940 Ireland faced possible invasion from either Great Britain or Nazi Germany. The Marine Service could do little to deter either an overland invasion from Northern Ireland or a German airborne invasion. The three MTBs could have offered some resistance in the environs of Cork harbour, but otherwise Ireland's maritime defences were too feeble to deter any invader. In reality Ireland's greatest asset against German invasion was her proximity to Great Britain, and therein the might of Britain's Royal Navy and Royal Air Force. Any German seaborne invasion fleet directed against Ireland would have been annihilated by the combined might of these forces. Also, Ireland's relative geographic isolation from German-occupied Europe greatly helped her. In view of the limited range and capacity of German military transport aircraft in 1940, an airborne invasion mounted from airfields in north-west France would have been a hazardous undertaking. In contrast, Ireland's geographic proximity to Great Britain, including sharing a land border with Northern Ireland, undermined the ability of the country to repell a British invasion.

Throughout the war years, Ireland's armed forces were under-resourced. In reality the only hope of obtaining adequate quantities of modern weapons was to seek assistance from overseas. The Allies would have done so, but at the price of surrendering Irish neutrality. However, had Ireland entered the war before 1943, it is likely that Dublin would have shared the fate of Warsaw, Coventry and Rotterdam. In 1941, Belfast, a city which enjoyed the protection of the RAF, suffered two devastating German air raids. More than 1000 people were killed in these two raids.

Ironically, the German foreign minister, von Ribbentrop, offered to help the Irish defend their neutrality without obligation. This aid was to comprise much needed artillery and small arms. On 13 April 1941 a shipment was made ready for delivery to Ireland. This comprised 46 field guns, 1000 anti-tank rifles, 550 machine-guns and 10,000 rifles, together with sufficient quantities of ammunition.[20] The source of this generous gift was the abandoned guns and munitions dumps of the British army at Dunkirk. It was a serious offer, but no Irish leader could have accepted it. The value of such weapons would have been outweighed by an under-standable sense of outrage in Britain. De Valera was still dependent on the embattled British merchant marine to keep his country supplied with vital imports. As de Valera correctly acknowledged, the fate of Irish neutrality was determined by two men (Adolf Hitler and Winston Churchill), neither of them was Irish.

The threat from Germany

In July 1940 it seemed likely that Germany might attempt to force Britain to sue for peace by mounting a Norwegian style invasion of neutral Ireland. To meet such a threat, the Irish government approved a plan to raise a regular army of 40,000 men. In September, 20,000 First World War Springfield rifles were obtained from the United States and a further 10,000 Lee-Enfield rifles were awaited from the British War Office.[21] Eventually over 50,000 regulars would be recruited. However, these troops were pitifully equipped to deal with the threat posed by the *Wehrmacht*. One of the main handicaps which Ireland suffered was a lack of long-range reconnaisance aircraft, which could provide early warning of a seaborne invasion. In most areas, maritime surveillance was the responsibility of the coastwatchers, whose range only extended as far as the horizon. The work of the coastwatchers was invaluable, as they kept local military command-ers informed of sightings of aircraft, surface ships and submarines. Maritime air patrols were mounted, but the limited number of serviceable machines from a pool of only nine aircraft severely degraded their ability to monitor offshore waters. The Marine and Coastwatching Service also found it very difficult to maintain a permanent presence at sea. The MTBs were ideal when operating within Cork harbour or in the milder waters of the Irish Sea, but elsewhere their employability was limited. In August 1940 the recently established Marine and Coastwatching Service only possessed two lightly armed patrol vessels and three MTBs. The coastal batteries were a serious deterrent to a seaborne invader wishing to capture any of the former Treaty ports, but they were very vulnerable. All of them lacked adequate hardened shelters, anti-aircraft defences and air cover.

The British military had calculated that a single German division would be sufficient to capture Ireland. Hitler had given serious consideration to a military operation against Ireland. The German navy's commander-in-chief, Admiral Raeder, advised that "the island (Ireland) has no defended bases or anchorages at all. Although the Irish might willingly open their ports to us, they would be open to the enemy pursuing us."[22] Implicit in this statement is Admiral Raeder's obvious belief that Ireland was defenceless. Within less than four weeks in April and May 1940 five neutral countries had been overrun by the *Wehrmacht*. There is little doubt that but for Ireland's fortunate geographic location, it would have shared the fate of these other European states. When the Allies occupied Germany in May 1945, their intelligence units came across a plentiful supply of maps of Ireland. In addition, documents seized by the Allies in this period confirm that had Nazi Germany succeeded in defeating Britain, the British Isles (including Ireland) would have been placed under a military government with administrative centres in London, Birmingham, Newcastle, Glasgow, Liverpool and Dublin![23] At the Wannsee Conference in January 1942 it was already decided that Ireland's community of 4000 Jews were to be murdered.[24] Had Hitler triumphed over the British in 1940/41, Ireland would have slipped with the rest of Europe into what Churchill correctly described as an abyss of a new dark age.

Fall Gruen: *The planned invasion of Ireland*

On 3 December 1940, during a situation conference, Hitler commented that: "The occupation of Ireland might lead to the end of the war. Investigations are to be made." Discussions were held with Gen. Kurt Student, the commander of the 11th Airborne Corps. Student's paratroops were instrumental in paralysing neutral Holland's defences in May 1940. The invasion of Ireland, code-named *Fall Gruen** (Plan Green), was to be have been a bold and extremely hazardous affair. From the French ports of Lorient, St Nazaire and Nantes, a force of five or six divisions were to be landed on a front along the south-east coast of Ireland. This was to have taken place, while the German 6th Army was mounting its invasion of southern England at Lyme Bay. The cancellation of Operation Sealion sealed the fate of *Fall Gruen*. However, Hitler, Goering and General Student did discuss the possibility of an airborne assault on Northern Ireland—*Operation Viking Raid*. Student had at his disposal over 20,000 paratroops and 12,000 glider troops. Hitler, always with a

* The invasion codeword did not have any intentional associations with Ireland's worldwide reputation for being the Emerald Isle; all German invasion plans had a colour code. Green was an unused colour code, as it had originally been the codeword for Hitler's intended invasion of Czechoslovakia in October 1938.

keen sense for historical anniversaries, had suggested the 25th anniversary of the 1916 Rebellion.[25] But the invasion did not take place. The German experience in Crete in 1941 and that of the Allies in Holland in 1944, would illustrate that large airborne operations can be very costly.

However, there were important practical difficulties for a German invasion force. The German navy had been badly mauled in the Norwegian campaign and was unable to guarantee the safe passage of an invasion fleet from the newly occupied French Atlantic ports to Ireland. This was especially valid, in view of the formidable strength of the Royal Navy's home fleet. An airborne invasion was also impractical, because without a follow-up seaborne landing to supply it with troop reinforcements, heavy weapons, munitions, fuel and medicines, the initial invasion would be doomed to failure. The RAF, in addition to its undefeated fighter groups, still retained a very large bomber force which could have devastated German strong points in Ireland. Even the poorly equipped Irish army could have delayed an invasion of German paratroops in time for British armoured and motorised formations to arrive from their bases in Northern Ireland. By April 1941 Germany's attention was focused on the crisis in the Balkans and on the forthcoming invasion of the Soviet Union. An invasion of Ireland now seemed less likely.

The threat from Britain

A British invasion from Northern Ireland was militarily feasible, and in the circumstances of July 1940 seemed likely. (In 1940 Britain showed a willingness to act decisively and occupy other strategically important Atlantic islands. On 10 April, British troops occupied the Faeroe or Sheep Islands. This was followed up by the occupation of Iceland on 10 May when a force of 4000 British troops landed without warning. Greenland was later occupied by US troops. They helped resident Free Danish sledge patrols to deter U-boats from surfacing in Greenland's coastal waters.) The highly-regarded *Economist* magazine argued in favour of immediate seizure of the former Treaty ports. However, the British army and government faced innumerable difficulties with regard to Ireland. The debacle at Dunkirk had denuded all the British army's fighting formations of their heavy weapons. What units were available could not be spared for an occupation of Ireland. The only fully-equipped division in Britain in July 1940 was not British but Canadian. The use of such a formation against Ireland would undoubtedly have created enormous difficulties for the Canadian government. In addition and most significantly, such an action would have had a detrimental effect on Britain's image in the United States, where isolationist sentiments were still prevalent. President Roosevelt was seeking re-election in November 1940. Therefore, a British invasion of Ireland would have had enormous repercussions in Washington, where the Irish–American lobby was well organised. Northern Ireland's participation in the war lessened the blow of losing the former Treaty ports. The convoys from Clydeside and Liverpool were now protected by escort ships and aircraft operating out of secure sea and air bases in Northern Ireland. In fact German control of the French Atlantic ports had made Berehaven and Cork redundant as potential convoy assembly ports. However, this didn't lessen the public perception widely held in wartime Britain that Ireland's neutrality was helping Germany to win the Battle of the Atlantic.

This view was later espoused by a former Royal Navy officer and veteran of the Atlantic convoys, Nicholas Monsarrat. According to Monsarrat, Allied merchant seamen and naval personnel "saw Ireland safe under the British umbrella, fed by her convoys and protected by her air force; her very neutrality guaranteed by the British armed forces."[26] Monsarrat's sentiments were of course coloured by his own harrowing experiences in the interminable Battle of the Atlantic. He saw ships sink and men die, who otherwise might have survived had Ireland allowed the Royal Navy to operate deep-sea rescue tugs from its west coast ports. But Monsarrat failed to acknowledge that the Treaty ports were returned to Ireland by a British government on the advice of the Chiefs of the Imperial General Staff; the Irish never seized them. Had this same government had the foresight to stand up to Hitler in 1938, instead of signing away the Czech army, the Skoda armaments works and the Irish ports, then the Battle of the Atlantic might never have taken place. Monsarrat acknowledged the right of the Argentines and Spanish to remain neutral but insisted that "this was Ireland's fight".[27] There is much truth in this observation, as a Nazi victory would have doomed Ireland as well as Britain. According to Helmut Clissman, an *Abwehr* agent stationed in Ireland during the war, "in the event of a German victory, Hitler would have sold the Irish down the river. Northern Ireland would have been given to a Vichy-type government in London. Hitler did not want to harm the British Empire."[28]

However, Monsarrat, as with many English observers, lacked a necessary degree of sensitivity towards Anglo-Irish relations. Many Irish people sympathised with the Allied cause, but they resented being told by certain rather arrogant English individuals that it was their duty to rally to the King Emperor. Had Britain remained silent and allowed America and Canada to encourage and coax the Irish into a Portuguese type of neutrality, then the lives of many of Monsarrat's friends and colleagues might have been saved.

Monsarrat, as with most people in both Ireland and the United Kingdom, was unaware of the degree of Ireland's pro-Allied bias during the war. For example, RAF Sunderland and Catalina anti-submarine maritime patrol planes were permitted to fly from their bases in Northern Ireland over the territory of neutral Ireland via the Donegal air corridor. The Irish authorites greatly assisted the British Admiralty by announcing over the radio the location of German U-boats spotted by the Coastwatching Service. Irish weather stations sent detailed reports to London which was of great assistance to the Allies.[29] Also, after 1942 crashed landed Allied aircrews were allowed to quietly slip across the border to Northern Ireland; German military personnel were simply interned for the duration of the war. Finally, in the event of a German invasion of Ireland, British forces were to be allowed to cross the border under the provisions of *Plan W*. This was a mutual defence agreement worked out in advance by high-ranking British and Irish military officers.[30]

A British invasion would have tied down scarce troops in a guerrilla struggle, which Germany would no doubt have aided. Major-Gerneral Bernard Law Montgomery, who, as a divisional commander in 1940 was involved in the planning for a possible military seizure of Cork by the British 3rd Division, was relieved to discover that the plan had been shelved. Montgomery was a veteran of the the Anglo-Irish War (he had served in Cork in 1921 as a brigade-major). An invasion of Ireland would have had grave implications for the morale and loyalty of Irish regiments serving within the British army (memories of the Connaught Rangers' mutiny in India were still vivid); 40,000 Irish citizens volunteered for military service in Britain's armed forces, of whom seven would win the Victoria Cross. One of these VC winners was a distinguished RAF fighter pilot, B. "Paddy" Finucane, who by 1941 was a living legend in Britain. Over 200,000 Irish citizens left Ireland to work in Britain's labour-starved war industries. An invasion would have have prejudiced Ireland's significant but indirect aid to Britain's war effort.

Ireland may have supplied Britain with civilian munitions workers, military volunteers, agricultural foodstuffs, whiskey and stout, but it remained unyielding on the question of granting refuelling and basing rights for Allied warships and aircraft. As the Allies pointed out, other neutrals were more flexible: Portugal allowed the Allies use of the Azores in the western Atlantic; neutral Ecuador in South America allowed the US Navy use of the Galapagos Islands in the Pacific; and Peru allowed the Americans to build an important air base at Talara on the Pacific coast. In fact most of Latin America which was neutral in 1942 declared war on the Axis Powers without ever getting involved in the conflict. Only Brazil actively participated in the war. Turkey which like Ireland had come under enormous pressure to enter the war, only declared war on Germany and Japan on 12 February 1945, in order to attend the founding conference of the United Nations in San Francisco in April.

During the war, a number of imaginative propositions were submitted to de Valera. Initially, the British suggested establishing an Anglo-Irish force of anti-submarine trawlers to patrol Irish coastal waters. This was rejected by de Valera. The British then suggested garrisoning the Treaty ports with non-British troops, for example, Poles, Free French and soldiers from the London Irish Regiment. This too was rejected. De Valera responded by making a suggestion, which two years later would have delighted any British minister, that was, for the US Navy to deploy a squadron of warships in Irish waters. Understandably, the US, which was neutral, did not want to deploy any of its warships in European waters. In the wake of the Dunkirk debacle, Churchill's government was so desperate that it offered de Valera a vague offer of Irish unity in return for a wartime alliance. De Valera was reticent to accept, as Britain was facing probable defeat and would offer anything to acquire a short-term advantage. Had de Valera accepted, Dublin most certainly would have shared the fate of Coventry,[31] and there was no guarantee that the Ulster Protestants would not resist being incorporated into an all-Ireland state.[32]

The value of Ireland's former Treaty ports may well have been over estimated, especially as Northern Ireland was fully involved in the war effort. In 1943 the US secretary of state, Cordell Hull, sought the views of the US joint chiefs of staff regarding a proposal to put economic pressure on Ireland, in order to force de Valera to agree to American basing rights. The reply signed by Gen. George C. Marshall is of much significance. They concluded that "while the ports of the Bay of Biscay were in German hands, it would be inexpedient to route convoys to the south of England, and that air or naval bases in Ireland would not appreciably alter the situation."[33] The memorandum confirms the Irish government's opinion on the real importance of the ports. However, the Royal Navy and the RAF's Coastal Command, while acknowledging Gen. Marshall's views on convoy routings, would argue that greater successes could have been achieved against the U-boat had Ireland allowed Allied anti-submarine units to operate from its ports and air-fields. Had the Royal Navy been able to operate deep-sea rescue tugs from Berehaven, Limerick, Galway, and Lough Swilly, many damaged Allied merchant ships could have been saved. (During World War II, a single British rescue tug, the *Robert Hastie*, was permitted to operate from Killybegs.) The basing of long-range maritime aircraft along the southern coast of Ireland would have significantly degraded the ability of U-boats, surface ships and F/W Condor bombers to operate from the French Atlantic coast.

Table 2: Manpower Levels in Ireland's Maritime Defence Forces, 1939-45

	Officers	NCOs	Ratings	Total
A Marine Depot	27	82	141	250
Two patrol Vessels	6	20	22	48
Six MTBs	12	72	18	102
A Mine Planter	2	8	13	23
A Training Vessel	1	6	3	10
A Minefield Section	4	24	36	64
A Port Control Service	13	49	69	131
A Coastwatchng Service	30	95	605	730
The Maritime Inscription	14	137	992	1143
Grand Total:	109	493	1899	2501

Source: Naval Policy Memorandum, 1961

THE END OF THE EMERGENCY

Ireland remained neutral up until the end of hostilities in May 1945. The German embassy was allowed to function and strict news censorship was still applied. (Irish newspapers were not allowed to report the deaths of Irish citizens serving with Allied forces. For example, if an Irish-born sailor was killed aboard a British warship, it was simply reported that he had died in mysterious circumstances in distant waters. No mention was made of the deceased's connection with the Allied war effort.) The Irish government's refusal to expel Axis diplomats in the period 1943-4 was a great source of concern to General Eisenhower. Understandably, he was worried that intelligence relating to the planned second front—the Normandy landings—might leak out via Dublin. In view of this concern, the Irish compromised by closing down the German embassy's radio transmitter. When Hitler committed suicide on 30 April, the Irish leader de Valera did what even the Spanish dictator General Franco refused to do: he went to the German embassy to express his condolences. Officially, this act of condolence was in accordance with diplomatic protocol. Less than two weeks earlier, on hearing of the death of President Roosevelt, de Valera paid a similar visit to the United States embassy in Dublin. However, with the exception of Portugal, Ireland was the only neutral country to acknowledge Hitler's death in such a manner. (Sweden and Switzerland, countries which out of necessity had supplied the German war economy with raw materials, ball bearings and precision instruments, made no effort to acknowledge Hitler's death.) This visit took place less than two weeks after Anglo-American troops had liberated the notorious concentration camps of Dachau, Belsen and Buchenwald; three months earlier Auschwitz had been overrun by the Russians. It is not surprising that the Soviet Union, a country which had suffered so grievously in Hitler's eastern war, should now wish to exclude Ireland from the newly founded United Nations Organisation.[34]

Once the war in Europe had formally ended the process of demobilisation began. By 15 May 1945 all emergency orders were revoked. Military courts, press, postal, telegraph and wireless censorship, registration of foreign residents and emergency censorship of films were terminated. Ireland's defence forces had succeeded in preserving the country's independence. The high regard in which Ireland's military were held, even prompted the United States government to offer high military awards to Gen. Dan McKenna and two of his senior colleagues. This was in view of their co-operation during the war years. However, the offer was politely declined as it would prompt much spectulation about the real level of Ireland's pro-Allied bias during the war.

The war also illustrated the country's need for a naval force to defend its ports and patrol its territorial waters. The 300 officers and ratings of the Marine Service had made a significant contribution to Ireland's defence of her neutrality and independence. The Irish coastline was not left unguarded or unobserved; the country's harbours were policed, and the main ports were heavily guarded and fortified. On 15 March 1946 it was finally decided that the Marine Service should become a permanent component of the defence forces and that it be reorganised and re-equipped to provide a small naval force to patrol territorial seas, cover prinicipal harbours and provide the state with a fishery protection service.

4

THE NAVAL SERVICE, 1945-70

When the war in Europe ended on 8 May 1945, Ireland's defence forces could look forward to early demobilisation. The maritime defence forces were among some of the first to disband: the Port Control Service on 1 June and the Coastwatching Service on 19 October. In May 1945 the Marine Service had its sea-going fleet of ten vessels reduced by the sale of the training schooner *Isaalt*. Three of the Service's six MTBs were inoperable because of a shortage of spare parts, and the two inshore patrol vessels, *Fort Rannoch* and *Murichu*, although still in commission, would eventually be released from military service. With demobilisation, the Marine Service's strength was reduced from a wartime peak of over 300 officers and men to 163 in early 1946—20 officers, 73 NCOs and 70 ratings. This level of manning was to be further reduced. In the wake of the Second World War, Ireland's *ad hoc* navy was quickly fading away.

In view of the important role performed by Ireland's coastal and marine forces during the Emergency, the Irish government decided to retain the Marine Service as a permanent component of the defence forces. This decision was taken on 15 March 1946 by the Irish defence minister, Oscar Traynor. The new navy's role would be to "patrol the territorial seas, protect principal harbours and provide the State with a fishery protection service". After 24 years of independence, Ireland would finally have a permanent naval defence force. Under the 1947 Defence Forces (Temporary Provisions) Act, the new navy would no longer be known as the Marine Service, but as the Irish Naval Service.[1] In addition, all ranks and titles would have a naval form. However, the new navy would not be independent, rather it was to be regarded as a separate military command of the Irish defence forces. Militarily, the country was subdivided into four territorial command districts—Eastern, Western, Southern and Curragh. In essence the Naval Service was to be regarded as an offshore or maritime command. The problem which faced the new navy was a shortage of manpower and sea-going naval vessels.

RECRUITING FOR THE NEW NAVY

With the demise of the Marine Service, all former marine officers were allowed to apply for commissions in the new Naval Service. Unfortunately age limits prevented many from being eligible. The number of officers in Ireland's embryonic navy was reduced from 23 in the former Marine Service to just seven (five executive and two engineers). In view of these manpower problems, temporary five-year commissions were offered to former Marine Service officers who for reasons of age were previously ineligible. This allowed 14 additional sea-going officers to be recruited. Five former army officers were also recruited to work in administration and supply. The Naval Service's complement of ratings stood at 143, but with an intense recruitment campaign this figure was increased to 304 in August 1946, and in 1947 it was raised to over 400.[2]

The Naval Service wanted to restrict recruitment for executive officers to those eligible for cadetships, but the time lag between training a cadet and fulfilling the immediate needs of the Service, obilged the navy to recruit a further intake of temporary officers from the merchant service. Similarly the navy relied on the merchant marine service for its engineer officers.

The Naval Service did recruit three cadets in December 1946 and these were sent to the Royal Naval College at Dartmouth in England to undergo the international midshipman's course. Their training included the Royal Navy's long gunnery course, as well as navigation, anti-submarine and minesweeping courses. One officer who benefited from one of these specialised RN courses was actually from the army's signals corps. He attended the Long Communication course at HMS *Leydene* and "passed with flying colours"! To this day, all Irish naval officers receive part of their training at the Britannia Royal Naval College, Dartmouth.

In 1946 the temporary officers who had come from the merchant marine were given additional training by the Royal Navy at various training establishments in Britain. These courses covered such varied areas as naval gunnery, radar, anti-submarine and machinery courses. In addition, the Royal Navy also seconded highly-trained chief and petty officers to assist the newly created Irish navy to become acquainted with naval skills.

The new Service also required a professional naval officer to command it. Many of the Marine Service officers were recruited from the merchant marine, and although extremely competent as sea-going officers, they lacked the formal naval training and experience. Early in 1946 enquiries were made and a suitable officer was located. Commander H.J.A.S. Jerome was a British naval officer who had just retired from the Royal Navy. During the war he had served as a senior adviser to the South

African navy. In 1946 he was offered the post of commanding officer and director of the Irish Naval Service. He accepted, and was commissioned into the service as a naval captain on 1 December 1946. It was an exciting opportunity for a retired naval officer, namely, to establish and oversee the growth of a new navy. Capt. Jerome's contract of employment was initially for five years, but this was extended to ten years.

Two other senior appointments were also made in 1946. A former engineer commander in the Royal Indian Navy was commissioned into the Naval Service as a commander and appointed engineer manager of the naval dockyard. An ex-Royal Navy instructor was commissioned into the Service as a lieutenant commander and appointed as naval education officer at the naval school.[3]

ACQUIRING SHIPS FOR THE NEW NAVY

The Naval Service's most immediate requirement was for sea-going naval vessels which could patrol all of Ireland's territorial waters regardless of season and weather conditions. The MTBs although visually impressive were not at all suited to the country's needs. Fortunately for the Naval Service, the world in 1946 was very different from 1939; the navies of the victorious Allied powers possessed an abundance of surplus naval shipping. The obvious supplier was Ireland's neighbour Great Britain. The British Admiralty had hundreds of warships mothballed in ports awaiting their fate—to be sold or scrapped. Among the most abundant variety in storage was a type of ocean-going convoy escort, the *Flower* class corvette.

The Flower *class corvette*

The type of vessel which was to constitute Ireland's sea-going navy for the next 25 years was the *Flower* class corvette. The vessel's design was based on that of a whalecatcher, the Southern Pride, which had been built in the late 1930s by Great Smith Docks Co. Ltd in South Shields in north-east England. This Company specialised in building whalecatchers for the Norwegian market, and during the Great War they had supplied the Royal Navy with escort vessels. In 1940 they hurriedly adapted the whalecatcher design and produced the *Flower* class corvette, so named because the first vessel of this type, HMS *Gladiolus*, as with all the others, was named after a *Flower*. The *Flower* class corvette was a cheap, easily constructed and robust convoy escort vessel. They were built to civilian specifications and from a distance looked like a merchant vessel. This had its advantages as surfaced U-boats always dived when they encountered a distinctive naval silhouette; the whaler-like appearance of the *Flower* class corvette allowed its crew to give an unsuspecting surfaced enemy submarine a nasty jolt with its four-inch gun. The initial vessels were costed at £90,000 each.[4]

In the novel *The Cruel Sea*, by Nicholas Monsarrat, the author describes the a *Flower* class corvette as being:

> 200 feet long, broad, chunky and graceless: designed purely for anti-submarine work, and not much more than a floating platform for depth-charges. Her mast, contrary to Naval practice, was planted in front of the bridge, and a squat funnel was planted behind it. The depth-charge rails aft led over a whaler-type stern—aesthetically deplorable, but effective enough at sea. She would be hot in summer—there was no forced-draught ventilation, and no refrigerator—and cold, wet and uncomfortable at most other times. She would be a natural bastard in any kind of seaway, and in a full Atlantic gale she would be thrown about like a chip of wood.[5]

They were approximately 204 feet long and had a standard displacement of 940 m/t (1140 m/t full load). With a fuel capacity of over 200 tons, they had a range of 4000 miles and could steam at 16 knots. They were fitted with a 4-cylinder triple expansion steam engine, the only design which was readily available in the early 1940s. This drove a single-line propellor. Although fast enough to escort merchant convoys, *Flower* class corvettes were actually slower than a surfaced U-boat. They were never intended for long range patrols, as they were designed for coastal escort work. But the demands of the Battle of the Atlantic obliged the Royal Navy to press them into service on Atlantic convoys. After 1942 improved *Flowers* came into service, and in view of the original design's excessive rolling, new and better designs followed, for example, the *Castle* and *River* classes. All of the Irish corvettes were of the unmodified, pre-1942 variety.

The wartime variants of the *Flower* class corvette had a complement of 85 officers and men. The excessive size of these crews was dictated by the pressures of wartime, when there was a constant need to have fresh reliefs to man the vessel's weapon systems and engines. Fortunately, the Irish corvettes were not obilged to work under such pressures. The sheer unpleasantness associated with life aboard a *Flower* class corvette is best encapsulated in Monsarrat's famous novel, which was later (1954) adapted to screen in the film of the same name.

Many of the complaints voiced by Canadian and British wartime crews about conditions on *Flower* class corvettes were still applicable during their peacetime service with the INS. Although a good sea boat, the corvette floated like a cork; in fact the corvette's hull contributed significantly to its reputation for rolling. In the words of Monsarrat, "a corvette would roll on wet grass".[6] He claimed that this ceaseless rolling became a special form of torture. Sea sickness was a constant problem, this being aggravated by poor ventilation and over crowding. Another irritant which plagued Irish as well as wartime Allied crews was the persistence of water and damp. Water dominated a corvette sailor's existence. Water covered the decks inside and out and dripped incessantly from condensation on the deckhead. Even in the ship's toilet, the crewman could not escape sea water, as there was a straight pipe which ran from the toilets to the sea. In the words of Harry Shorten, a telegraphist aboard the corvette *Dundas* in 1942, "if you happened to be sitting on the seat and she rolled, you got a four-inch jet of Atlantic up your stern."[7]

The *Flower* class corvette was the most heavily armed vessel ever to enter the service of the INS. The vessel's main armament consisted of a single four-inch BL gun with 100 rounds of mixed HE and AP ammunition aboard. This weapon was positioned on the forward bandstand mount; it was the same type of gun which was mounted on the *Hunt* class minesweepers during World War I. It required a five man gun crew to operate this weapon regardless of weather conditions. Unfortunately the gun shield only gave the crew partial shelter from the elements. The weapon had a maximum range of approximately 4000 metres; separate charges and shells were employed. The vessel's secondary armament consisted of a single two-pounder Pom Pom anti-aircraft gun mounted on the aft gun mount. In addition the vessel had two single 20mm Oerlikon anti-aircraft guns, one on either bridge wing.

To this day the *Flower* class corvette was the only type of warship used by the INS which was equipped with an anti-submarine weapon (ASW) system. These comprised depth-charges and a Hedgehog mortar. A total of 45 depth charges were carried, and these could be launched from four throwers and two depth-charge rails. A hydrostatically controlled pistol detonated the depth-charge at a pre-selected depth. These bombs were devastatingly effective if they exploded within 20 feet of the hull of a submerged submarine, but they had their limitations. First, to be effective the corvette had to physically pass over the enemy submarine, in order for the depth-charges to be released. Such proximity was difficult to achieve. Second, the depth-charges' rate of sinking after launch was seven feet per second; a submerged submarine could easily move a distance equal to three times the lethal radius in just ten seconds. In addition, the ship's anti-submarine detection device Asdic could not function during the depth charge bombardment.

The corvette's other ASW system was Hegdehog. This was an ahead-throwing weapon which could fire 24 65lb contact fuse bombs over 200 yards ahead of the ship in an intricate circle pattern about 100 feet in diameter. Each bomblet was loaded with 30 pounds of Torpex and any one of them, dropping straight down through the water, would explode on contact with disastrous results for a submarine. This system greatly resolved the problem associated with the lag between target detection and the depth-charge arriving within the vicinity of the enemy submarine. Hedgehog was accurate, except in heavy seas; its main advantage being that the enemy submarine commander had no warning of attack. However, this system was also plagued by its limitations: the warheads themselves were armed by a propellor screw on entering the water. In service they sometimes failed to leave the firing spigots, or much worse armed themselves and exploded on board.[8]

In all, 258 *Flower* class corvettes were built, of which 151 were constructed among 16 British yards and 107 in Canada.[9] After 1945 many of the surviving corvettes were either scrapped, converted into weather ships or sold off to merchant shipping companies. Some were sold to foreign navies, of which Ireland purchased three. In 1971 the INS was one of the last navies in the world to operate this type of vessel. The only other naval operators of the *Flower* class corvette were the Dominican Republic and Egypt. The latter had one *Flower* class in service, the *El Sudan*. Built in Harland and Wolf shipyard, Belfast, this vessel had seen service with the British and Yugoslav navies before being sold to Egypt in 1949.[10]

Early in 1946 an order for six *Flower* class corvettes was placed with the British Admiralty. In view of the acute shortage of trained manpower, the intention was to acquire three vessels immediately and then take delivery of a further three two years later. The Royal Navy initially nominated three vessels—HMS *Saxifrage*, HMS *Oxlip* and HMS *Bellworth*—to be transferred to Ireland on purchase. All of these vessels were on the reserve. However, later on HMS *Borage* was substituted for HMS *Saxifrage*, as it was then only coming into the Reserve, and in operational condition. The names for the new Irish corvettes were derived from Irish mythology; to this day all Irish naval vessels are named after female figures from Celtic mythology. An army order allotted the names Macha, Maev, Cliona, Banba, Fola and Grainne to the new corvettes. The first batch of three corvettes were purchased at a total cost of £200,000,[11] while the remaining three were not bought because of a continuing shortage of trained manpower. The names Banba, Fola and Grainne were retained in anticipation of future procurements. In 1971 these names were indeed allocated to the corvettes' replacements.

The first corvette to be delivered to the Naval Service was LE *Macha* (ex HMS *Borage*). She was taken over and commissioned with full ceremonial in Devonport Naval Dockyard by Lt. W.J. Reidy on 15 November 1946. Five days later, after delivering LE *Macha* to Cobh, where she was handed over to her new commander, Lt. F. White, Reidy returned to Devonport. The second corvette, *Maev* (ex HMS *Oxlip*), was

9 Corvettes LE *Cliona* and LE *Maev* on patrol in the late 1940s. The photograph is taken from LE *Macha*.

Table 3: Selected Force Levels in
Ireland's Marine/Naval Service, 1939-50

Year	1939	'40	'41	'42	'43	'44	'45	'46	'47	'48	'49	'50
Corvettes	0	0	0	0	0	0	0	2	3	3	3	3
Patrol vessels	1	2	2	2	2	2	2	2	0	0	0	0
Minelayers	0	0	1	1	1	1	1	1	1	1	1	1
Motor torpedo boats	0	3	3	4	6	6	6	6	6	2	2	2
Sail training craft	0	0	1	1	1	1	1	0	0	0	0	0

commissioned on 20 November 1946, and steamed for Cobh, where she was handed over to Lt. A. Thompson. The third and subsequently the final corvette, LE *Cliona*, was not taken over at Devonport until 3 February 1947. This vessel was retained by Lt. Reidy as his own command.

The purchase of a fourth corvette was cancelled because of the Naval Service's inability to provide trained crews for both this vessel and an intended hydrographic survey ship. Hydrographic survey was a role which the new Naval Service was obliged to undertake. Costings were received from the British Admiralty regarding suitable vessels. The figures quoted by the Admiralty were quite daunting for a country in Ireland's economic circumstances in the late 1940s: £250,000 for one ex-RN *Algerine* class ocean minesweeper, or £655,000 for a purpose-built hydrographic survey ship.[12] The latter would take two and a half years to build. In the end, the Naval Service got neither a survey ship, or a fourth corvette. However, regardless of these setbacks, Table 3 illustrates the significant development of Ireland's maritime defence forces since 1939.

Within 11 months of the official birth of the Irish Naval Service on 15 March 1946, the new navy had accomplished three important objectives. First, the chronic drain on manpower had been reversed and the navy now had over 450 officers and men in regular service. Second, the absence of trained naval officers had been rectified by the recruitment of Capt. Jerome and other former Royal Naval officers. Finally, the lack of sea-going naval vessels which were capable of operating in all weathers off Ireland's coasts had been resolved by the purchase of admittedly only three out of an intended six ex-RN corvettes. The necessary ingredients for any viable navy were now in place: sea-going vessels, experienced senior officers and trained manpower.

The Naval Service's home base and training centre was the former Marine Service centre on Haulbowline Island. On this island was located

10 A gun crew undergo anti-aircraft drill on one of the corvettes.

the navy's only operational base, dockyard and training centre—the Naval School. At the island's former Royal Naval dockyard, new buildings were erected and the slipway reactivated. At this dockyard, the Service's patrol vessels and MTBs were repaired and refitted. Training bays were established at the Naval School, which encompassed such areas of naval education as fire and damage control, TAS (torpedo anti-submarine), gunnery, navigation, seamanship and communications. By 1948 the Naval Service was firmly established.

Disposing of wartime craft

When the war ended in May 1945, Ireland's maritime defence forces no longer required many of their harbour craft and patrol launches. Dublin's port control launch, the *Noray*, was sold back to Dublin Port and Docks Authority. The various harbour launches and work boats used by the Port Control Service were quickly sold off. One of the Marine and Coastwatching Service's first acquisitions, the armour-plated target boat, was released from its river patrol duties on Lough Derg in May 1945. While being escorted back to Cork by the *Murichu*, the unfortunate craft caught fire. Although it did not sink, it was eventually sold off. Also in the same month the training vessel, *Isaalt*, was condemned as being unseaworthy and was sold. She later foundered off Wicklow Head in December 1946 with the loss of five lives. The *Murichu* remained in service until 1947, when she was condemned as being "unseaworthy"; she was decommissioned and sold for breaking up. On 8 May 1947 the venerable old steamer foundered off the Saltees, Co. Wexford on her last voyage to the Dublin breakers yard. It was only fitting that a veteran of two world wars, one civil war, one anti-British rising, and numerous encounters with foreign trawlers should end its days at sea. Her sister vessel, the patrol vessel *Fort Rannoch*, was classified as being unsuited for continued naval duties, and was sold to Dublin Steam Trawling Co. in 1947. The minelayer *Shark* was retained as a stores' ship and harbour transport until its disposal in 1952. The MTBs remained in service until 1948, when four of the boats (M1, M2, M3, M6) were sold to a private company headed by Col. James Fitzmaurice for conversion into houseboats. The last two were sold off to Fitzmaurice in 1950 for the same purpose. Their eventual disposal was dictated by the fact that dry rot had set in and the engines were worn out.[13]

By 1952 the Naval Service was reduced in size to a sea-going fleet of three ex-RN *Flower* class corvettes and one small harbour launch, the *Colleen*. The department of defence also maintained a small fleet of harbour and coastal auxiliaries.

THE NEED FOR ADDITIONAL SHIPS

By 1952 Ireland's navy had been reduced to three sea-going vessels. The small squadron of wartime MTBs had been scrapped, as had the two patrol vessels, the sail training vessel, *Isaalt*, and the harbour stores ship, *Shark*. The intended flotilla of six corvettes never materialised, and the hydrographic survey vessel was never purchased. However, throughout the 1950s both Captains Jerome and McKenna NS made it clear through the submission of repeated memoranda that additional ships and craft were urgently needed if the Naval Service was to be able to carry out its designated primary and secondary roles.

The need for additional vessels was recognised in 1951 when the then defence minister, Oscar Traynor, held discussions on the future direction of the Naval Service. These discussions, which were held on 4 May, can be traced back to a cabinet discussion in June 1949 on this same subject. At that time, no firm decision had been taken as to whether the Naval Service should be a non-military fishery protection force or form part of the defence forces. In 1951 Traynor stated that he was satisfied as to the necessity for an effective Naval Service within the structure of the IDF.

In view of this new and definite commitment to build up a regular navy, Traynor stated that he would approach the government for additional funding in order to buy suitable vessels and equipment. An official delegation was sent to the British Admiralty in February 1952 to discuss and secure information on the type of hostile naval threat anticipated and possible methods of defence, and suitable vessels and equipment. The Admiralty's advice was that the Naval Service should concentrate on the seaward defence of Ireland's most important ports, in addition to carrying out peacetime fishery protection duties.[14]

Seaward defence craft

The need for seaward defence boats had been clearly illustrated during the Emergency. During this period the Marine Service was not equipped with any vessels that had the capability to detect, pursue and destroy hostile submarines in offshore waters. The MTBs were equipped with depth-charges, but they lacked any submarine detection equipment. Also, in addition to being unable to operate in rough weather, they lacked endurance, the ability to stay at sea for any significant period of time. The Naval Service's requirement was for a specially designed seaward defence boat or a converted inshore patrol craft that could carry out a dual role of fishery protection and seaward defence training.

The Naval Service's specification for a seaward defence boat was as follows:

11 A depth–charge explodes astern of LE *Cliona* during anti–submarine warfare training in the late 1940s.

displacement	70/100 tons (of wooden construction)
draft	max. 6 feet
fuel endurance	2000 miles
speed	18 knots
armament	40mm or 20mm AA guns, depth-charges and flares
accommodation	3 officers, 4 petty officers, 12 ratings. Rations for 5 days' patrol duty[15]

Initially, the aim was to provide one seaward defence boat for each of the four defended ports, those ports protected by, admittedly, obsolete coastal defence batteries. This would enable An Slua Muiri naval reservists in each of these ports to receive adequate training. In July 1953 Lt.-Cdr. A. Thompson, the officer instructor to An Slua Muiri in Southern Command was sent to Portsmouth to attend a five-day introductory course on seaward defence. In October the Admiralty forwarded details of suitable RN craft that were available for purchase. In May 1954 Capt. Jerome NS and the department of defence's contracts officer, Mr Collins, flew to England to inspect the available craft. In September of the same year the Irish department of defence asked the Admiralty to select a contractor for suitable refit and conversion work. The prospect of the Naval Service acquiring two ex-RN patrol craft seemed about to be realised. On 31 January 1955 Capt. Jerome again returned to England to inspect two of the most suitable boats—MFV 1531 and MFV 1507. These were large harbour defence launches.

During the course of his visit to England, Capt. Jerome discussed the training of Irish cadets with the commandant of BRNC Dartmouth, Vice-Admiral Ben Bryant. At the time Dartmouth was under pressure to take an unusually high quota of cadets from the Royal Australian navy, but Vice-Admiral Bryant assured Capt. Jerome that the Royal Navy would ensure that Irish naval cadets would not be excluded by reason of pressure of numbers. In 1956 the British Admiralty refused to take further Irish naval cadets unless the educational standard was increased to honours mathematics and physics. Advertisements to fill four vacancies in 1956 only brought one application with the necessary qualifications. In view of this situation, the Naval Service decided to train its own cadets with one year in the Military College, one year in the Naval School and two years at sea. In 1961 the first Irish-trained naval cadets received their commissions.

The intended purchase of the two seaward defence boats was undermined when it became apparent that the cost of refitting them had increased by £20,000. The initial total costing for both boats, including all necessary conversion work, was £92,000. The price increase was attributed to wage inflation in the UK. This price increase doomed any prospect of the Naval Service taking delivery of specially designed inshore patrol craft. For Capt. Jerome it was a bitter blow. He went on to note in an official memorandum: "An enormous amount of work has been done by the British Admiralty on our behalf over the past three years. They have taken great trouble to assist us by way of advice, technical discussions, selection and examination of vessels, provision of drawings and redrawings, and securing of tenders."[16] The purchase of the SD boats was deferred indefinitely.

Training and supply ship

The scrapping of the antiquated stores ship, *Shark,* was a loss that was supposed to have been rectified by the acquisition of a dual-purpose training and supply vessel. Capt. Jerome identified the absence of a training vessel as a major deficiency: "our most serious problem is sea training—the most important part of Naval training, and this can only be properly carried out in a training ship, which the Service has not got." Capt. Jerome went on to comment: "since the condemnation of the *Isaalt,* we have had to depend on diluting corvette crews with trainees to achieve any sea training. A suitable training vessel with accommodation for 50 trainees is essential. Such a vessel could serve in a dual purpose role as a training and stores' ship, with special fittings for the carriage of warlike stores etc.—thus supplying a further gap in the Service's requirements. A gap which has existed since the *Shark* was scrapped."

The Naval Service's general specification for such a vessel was:

- Sufficiently large to be seaworthy around the coast of Ireland, and to carry out voyages to continental Europe in chosen weather

- Able to transport 100 tons of cargo

- Dimensions: Length: 160'; beam 30'; draft not more 11/12'

- Speed not less than ten knots

- Accommodation for 22 crewmen and 36 trainees, equipped with modern navigation aids and AA guns

- Boats: one 25' motor boat; one 27' whaler boat.

Efforts to acquire such a ship began in 1947. In 1951 the department of finance gave approval for the drawing up of specifications and estimates, in consultation with Irish Shipping Ltd. Two years later, sanction was given for expenditure of £152,000 on the construction of a suitable vessel. However, this was suddenly followed by a demand from the department of finance that economies had to be made. According to Capt. McKenna, "alledged financial stringency and a need for economy measures brought the project to an end." The size and cost of the vessel were to be reduced. The consultants, Irish Shipping Ltd, lost interest in the project stating that due to ongoing commitments they were unable to comply with the new requests. The project was suspended indefinitely. Although in 1963 official interest was resurrected momentarily, the estimated cost of £209,000 for a suitable vessel was sufficient to stifle this.

Hydrographic survey vessel

The need for a hydrographic survey vessel was recognised as "a must" throughout the 1950s. The most suitable type of vessel recommended for such tasks was an ex-RN inshore minesweeper. Such a vessel could have been purchased from the British Admiralty for £60,000. However, to provide for such a service would have required significant funding to cover the costs of buying and converting a suitable vessel; providing for a crew; and training a survey team. On 5 July 1963 the Irish government made an undertaking that "in principle an Irish Hydrographic Service should be established as part of the Naval Service, but that the implementation of this decision should be deferred until such times as the staffing resources of the Naval Service and financial considerations permit". The Naval Service was never to acquire a survey vessel.

Patrol vessel

In 1959 the government made enquires via the British Admiralty to acquire a fourth vessel to assist the three corvettes in their fishery protection patrols. Their requirement was for an all-weather vessel with a draft not exceeding 12–14 feet and a speed not less than 16 knots. It was to be moderately armed. The need for new patrol vessel was dictated by the radical changes which had taken place in the fishing industry after 1945.

Prior to 1939 the largest fishing vessel on the British register was the *Gatooma*. She had a displacement of 307 tons and was powered by a 85 HP engine. The next largest was the *Imperialist* at 226 tons with a slightly more powerful 99 HP engine. All others were under 200 tons and only 15 had engines in excess of 100 HP. After 1945 a revolution occurred in both the size and types of ships, as well as the methods of fishing. By the late 1950s, fishing vessels were in the 500-1000 m/t category, with engines ranging in size from 500-3400 HP. By the end of the 1950s some fishing vessels operated within self-supporting fleets, in which there were repair vessels, factory and mother ships.

In response to the Irish enquiry for a fourth patrol vessel, the Admiralty offered HMS *Niger*, an *Algerine* class ocean minesweeper.[17] In addition, they also offered some mid- and late 1940s vintage frigates which were up for disposal. The decision to purchase a patrol vessel was postponed.

12 LE *Cliona* at anchor off Haulbowline Island, Cork

IRELAND AND THE NAVAL SERVICE IN THE FIFTIES

The 1950s was a period of economic privation and recession in Ireland. Emigration levels were increasing, which resulted in many of the country's youngest and most talented citizens leaving for Great Britain, Canada, USA, and Australia (between 1951-61, 400,000 people emigrated from the Republic of Ireland). Ireland's poor economic circumstances were compounded by her diplomatic isolation. The country had attempted to join the newly founded United Nations Organisation, but to no avail. Ireland's wartime neutrality had rankled many allied nations, and de Valera's message of condolence did not help matters. But Ireland's exclusion from the United Nations was not only unfair but hypocritical. Sweden was permitted to join, even though she too had a pursued a policy of wartime neutrality, which at times bordered on being pro-Axis. (During the Second World War, the German army of occupation in Norway was allowed free right of passage through Swedish territory.) In 1955, two years after Stalin's death, the Soviet Union agreed to let Ireland join the UN. The only condition attached to her joining was that Romania be granted entry as well.

The passing of the Republic of Ireland Act in 1949 severed the final link between the United Kingdom and Ireland. However, this important episode in modern Irish history only increased the country's diplomatic isolation. Ireland had refused to remain within the British Commonwealth, a decision about which even de Valera was critical. India's decision to become a republic, yet remain within the Commonwealth, had shown that another path was possible. Excluded from the United Nations and voluntarily withdrawing from the British Commonwealth had left Ireland an independent, neutral, yet economically- stagnant state on the periphery of Europe. Invitations to join the newly-founded trans-Atlantic defence organisation NATO were turned down. So long as the island of Ireland remain partitioned, no security alliance involving Britain could be contemplated. However, this concern over partition sounded rather hollow in view of Mr Costello's decision to accentuate the partition of Ireland by withdrawing from the Commonwealth. In the words of Britain's prime minister, Clement Attlee, "the government of Éire considered the cutting of the last tie which united Éire to the British Commonwealth a more important objective than ending partition."[18]

At the beginning of the 1950s Irish defence expenditure increased slightly. The Cold War had become "hot" in north-east Asia with the onset of the Korean War in June 1950. Europe too was traumatised by the ideological divide which had split central Europe from Rostock on the Baltic to Trieste on the Adriatic. Although Ireland remained geographically isolated from these cold and hot conflicts, defence expenditure was

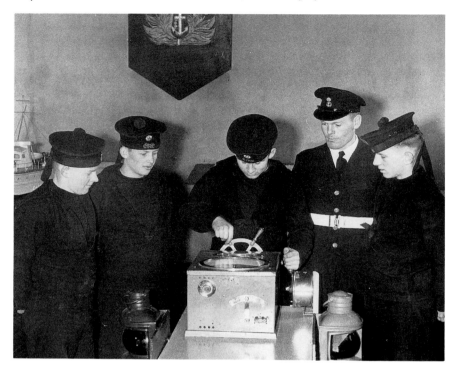

13 Young recruits under instruction in the 1950s

increased. However, the Naval Service did not benefit from any of this additional expenditure.

Although Ireland had decided to remain outside of NATO, this did not prevent the IDF from maintaining or developing contacts with the armed forces of other countries. In 1951 a team of senior Irish military officers, lead by Major-General Liam Archer, chief of staff of the IDF, visited United States Army units in Germany. Three years later senior Air Corps officers visited USAF bases in Germany.[19] To those who visited, it was quite clear that the years of military penury would end immediately if Ireland agreed to join NATO or establish a bilateral defence agreement with the USA. The Americans had already shown how they had lavishly re-equipped the land, air and naval forces of Greece, Turkey, Spain, Portugal and West Germany. Had Ireland signed a military assistance treaty with the USA, it is very likely that the Irish Naval Service would have been transformed out of all recognition.

With the exception of the five visits to overseas ports, the Naval Service settled into a routine of training and providing the State with a fishery protection service. The navy's area of responsibility was 8950 square miles. The task of policing these territorial waters rested with the navy's only seagoing vessels, the three corvettes. Although the Air Corps still retained some Avro Ansons, fisheries/maritime surveillance flights were not undertaken. The only modern twin-engined aircraft available to Ireland's military air arm was one newly-acquired DH Dove. However, this light transport aircraft was not configurated for coastal patrol operations. In fact the Irish Air Corps was not to be involved in fishery protection/maritime surveillance operations until 1977.

In the early 1950s more cadets were recruited, one of whom was a Joseph Deasy from Dungarvan, Co. Waterford. He was sent to Dartmouth in 1951; 39 years later he would be appointed flag officer commanding the Naval Service with the rank of commodore. The Service which he had joined was still devoid of any port control craft, seaward defence boats or minesweeping vessels (see Table 4). Other branches of Ireland's defence forces were more fortunate. In July 1956 the Air Corps acquired not only their first jet aircraft, but Ireland's as well. The three brand new Vampire T55 armed trainers were flown to Baldonnel from the factory at Hatfield in southern England (a further three Vampire T55 aircraft were delivered in 1961). To meet the needs of the new jet aircraft, hardened (concrete) runways were constructed at Baldonnel. Four years later these runways were to be of great assistance to the United States Air Force during the Congo airlift.

In 1958 the Irish army acquired their first battle tanks. Eight ex-British Comet A3 tanks were delivered, thus enabling the formation of Ireland's first and only tracked armoured fighting unit—First Tank Squadron. The

Table 4: Selected Force Levels in the Irish Naval Service, 1951-62

Year	1951	'52	'53	'54	'55	'56	'57	'58	'59	'60	'61	'62
Corvettes	3	3	3	3	3	3	3	3	3	3	3	3
Minelayers	1	1	0	0	0	0	0	0	0	0	0	0
Motor torpedo boats	2	2	0	0	0	0	0	0	0	0	0	0

Comets joined four Churchill tanks which had been delivered in 1948. The Naval Service did not benefit from any of these acquisitions. Naval gunnery practice was restricted to surface shoots; aerial anti-aircraft shoots were out of the question. Since the scrapping of the Martinet in 1953, the Air Corps had lost its last target-towing aircraft. This situation would not be rectified until October 1972, when the IAC acquired eight Rheims Cessna 172 aircraft.

In 1956 Capt. Jerome retired after spending nearly ten years overseeing

14 Cmdr. Thomas McKenna in 1973

the Naval Service during its formative years. The new director of the
Naval Service was Capt. Thomas McKenna NS. He had been involved
with Irish governmental and naval shipping since 1936; he was a former
officer on the fishery protector *Murichu*. Prior to this Thomas McKenna
had served in the Far East and Latin America in the merchant marine.
During the war he commanded one of the motor torpedo boats, before
becoming involved in the foundation of the new Naval Service. He had
formerly held command of the naval base and dockyard, before being
appointed Commanding Officer of the Naval Service.

1956 annual inspection of the naval base

One of Capt. McKenna's first official duties as the new CONS was to
inspect the naval base and dockyard which he had so recently commanded. The official record of the visit gives an outsider a fascinating
insight into life in the INS during the mid-1950s. The inspection started
on Tuesday 5 June 1956 and lasted three days. It was an exhaustive
process, whereby the CONS, literally inspected every office, barrack block,
workshop, storehouse, training bay and classroom on the island. The
naval magazines on Spike Island were not exempted, nor were the
corvettes or the department of defence transport vessels. Capt.

McKenna's comments in general were positive. He noted that the guard of honour was well turned out, but that their uniforms were noticably worn. However, he also mentioned that "I noticed irregularities in saluting." Furthermore, he went on to state that "some individuals did not come to attention when spoken to and had to be corrected." Capt. McKenna's report of the visit, which was forwarded to the IDF's chief of staff, mentions that the Naval Service was still underfunded in many areas. His report mentions that due to undermanning, officers did not have time to undergo any revolver training in 1955-6. Similarly, grenade training was not conducted for the same reason. No endurance training was conducted as well, presumably for the same reason. The absence of a physical training instructor or a qualified NCO from the army's school of physical culture was noticed. Unlike the army, the Naval Service had still to receive the new Swedish-made Carl Gustav sub-machine gun.[20]

Capt. McKenna went on to comment about recreational facilities on Haulbowline Island. He mentioned that recruits could participate in organised team sports such as Gaelic football, association football, hurling and basketball. Every recruit had to box on wet Wednesday afternoons. Any talent noticed was picked out for a novice tournament. In 1956 no such tournament was held. For those not interested in sport, the naval

15 Capt. Jerome and Maj. Gen. Archer congratulate a newly commissioned ensign on board LE *Maev* in November, 1949.

base had a cinema, with four films being shown per week. Evening classes (voluntary) were available for recruits, but as Capt. McKenna commented "numbers have dwindled".

The Argentine offer

In March 1957, the Argentine navy celebrated the centenary of its founder, Irish-born Admiral William Brown. On this occasion a three-man delegation was sent to represent Ireland at the official commemorative ceremonies in Buenos Aires. The delegation comprised Mr Kevin Boland, the Irish defence minister, Major-General P. Mulcahy, the IDF's chief of staff, and Capt. McKenna. During his visit to Argentina, Capt. McKenna was awarded the Argentine Cross of Naval Merit. The Argentine navy also offered the Irish delegation two scholarships for suitable Irish officers to study at the Argentine Naval Academy. In addition, Captain McKenna was invited to send a party of Irish naval officers to tour Argentine naval establishments.

The Irish response to these two offers of assistance was negative. Although Capt. McKenna was understandably enthusiastic, IDF's chief of staff, Major-General Mulcahy, was more circumspect. He commented that " I am not disposed to take the initiative in this matter. Such a tour will be of great interest to the officers selected, but I do not see a real necessity for it. Although it is suggested that the Argentine government would bear the expenses, it is not clear whether the offer covers travel from and back to Ireland." Finally, Major-General Mulcahy made his intention clear when he stated that "we should not put ourselves in the position of accepting costly favours, unless we are prepared to return hospitality on the same scale".[21] The Argentine offers were not followed up.

The following year, 1958, the corvettes *Macha* and *Cliona* had a major refit. They were now over 16 years old and were showing signs of the strain imposed on them by wartime service in the Atlantic and peacetime duty off Ireland's turbulent coasts. In 1959 the Irish Defence Forces underwent a radical overhaul. The objective of this programme was to enhance the morale and combat efficiency of the reserve forces, by merging regular and reserve units into common formations. For example, an infantry brigade would now be comprised of one regular and two reserve (FCA) battalions. In practice the system was unpopular and impractical; it was eventually phased out in 1977. The 1959 reforms did not effect the Naval Service, as it would have been impossible to man the corvettes and the naval base on the basis of one-third regular personnel and two-thirds second-line reservists.

OVERSEAS VISITS

Although very small, the new Naval Service now had the capability to mount overseas visits. This was something which the Marine Service could never have accomplished with their MTBs and inshore patrol vessels. In 1948 the Naval Service was called upon to carry out its first overseas mission. The distinguished writer W.B. Yeats had died in exile in wartime France. The German occupation had raised obvious difficulties in returning his remains to his native Co. Sligo. However, in 1948 the Irish government arranged for the Naval Service to send one of their newly acquired corvettes to Nice in southern France to collect Yeats' remains and transport them back to Ireland. In June of that year LE *Cliona* left Haulbowline for Nice, calling in on Gibraltar on the outward and return journeys. According to the late Cmdr. McKenna NS, who went on this vovage, the sight of an Irish warship on her first overseas voyage was a notable event. He went on to remark that the reception at Gibraltar was "fantastic . . . the British were all Irish".[22] Regardless of the historic antagonisms between England and Ireland, the genuinely friendly and professional relations between the Royal Navy and the Irish Naval Service

16 French Alpine troops provide a guard of honour for W.B. Yeats' coffin.

17 W.B. Yeats' coffin aboard LE *Cliona*

transended these differences. On arriving at Nice, Yeats' body, which was given an honour guard by French alpine troops, was carried aboard the corvette. Seventeen days after leaving Ireland, the *Cliona* arrived in Sligo Bay.

The previous year the Naval Service took the Irish prime minister, Eamon de Valera, on a cruise around Ireland. (Only two Irish prime ministers have embarked on such voyages—Eamon de Valera in 1947 and William Cosgrave in 1975.) LE *Macha* sailed from Cork up to the west coast, stopping off at the Aran Islands. The vessel then proceeded to the west coast of Scotland and then down towards Dublin stopping off at the Isle of Man.

Foreign training cruises continued with the corvette, *Maev,* paying visits to Milford Haven, Devonport and Cherbourg in 1950. This was followed by a visit to Copenhagen in 1952. On that occasion LE *Maev* was sent to represent the Naval Service at the International Council for the Exploration of the Sea. In September 1951 LE *Macha* went to Brest and Vigo in north-west Spain. Three years later, LE *Macha* again went overseas, with Capt. Jerome NS as senior officer. The ports visited were Antwerp, Stockholm, Amsterdam, Portsmouth and Fishguard. After 1954, with the exception of a weekend visit to Brest, foreign training cruises were not undertaken. This can be attributed to the smallness of

Ireland's navy and the repeated demands from the department of finance for economic stringency. In 1956 *Macha* was temporarily decommissioned, thus reducing the size of the fleet to two corvettes. Three years later Capt. McKenna raised the subject of overseas visits in a memorandum submitted to the chief of staff. In it, he recommended that a foreign visit should be arranged on an annual basis for each of the corvettes. Capt. McKenna stressed the importance of such visits for crew morale and image projection. In that year he recommended that the re-commissioned *Macha* should be sent to Iceland, and LE *Cliona* to Denmark and the Channel Islands.[23] The suggestion was not followed up.

It would not be until 1961 before one of the corvettes would venture abroad again. On that occasion the visit would be dictated by the need to collect batches of the new Belgian FN self-loading rifle for use by Irish UN troops in the Congo. Both in May and June 1961 the corvette *Cliona*, under Lt. Cdr. Moloney, went to Antwerp; the rifles were then transported back to Ireland. Fourteen years would pass before an Irish naval vessel would be able to go overseas again.

18   Eamonn de Valera (far right) going ashore to the Scottish island of Iona on one of LE *Macha*'s open launches in 1947

THE SIXTIES

The Naval Service entered the new decade without a fourth patrol ship, seaward defence craft, minesweeping vessels, or a training and supply ship. The three corvettes were not only obsolete as anti-submarine patrol vessels, but they were wearing out. The recent refits in 1958-9 had extended their seaworthiness by another seven years. However, their value as naval vessels was now limited. In view of this critical situation, Capt. McKenna CONS submitted to the chief of staff and the department of defence a memorandum on naval defence. The contents of which clearly illustrated the enormous gap between what the INS possessed in 1961 and what they would require to defend Ireland's ports and territorial waters.

1961 Naval Policy Memorandum

Role The role of the Naval Service in wartime is as follows:

- anti-submarine patrol of territorial seas;
- minesweeping in the approaches to ports and passage sweeping in territorial waters;
- the seaward defence of the four defended ports.

Organisation To carry out this role would require the following organisation:

- A Naval Headquarters complete with a naval intelligence section; its own communications station, merchant navy and port liasion section.
- The division of the coast into three distinct naval districts with bases at Dublin, Cork, and Limerick. The suggested naval districts were:
  Eastern District—Carlingford to Mine Head
  Southern District—Mine Head to Brandon
  Western District—Brandon to Inishowen
  These districts were to be responsible for the coasts in their area; for the naval side of seaward defence of the ports in their area; and repair and supply of ships.
- The establishment of a supply sub-base at Killybegs or Lough Swilly under the control of Western District.
- Seaward defence port headquarters, in each of the defended ports: Dublin, Cork, Limerick and Waterford.

Vessels and craft needed for such a task The memorandum stated that in order to provide Ireland with an adequate naval defence, four different categories of naval vessel would have to be purchased. They were as follows:

    8 all-weather fast anti-submarine frigates
    6 coastal minesweepers
    11 inshore minesweepers
    12 seaward defence boats

The suggested type of fast ASW vessels that were then available on the market were the Royal Navy's *Blackwood* and *Loch* class frigates. The *Loch* class frigates were nearly as old as the corvettes, having been built in the period 1944-6. However, the *Blackwood* class vessels were more modern, being built between 1955 and 1958. According to the memorandum, the force of eight frigates would be sub-divided into the following patrol units: two frigates to patrol the east and SE coast; two to patrol the south coast; and four to patrol the SW, west and NW coasts.

The memorandum recommended that the most suitable type of coastal minesweeper currently on the market was the British *Coniston* or Ton class. Ironically, ten years later, the INS would acquire three ex-RN *Coniston* class minesweepers, but for very different reasons. In 1971 they were purchased as a desperate stop-gap to prevent the Naval Service from dying for lack of any sea-going fishery protection vessels.

The type of inshore minesweeper which the memorandum recommended was the Royal Navy's *Ham* class. According to the report, approximately 70 of these vessels were built between 1952 and 1958. They were 100 feet in length, had a displacement of 120 tons, and were armed with either a single 40mm Bofors or 20mm gun. The vessel required a crew of 15 in peacetime or 22 in wartime. The Naval Service's requirement was for 11 vessels, that is, two vessels for each of the four defended ports, with a reserve of three.

The type of seaward defence boat, which, according to the report, appeared to be the most suitable, was the Royal Navy's *Ford* class. The *Ford* class was designed to detect, locate and destroy submarines, including midget submarines, in the approaches to a defended port. They were 110 feet length and had a displacement of 120 tons with armament comprising a single 40mm Bofors gun, flares and one Squid triple barrelled depth-charge mortar or depth-charge rails.[24]

The memorandum's recommendations were not undertaken. To do so, would have imposed an enormous burden on the Irish economy. In addition to carrying out the primary peacetime role of fishery protection, the navy would be called upon to fulfill additional functions without extra manpower or ships. One of these tasks had actually been decided upon in the 1950s, but it was not until October 1966 that the Naval Service undertook the role.

Defence of Merchant Ship Courses The task in question was to provide the personnel from the Irish Merchant Service with Defence of

Merchant Ship Courses. These were undertaken twice yearly at the naval base. Between October 1966 and June 1973, 125 superintendents, masters, deck officers and engineer officers underwent these stringent courses.[25]

Training of Boy Fishermen Another function which the Naval Service was asked to carry out was the training of boy fishermen. This was done on behalf of the department of agriculture and fisheries. The course lasted three months; six weeks of which were spent with the Naval Service, the remainder at Cobh Vocational School. At the latter centre of tuition, the apprentice fishermen studied engineering, mathematics, accounting and domestic science, that is, cooking. Naval instructors (normally chiefs and P.O.s) under the commandant of the Naval School gave the boys an insight into naval life: they underwent physical training and military drill every morning. During their three month course, the navy provided the youths with accommodation and their meals. In the four-year period from its commencement in 1964, 128 boy fishermen attended this course. The scheme was terminated in March 1968, when the department of fisheries opened their own training centre in Greencastle, Co. Donegal.[26]

UN SERVICE

Ireland's entry into the United Nations in 1955 offered her defence forces the prospect of overseas service. Indeed in 1958, 50 Irish army officers were sent to monitor the ceasefire in Lebanon's mercifully-brief civil war of that year. The prospect of Naval involvment in any of these operations was out of the question. However, when in 1961 Ireland sent two reinforced infantry battalions to serve with the UN in the Congo, a Naval Service officer accompanied them. He was Lt. Cdr. Brunicardi, who had previously been attached to the naval base on Haulbowline. In the Congo, he was assigned as a staff officer to the Headquarters Group of the Irish contingent. Unfortunately, this very successful experiment in assigning an naval officer to an Irish UN Group was not followed up. This was despite the fact that Irish army personnel continued to serve throughout the 1960s with the UN in Cyprus and in the Middle East. In fact it was not until 1978 that another Naval Service officer was permitted to serve with the United Nations.

In June 1962 President John F. Kennedy paid a three-day official visit to Ireland; the first by any American president. During the course of his visit President Kennedy unveiled a memorial in Wexford to Commodore John Barry, the founder of United States Navy. While in Wexford, President Kennedy inspected a Naval Service guard of honour drawn from the crew of the corvette LE *Cliona*.

19 President John F. Kennedy unveils a memorial in Wexford to Cmdr. John Barry, founder of the United States Navy.

The visit of Captain McKenna to the US Sixth Fleet

Early in 1963 the commanding officer of the Naval Service received an invitation to visit the United States Navy's Sixth Fleet which is permanently based in the Mediterranean. The term "based" is inappropriate, as this fleet is self-supporting and in time of war or crisis can operate independently without recourse to port facilities. This is made possible by the impressive array of supply vessels, oilers, depot and repair ships which accompany the main body of warships.

The visit commenced on 17 March 1963, St Patrick's Day, when the US Navy sent an aircraft to Collinstown (now Dublin) airport. Capt. McKenna was flown to the French Mediterranean port of Nice, where he was conveyed by car to the Cannes. At Cannes Capt. McKenna was welcomed aboard the USS *Willis A. Lee*, a destroyer leader and flagship of Rear-Admiral Smith, commander of the fleet screen. Once aboard the *Willis A. Lee*, Capt. McKenna received a signal from Admiral Burke, chief of naval operations from the United States Navy:

> It is particularly fitting to have you visit our Sixth Fleet on this glorious St Patrick's Day. Near you in the Mediterranean is the United States Ship *Leary*. Out in the Atlantic are the *J.P. Kennedy* and *The Sullivans*. In the Pacific are the *Colahan* off the California coast. *O'Bannon* in Hawaii and *Rowan* in Philippine waters. All of these and other fine ships of our navy are maintaining the peace around the world, with friendliness backed up by the determination, courage and readiness for the fray so typical of those heroes of Irish descent for whom these ships are named.

A further signal from comm sixthflt (Commander of the US Sixth Fleet) was addressed to all the above mentioned ships:

> Best wishes to all hands on this glorious St Patrick's Day. May you continue to serve with energy and devotion in the tradition of St Patrick as indefatigable Missionaries of World Peace—Arleigh Burke, chief of naval operations of the US Navy.

It was a very thoughtful touch, or in the words of Capt. McKenna, "A real cead mile fáilte" (Irish for "a hundred thousand welcomes").[27] During the course of his ten-day visit to the Sixth fleet, Capt. McKenna observed intricate fleet manoeuvres, including refuelling at sea during a 60-knot gale. In addition, he was shown the US Navy's latest (1963) naval guns and anti-submarine weapon systems. The naval forces which Capt. McKenna visited in March 1963 comprised only a small part of the world's largest navy; a navy which in that year possessed 25 aircraft carriers. Indeed 1963 was the highpoint of *Pax Americana*; in December of the previous year the USSR had been forced to withdraw its missiles from Cuba, the Soviet navy was still primarily a coastal defence force, and America's disastrous involvement in the Vietnam War was yet to come.

During the course of his command of the Naval Service, Capt. McKenna would make other overseas visits to his naval counterparts in Argentina, Italy, Spain and West Germany.

THE PROBLEM OF MAINTAINING MORALE

The most pressing problem which faced the Naval Service in the early 1960s was the near collapse of morale. On 4 October 1962 a conference was held at the naval base to ascertain "why men leave the Service and the failure to attract new recruits". The conference was attended by Capt. T. McKenna CONS, the commandant of the Naval School, the commanding officers of the corvettes and other senior grade officers. The discussion was completely candid. The following observations were recorded by Capt. McKenna, as to why the Naval Service had a morale problem. The reasons cited were:

1. Pay.
2. Men join the Naval Service for adventure, and find instead a life of deadly monotony and genuine hardship.
3. Morale of Seamen's Branch completely collapsed due to consistent downgrading of status; chased from "Billy to Jack and given all the menial tasks".
4. Gunners—lynch pin in any Naval Service—now humping coal parcels etc.—complete lack of status.
5. In these days of full employment men need not accept these conditions for a comparative pittance.
6. Food, while not a governing factor, is well below the standard in other navies and the merchant service; lacking in variety—only two slices of butter per man
7. Absence of foreign cruises.

During the one-day conference Capt. McKenna was informed that the contrast between conditions in the Irish Naval Service and those in other navies and the merchant marine were a source of particular irritation. Sailors who boarded foreign fishing vessels and merchant ships saw for themselves how poor their circumstances were. Merchant and fishing personnel gladly told inquisitive Irish sailors how much they earned. Similarly, when foreign naval vessels visited Cork it was clear that pay and conditions in the INS were inferior to those in other European navies.

Finally, every Irish sailor knew that he always had the option to join the Royal Navy. In 1962 pay and conditions in the Royal Navy were far in excess of those in the INS. Opportunities for advancement were far greater, especially as the RN still had operational fleets and squadrons in Singapore, Hong Kong, Malta, Gibraltar and elsewhere.

During the conference, Capt. McKenna was told that it was humiliating for highly-trained and yet underpaid Naval personnel to go ashore and see "kids of 17 and 18 flashing £5.00 notes". These same youngsters had access to television, radio and library facilities, while the Naval Service had not any of these. The absence of any facilities on Haulbowline obliged the Irish sailor to either "remain in his bunk or go ashore and window shop". In such circumstances, it was not surprising that some naval personnel opted to buy themselves out, or, in desperation, desert. Two sailors opted for the latter drastic course of action and went to England to form a syndicate to help others buy themselves out. While in England the deserters obtained employment as construction workers and raised the necessary £40 to help a colleague buy himself out.[28]

Capt. McKenna reported his depressing findings back to the chief of staff and the department of defence. No significant measures were taken immediately to reverse the decline. However, in the autumn of 1963 an extensive recruitment drive was undertaken throughout the whole country. According to Capt. McKenna, "it was a complete failure". Only 23 recruits enlisted between 1 January and 30 September 1964.[29] At the time it seemed that the INS was slowly haemorrhaging to death. In 1959 there were 436 officers and men in the regular navy, the following year there were 397. In 1962 this fell to 302 and by 1965 this had fallen to only 283 (see Table 5). The severe shortage of fully-trained officers was undermining the ability of the INS to keep more than one of its three corvettes in commission. In 1964, of the five applications received for cadetships in the Naval Service, not one was found to have been suitable. In that year, it was only possible to keep one ship in commission. This was because the five officers needed to man a second corvette were away on extended courses and would not be available for sea duty until January 1965.

In 1965 the IDF's chief of staff, Lt.-Gen. Sean MacEoin, reported that, "it is apparent that the Naval Service has not the capabilities either at present or potentially to meet its war and peace commitments. It has no potential or capability in war either as a neutral or belligerent and can

Table 5: Manpower Strength in 1965

	Officers	NCOs	Ratings	Total
Established strength	45	285	281	531
Active strength	38	122	123	283

meet part of its peacetime committments, particularily fishery protection, only in a very limited way." Lt.-Gen. MacEoin went on to comment: "in the circumstances, it is very difficult to maintain morale and the continuous fall in strength is an indication of this."

The chief of staff's report also made reference to the state of Ireland's naval reserve. He noted that manpower levels were satisfactory with 403 officers and men in the second line reserve, but that they had no equipment to train with. They lacked any sea-going craft and that the defence of Ireland's four main ports was reliant on five whaler boats. In summary, his comment on An Slua Muiri was understandably direct: "They are in no better condition than the sea scouts."[30]

As the 1960s progressed it became evident that the Naval Service would eventually require replacements for the corvettes. By 1965 they were already over 24 years old. All three corvettes had benefitted from a comprehensive survey and refit between 1958 and 1960. This had extended their lifespan by another eight to ten years. The Service was faced with several options: to purchase or lease suitable offshore patrol vessels from overseas; to purchase second-hand coastal warships from a friendly navy, or to design and build a patrol vessel suitable to the Service's needs in Ireland. Indeed in 1959 an Irish shipbuilding company had been established in Cork. The Verolme Cork dockyard was a joint Irish-Dutch venture which was located at Rushbrooke near Cobh. This company had the necessary professional staff, skilled workers and international contacts to enable them to build a suitable type of patrol vessel. Verolme's yard had a capacity to build vessels up to a weight of 50,000 metric tonnes. On nearby Haulbowline Island was located the furnaces and foundry of Ireland's only steel manufacturer, Irish Steel Ltd. The necessary ingredients were in place should the Naval Service be authorised to build the corvettes' replacements in Ireland.

OPERATION TUSKAR

However, no immediate action was taken to remedy the situation. The corvettes were maintained in working order for as long as possible. Obviously, this situation placed an enormous strain on their engines, which required constant attention. In March 1968 an air accident occurred which illustrated the Service's inability to provide necessary seacover. On 28 March an Aer Lingus Viscount airliner crashed into the sea between Wexford and the Welsh coast. There were no survivors. The bodies of the deceased had to recovered as quickly as possible. Unfortunately, the Naval Service was unable to provide any of the corvettes for this purpose, as none of them were at sea. LE *Macha* was in Killybegs, in

Co. Donegal; LE *Cliona* was on leave in Haulbowline, and LE *Maev* was undergoing a refit. It was left to two Royal Navy warships, HMS *Hardy* and HMS *Penelope*, and the RNLI lifeboats to deal with the unpleasant task of collecting the bodies of the deceased. LE *Macha*, after having promptly departed from Killybegs, arrived on the scene to relieve HMS *Hardy* as the search controller.

The next task was to recover the wreck of the ill-fated Viscount. The Naval Service's commanding officer, Capt. McKenna, was appointed the search and recovery coordinator by the accident inspectors from the department of transport and power. This involved liasing with a myriad of Irish and British agencies: the Air Corps, Naval Service, RNLI, the RAF, the Royal Navy, the Gardaí, and CIE (Irish State Railways) who owned the port of Rosslare. What became knowm as Task Force Rosslare was one of many examples of Anglo-Irish naval cooperation in action. The Royal Navy provided the following vessels: HMS *Shoudton*, HMS *Clarbeston*, HMS *Iveston*, HMS *Nurton*, HMS *Bronnington*, HMS *Reclaim* (diving and rescue) and the RN salvage vessel *Uplifter*. The Irish provided their only two operational corvettes LE *Macha* and LE *Cliona*, the Lighthouse tender *Atlanta*, the fisheries research vessel *Cú na Mara*, and the fishing vessel *Glendalough*. A DH Dove from the Air Corps's general purpose flight was on hand as well. The Army provided transport for the recovered wreckage. Shoreside cooperation was organised by Lt. J. Deasy from the Naval Service and Lt. Cdr. Chapman RN.[31]

The search for the wreckage of the Aer Lingus Viscount was conducted on a daily basis from 28 March to 5 June 1968. On that day the skipper of the trawler *Glendalough*, W. Bates, hauled up wreckage from the Viscount. Royal Naval divers from HMS *Reclaim* confirmed that *Glendalough's* area of trawling was the location of the wreck. The Royal Navy assisted in the recovery of the wreckage, weather permitting, until 21 August. From then until 4 October the Naval Service and other Irish agencies continued the search. At 16.45 hours on 4 October Operation Tuskar was terminated; Task Force Rosslare was disbanded. Approximately 56 per cent of the wreck had been recovered.

DISPOSING OF THE CORVETTES

The corvettes LE *Macha* and LE *Cliona* made a valuable contribution to Operation Tuskar, but they were evidently wearing out. In 1968 all three corvettes were stripped of their secondary armaments: the two-pounder pom pom gun, the two single 20mm Oerlikon guns, the Hedgehog mortar and the depth-charge systems. They were now armed only with a single World World I vintage four-inch gun.

On 9 December 1968 a meeting was held at the department of defence in Dublin to seek out possible solutions. Capt. McKenna CONS informed the meeting that the options available were to buy suitable naval patrol vessels from an overseas source; to buy trawlers and convert them; or to build specially designed all-weather offshore patrol vessels. If they were to buy trawlers, they would have to meet the following minimum requirements: Length 160-70 feet; draft 12-14 feet; tonnage 800-1000 tons; speed 16 knots. In addition, Capt. McKenna informed the meeting that because of chronic manpower shortages, it was only possible to keep two corvettes at sea by closing the Naval School. The shortage of officers available for sea-going duty was perilous. In April 1969 the Irish Naval Service had only one captain, two commanders, five lieutenant-commanders, seven lieutenants and two sub-lieutenants.

Although Capt. McKenna advised that armed trawlers could carry out fishery protection duties, as in Iceland, he cautioned that they would have "zero naval potential".[32] Enquiries were made and it was ascertained that there were no trawlers of these dimensions in Ireland. If such trawlers were to be purchased from overseas, they would require an expensive programme of conversion. In order to mount a gun, the trawler's keel would have to be reinforced to support the weight of a gun platform. A magazine would have to be constructed, as well as the means to flood it. The overall cost of purchase and conversion was estimated to approach those of building a new and specially-designed patrol ship.

The option of purchasing a naval all-weather patrol vessel from overseas was looked into, but no such suitable vessels were available. The international shipping market was examined for suitable vessels, particularily in Britain and Norway, but to no avail. A suggested contender was the French *L'Agile* class inshore patrol vessel, but at 267 m/t, it was too small to be able to operate off Ireland's coasts in all weathers. Originally, the intention had always been to acquire two fishery-protection vessels and one fast naval vessel with an anti-submarine capability. However, the prohibitive costs of such modern warships obliged the department of defence to focus exclusively on acquiring fishery protection vessels.

In December 1968 *Macha* was taken out of service. Eight months later, in July 1969, *Cliona* was withdrawn from service as well. Both were eventually sold to Haulbowline Industries Ltd and promptly scrapped. By high summer 1969 Ireland's navy constituted a single World War II-vintage corvette, which regardless of a refit in 1968, was due for replacement.

This 26-month-long period between December 1968 and January 1971 must constitute one of the bleakest periods in Ireland's naval history. The already undermanned and grossly under-equipped navy was facing extinction (see Table 6). In order to give the Naval Service some form of sea-

Table 6: Selected Force Levels in the Irish Naval Service, 1962–70

Year	1963	'64	'65	'66	'67	'68	'69	'70
Corvettes	3	3	3	3	3	3	2	1

going capability, the government-owned fisheries research vessel, *Cú Feasa*, was taken over as an unarmed patrol vessel. Although an excellent platform for marine research, she had her limitations. The *Cú Feasa* was only 80 feet long and had a gross weight of 93 tonnes—less than one-tenth that of a *Flower* class corvette. She had accommodation for a crew of eight and four scientists.

In this period the Icelandic coast guard was equipped with much more impressive and suitable vessels. Their *Aegir* and *Odinn* class patrol ships were based on conventional trawler designs. These were ideally suited to the sometimes atrocious weather conditions in the North Atlantic. They had a range of 2000 miles and were armed only with a single 57mm gun, which was quite adequate for their fishery protection duties. These were the type of vessels which Ireland's navy would require—robust and relatively inexpensive, certainly when compared with conventional warships. The disparity in size between the fishery protection services of both of these Atlantic islands is quite staggering. In 1969 Iceland, with a population of only 201,975, had a fleet of six patrol ships, ranging in size from 1150 m/t to 200 m/t. Most of these ships were very modern, two having helicopter flight decks. Ireland in contrast with a population of 2.9 million had a navy comprising one ship, and maritime aerial surveillance was non-existent.

In view of the absence of any suitable vessels on the world market, a decision was taken to build the navy's new patrol ships in Ireland. Irish Shipping Ltd were retained as consultant and Verolme Cork Dockyard were successful in 1971 in tendering to build the first vessel. The Naval Service would eventually obtain a modern purpose-built patrol vessel, which would meet the Service's special requirements. However, in the interim period the Naval Service would have to struggle on with one worn out 30-year-old corvette.

THE NAVAL SERVICE, 1970-90

In January 1970 the Naval Service entered the new decade with only one ship in commission, LE *Maev*. There was no prospect of any new vessels becoming available in the immediate future; the first of the three proposed all-weather fishery protection vessels would not be in commission for another two and half years. With only one worn out and disarmed corvette, Ireland's navy was faced with the humiliating prospect of not being able to go to sea.

The Naval Service's situation, although extreme, was not unrepresentative of the condition of Ireland's armed forces in the late 1960s. This was an inevitable consequence of consistently low defence expenditure throughout the post-war period. There was even a suggestion that Ireland, like the Central American state, Costa Rica, should disband her armed forces. When in August 1969 communal violence erupted in Northern Ireland, the Irish Prime Minister, Jack Lynch, promised his compatriots that "he would not stand idly by"—the inference being that Irish military intervention was possible. However, there was little that Mr Lynch's government could have done. The Irish Defence Forces were under-equipped and under-manned: the Naval Service had one disarmed corvette; the Air Corps had six jet trainers, three helicopters and an assortment of unarmed light trainer and utility aircraft; and the 8000-strong Irish army did not have any permanent military posts on or near the border (prior to August 1969 there were no permanent military posts north of a line stretching from Gormanston Air Station to Galway). The Army's only modern armoured vehicles were 16 Panhard AML 60 light armoured cars, (eight of which were in Cyprus with the UN). With the exception of the eight Panhards in Ireland, the Army's thin sprinkling of wheeled armoured vehicles consisted of obsolete Second World War-vintage Landswerk and Leyland armoured cars. (According to Lt.-Col. John Duggan, the Landswerks were valueless, except for scrap. None of the armoured cars in service mounted a gun capable of penetrating 6mm armour plate.) It would not be until 1972 that the Irish army would acquire its first armoured personnel carriers (wheeled). Finally, the Irish army's sole tank unit, 1st Tank Squadron, was still equipped with eight elderly Comets and four Churchills. (Duggan went on to comment that the Comets were of no operational value and that the Churchills were not worth maintaining. In fact because of a design fault in the ammunition, the Comets could only fire solid shot.)[1]

The Northern Ireland crisis obilged the government to call up 2000 reservists; field hospitals were established near the border, but military intervention was not undertaken. The arrival of British troops in Belfast and Derry prevented further bloodshed. However, the violence and political instability which grew out those riots of August 1969 would eventually have a significant effect on the defence policies of both Ireland and the United Kingdom.

Without doubt 1970 was the bleakest year in Ireland's naval history. The Naval Service's sole vessel, LE *Maev*, was non-operational for several months, leaving Ireland's territorial waters open to all and sundry. The situation was actually worse than in 1940. At least at the beginning of the Emergency, the Marine Service was capable of going to sea with its small force of two armed patrol vessels and three modern motor torpedo boats. In addition, the Marine Service had the benefit of aerial surveillance, thanks to the Air Corps' seaplanes and maritime patrol bombers. Thirty years later, Ireland's navy did not have any of these luxuries: there were no port control craft, no armed trawlers in service and no maritime patrol aircraft—just one worn out corvette armed with a World War I-vintage gun. The effect on morale was an increase in those seeking careers outside the Naval Service.

This potentially catastrophic situation was rectified in late 1970, when the government decided to buy three minesweepers from the United Kingdom. The period of near terminal decline had finally been halted. Ireland's navy could once more be assured of having the means to police the country's coastal waters.

The Coniston *class minesweeper*

The type of vessel which saved Ireland's navy from disappearing into oblivion was the *Coniston* class coastal minesweeper. The Tons, as they are commonly described, were built by J.I. Thornycroft Co. in Southampton in the 1950s to meet the Royal Navy's urgent need for minesweeping vessels with a very low magnetic signature. (HMS *Coniston* was the first vessel of this class to be commissioned into service with the Royal Navy. All other *Coniston* class minesweepers were named after English villages ending in "ton", for example, Alverton.) Consequently, they had a composite hull of double mahogany planking on aluminium; the superstructure being made of aluminium as well. The underwater hull was originally sheathed in copper, but this was replaced by Cascover nylon.[2]

They were 153 feet in length and had a displacement of only 360 tons. With a fuel capacity of 47 tons, the Ton had a range of 2300 miles at 13 knots. However, they were primarily intended for use in coastal waters. The quality of accommodation for the 4 officers and 35 crewmen was far in excess of anything available on the old corvettes. In every respect these vessels were a generation ahead of the *Flower* class corvettes. While the remaining corvette, LE *Maev*, was powered by steam engines, the Tons had diesel engines. The minesweeper's armament was modern as well— one 40mm L60 Bofors gun on a power operated mount and two 20mm Oerlikon guns on a twin mounting.

In all, 118 of the *Coniston* class were built between 1954 and 1962. Although intended for service in a minesweeping capacity in European waters, the Tons proved to be highly ubiquitous. They were economical and sturdy seaboats which, thanks to their armament systems, could perform fishery protection, as well as coastal patrol duties. Up until 1985 five Tons were permanently on station in Hong Kong as patrol boats. They were also used by the Royal Navy for internal security work in the waters off Northern Ireland.

Many of them were eventually sold off as dual-purpose patrol/ minesweeping vessels to the navies of Argentina, India, Ghana, Australia, Ireland, and South Africa. Forty years after they were first built, the *Coniston* class is still in service with the South African navy. In 1993 the Royal Navy retired its last two operational Tons—HMS *Sheraton* and HMS *Brinton*. A single Ton, HMS *Wilton*, is still retained in service as a training vessel in Portsmouth.

Taking delivery of the Tons

The *Coniston* class minesweeper was a logical choice for Ireland's navy. They were robust seaboats which could perform a limited fishery protection role, as well as provide the Naval Service with a minesweeping capability. Also, it was fortunate for the Naval Service that Britain had several *Coniston* class vessels available for immediate purchase. The fact that the vessels were British built and owned facilitated their eventual use by Irish naval personnel; there were long and established links between the navies of both countries and, more importantly, all the necessary training manuals would be in English.

After inspecting a selection of available minesweepers in Britain and Gibraltar, three vessels were chosen. One minesweeper, HMS *Oulston*, lay at Hythe (Southampton) and the other two, HMS *Blaxton* and HMS *Alverton*, lay in Gibraltar. The vessels were purchased as they lay with their spares and minesweeping gear. With financial economy always in mind, the Naval Service was allowed to take delivery of only one of the minesweepers under Royal Naval supervision. All the necessary depreservation work required to reactivate the remaining two vessels had to be accomplished by Irish naval personnel alone.

The only ships on which most Irish naval pesonnel had ever served on were the *Flower* class corvettes. By 1970 much of the equipment on this class of vessel had become completely obsolete. The minesweepeers were diesel powered and armed with much more modern weapon systems. Therefore, the Naval Service had to update the training of the designated crews for the new minesweepers. Between November 1970 and February 1971 the Naval Service sent seven officers and 26 senior ratings to Britain for specialised courses. These covered such areas as electrical, basic diesel, gunnery, radio, radar, mechanics and basic communications.

On 8 December 1971 the first vessel was taken over at Hythe by the CONS, Capt. McKenna. She was towed initially to Vosper/Thornycroft in Southampton, before being towed to Portsmouth. At Portsmouth all the necessary depreservation work and storing was accomplished. On 30 January 1971 LE *Grainne* was commissioned by her new commanding officer, Lt.-Cdr. J. Deasy. Nine days later she left for Cobh, where she arrived on 10 February. On 12 February, at Haulbowline, she was formally named LE *Grainne* by Mrs Cronin, wife of the Irish defence minister, who was also present. The British ambassador and the defence forces' chief of staff were in attendance as well.

The ships' companies for the two remaining minesweepers were flown out to Gibraltar on a chartered Aer Lingus aircraft. Capt. McKenna formally took delivery of the vessels on 22 February. On the following day, and in the presence of the Flag Officer Gibraltar, Rear Admiral R.A. Sturdee RN, the minesweepers were blessed by Fr B. Devlin and named by Capt. McKenna's wife. In the words of the Capt. McKenna, the Royal Navy laid on "a whale of a reception" to mark the special occasion.

After depreservation work, the mineweepers were "worked up" in the Western Mediterranean, in order that they could complete HATs (Harbour Acceptance Trials) and SATs (Sea Acceptance Trials). On 20 March, both vessels, LE *Fola* and LE *Banba*, left Gibraltar for Cobh. *En route* they encountered bad weather, which obliged a stop-over in the Portuguese capital of Lisbon. Finally, on 29 March 1971 both vessels reached Cobh. The Naval Service's sea-going fleet now consisted of four ships. A significant transformation in the Service's fortunes had taken place.

The arrival of the *Coniston* class minesweepers saved the Naval Service from probable extinction, but there was still a need for an all-weather offshore patrol vessel. The intention to build a suitable vessel was confirmed and tenders were submitted to the department of defence. Irish Shipping Ltd were retained as consultants during all stages of the proposed vessel's creation—tendering, design and construction.[3] Eventually,

20 LE *Grainne*

in February 1971 a contract was signed with the Irish shipyard, Verolme Cork Dockyard Ltd. In the months following the signing of the contract, considerable design and model took place. The ship's hull was designed by NEVESBU* at the Hague and exhaustively tested in the Netherlands Ship Model basin in Wageningen.[4] These tests were necessary because the Naval Service had stipulated that they wanted a patrol ship, similar in design to those in service with Royal Norwegian navy. Such a vessel would have to be capable of mounting offshore patrols in all weathers. The latter was most important, as the *Coniston* class minesweepers were not suited to operating in bad weather, especially off Ireland's west coast. On 10 August 1971 the keel of the new patrol vessel was laid; the ship was launched on 10 December 1971 and named LE *Deirdre* by Mrs Cronin, wife of the Irish defence minister. After fitting out and intensive sea trials, the LE *Deirdre* was finally handed over to the Naval Service on 11 May 1972.

The Deirdre *class offshore patrol vessel*

The *Deirdre* was the Naval Service's first custom built ship; indeed she was the first vessel ever to be built in Ireland for the Service. All previous craft and sea-going vessels had been purchased from Britain, and these had already seen long service with the Royal Navy before being sold to Ireland. Truly, the arrival of the *Deirdre* was a milestone in Irish military and maritime history. For the first time in the history of the state, the country's navy would have a modern, purpose-built patrol ship which was capable of operating in all weather conditions off all of Ireland's coasts. The *Deirdre* was brand new and Irish built, something which contributed significantly to the restoration of morale and self-esteem in a navy which was faced with extinction only two years previous.

The *Deirdre* was not a warship, but an ingenious adaption of an enlarged ocean-going trawler design. Unlike most modern naval vessels, the *Deirdre* and the later P21 class OPVs did not have extensive watertight compartmentalisation. "The main engines and generators are all lumped together in one compartment."[5] This gives the ship no redundancy if that space is flooded or put out of action. The vessel's ability to survive any battle damage is very limited. Her sonar is a fish-finding type, akin to that found on most sophisticated deep-sea trawlers. The *Deirdre's* top speed is only 18.6 knots; this is fast enough to pursue foreign trawlers and terrorist/ drugs smugglers, but insufficient to escape from a modern naval vessel.

* NEVESBU (The Netherlands United Shipbuilding Bureau). Founded in 1935 and based in the Hague, NEVESBU is the design and engineering office for naval construction. NEVESBU performs three tasks: 1. design vessels and draw up specifications; 2. make all workshop drawings for the yard; 3. co-ordinate design and construction between authorities, construction yard and sub-contractors.

The *Deirdre* is 205 feet in length and has a displacement of 960 tons. With a fuel capacity of 67 tons, she has a range of 4000 miles at economical speed. The vessel's complement consists of four officers and 37 crewmen, although there is accommodation on board for an additional seven personnel. The quality of accommodation, catering and dining facilities on board the vessel was a quantum leap ahead of anything available on the old corvettes. Instead of the cramped, poorly ventilated and damp conditions on board the corvettes, the *Deirdre* was able to offer all the officers and senior petty officers single cabins. The petty officers had twin cabins, as did all of the naval ratings. There were separate mess decks for both junior and senior ratings, who were provided with cooked meals from a modern and spacious galley.

The vessel's armament was very modest. This consisted of a single open-sighted 40mm L60 Bofors gun on a power-operated mount forward of the bridge. The choice of this weapon system enabled the Naval Service to standardise ammunition, as this was the same type of gun system which was employed on the Service's three minesweepers. In addition, a limited quantity of small arms were carried on board for use by boarding parties. The vessel's modest armament was dictated by the need to keep costs as low as possible. Also, the vessel's armament was sufficient for its primary peacetime role, fishery protection. Eventually, the *Deirdre's* armament was slightly upgraded with the addition of two (single) 12.7mm heavy machine-guns.

The *Deirdre* remains in service to this day, although she is now the oldest vessel in commission. In the 21 years since her formal handover, she has undergone a survey and refit. The vessel's communications' systems have been completely updated, especially with the addition of satellite navigation systems.

By July 1972 the Naval Service had more ships in commission than at any other time since 1952. The sea-going fleet now consisted of one modern offshore patrol vessel and three coastal minesweepers. The Naval Service's remarkable reversal in fortunes was also experienced by other branches of Ireland's defence forces. Sadly, the reason for their expansion was related to the political turmoil and violence in neighbouring Northern Ireland. Since the beginning of the "troubles" in August 1969, politically-motivated violence had increased dramatically in Northern Ireland. By July 1972 there were over 35,000 British troops and armed police in a province with a population smaller than that of the English county of Hampshire. There was a real possibility that parts of Northern Ireland would disintegrate into anarchy and civil war. Such a doomsday scenario would not only be catastrophic for the people of Northern Ireland, but also for the fragile economy of the the Republic of Ireland. Even with the lavishly-equipped British army in Northern Ireland, there was the ever

21 LE *Deirdre*

present threat of terrorism spilling over the open and unmarked border. This threat of an overspill of violence compelled successive Irish governments to increase defence expenditure. From a low of £12.8 million in 1970, defence spending increased to £85.2 million by 1977.[6] Between 1972 and 1976, three new infantry battalions and a cavalry squadron were formed specifically for border duty. In a period of four years, the regular army had grown by nearly 30 per cent; a remarkable rate of increase in peacetime. The Air Corps acquired five more helicopters and eight Cessna army cooperation aircraft. More wheeled armoured vehicles were also acquired from various sources: in 1972 the Irish government bought 18 Unimog scout cars at a Swedish government auction. From the French firm of Panhard, they bought nine M3 armoured personnel carriers (APCs), four AML 90 and 16 AML 60 light armoured cars. Later on, 16 AML 90s and 51 M3 APCs were bought. Ten Irish-designed Timoney APCs were also acquired.

The seizure of the MV Claudia

By 1973 over 800 people had been killed in terrorist-related violence in Northern Ireland. With little prospect of the conflict coming to an end, it was inevitable that the main terrorist organisation, the Provisional IRA, would seek to import weapons and explosives from overseas in order to sustain a prolonged campaign of violence. If arms and explosives were to be imported in quantity, they would most certainly have to come in by sea. In March 1973 the Irish Naval Service would prove that it could perform critically-important roles other than fishery protection.

Early in March 1973, the 298-ton coaster MV *Claudia* left Cyprus on a journey that would eventually lead it to a dramatic confrontation with the Irish navy off Co. Waterford. The vessel sailed westwards, calling in at Tunis for repairs. During the course of her voyage, the *Claudia* picked up a cargo of arms off the Libyan coast. The events which followed were recounted by Herr Gunthur Leinhauser, the managing director of the *Claudia*'s German owners, the Giromar Shipping Company of Nicosia, when he spoke to reporters in Hamburg on 2 April 1973:

> The IRA contacted me and I arranged the transport. I went to Tripoli and arranged things with IRA men, but I was not present when the ship was loaded. It was the first and only deal with the Irish. The Libyans dealt direct with the IRA and the IRA paid me half my fee before loading. The Claudia was loaded outside Libyan territorial waters but the arms came from Tripoli.[7]

The *Claudia* sailed on, passing through the Straits of Gibraltar on Wednesday 21 March. On 24 March the Naval Service began its naval operation with the minesweeper *Fola*, under the command of Lt.-Cdr. Mike Murphy, quietly slipping out of Haulbowline naval base for Rosslare. On 25 March the *Fola* remained at anchor in Rosslare Bay for most of the day before moving off in the direction of the Saltee Islands. At the same time, two other naval vessels left Haulbowline: the navy's brand new offshore patrol vessel LE *Deirdre* and the minesweeper LE *Grainne*. The *Deirdre* was under the command of Lt.-Cdr. Brett, the senior officer afloat during the entire operation. The *Grainne*, under the command of Lt.-Cdr. Owen McNamara, had just returned from a fishery protection patrol, but was quickly refuelled and sent out to sea without delay. All leave had been cancelled. Aboard the LE *Deirdre* was the arresting officer from the Garda, Superintendent McGrath of Cobh, and the chief preventative customs officer, Patrick Kelly.

The *Claudia* had intended to meet up with a fishing boat off Helvick Point, Co. Waterford, in south-east Ireland. Three-quarters of Ireland's Naval Service lay in wait to intercept the arms ship. In Helvick Harbour and on the cliffs overlooking the sea, armed Irish troops with blackened faces took up prepared positions. The Air Corps was also held in reserve and on call if required. When the *Claudia* approached the rendezvous area off Helvick Point, she was intercepted by the *Deirdre* and the two minesweepers. No resistance was offered by the *Claudia*, as even the navy's modest 40mm and 20mm guns could have devastated the arms ship. However, the small fishing launch made a desperate attempt to escape and both minesweepers had to fire tracer shells across the bow of the launch to force it to surrender.[8] Eventually, armed naval personnel on board a high-speed dinghy caught up with the launch. Both the *Claudia* and the fishing boat were quickly boarded and six Irishmen were placed under arrest, including Joe Cahill, the former commanding officer of the Belfast Brigade of the Provisional IRA. The *Claudia*'s crew of three Germans and two Turks were then obliged to take their ship under naval escort to Haulbowline.

Once at Haulbowline the extent of the arms seizure became apparent. In total five tons of arms and explosives were confiscated. In Hamburg on 2 April the ship's owner, Herr Leinhauser, insisted that 100 tons had been loaded at Tripoli. However, this was discounted by the *Claudia*'s captain, Herr Hans-Ludwig Flugel. He maintained that the Libyans only loaded five tons of arms, and that, while off Helvick Point, none of ship's cargo of weapons and explosives were thrown overboard. What the navy had successfully seized was the illegal cargo in its entirety. The *Claudia*'s cargo of five tons of arms and explosives consisted of the following:

250 rifles with 850 rifle magazines
246 bayonets

244 Webley revolvers and 600 rounds of ammunition
250 sub-machine-guns and 14,000 rounds of ammunition
100 anti-tank mines
100 cases of anti-personnel mines
blocks of TNT and 5000 lbs of other explosives
a quantity of cortex fuse
500 high explosive hand grenades[9]

The seizure of the MV *Claudia* was an outstanding achievement for the Naval Service. During the course of the naval operation, the Irish defence minister, Patrick Donegan, monitored the ongoing developments at Naval Headquarters in Dublin. On the morning following the seizure, Donegan gave an ebullient account of the Naval Service's success at an international news conference held at Naval HQ. Later, Donegan, Major-General Thomas Carroll, the IDF's chief of staff, and Capt. McKenna CONS flew by helicopter to Haulbowline to congratulate the naval crews in person. In the words of Donegan, "they were a credit to the Irish armed forces".[10]

The operation attracted worldwide publicity, which was something quite new for the navy—although some comments were made about the size of Ireland's navy; an editorial in the *Irish Times* of 30 March 1973, for example, reported: "the British may realise with some incredulity that almost the whole of the Irish navy was committed to the exercise." The operation was not a chance encounter, but the product of cooperation between the security and police services of Britain and Ireland. The *Claudia*'s movements had been followed since she left Cyprus.

The seizure proved that a large island state such as Ireland could ill afford not to have a navy. The interception of the *Claudia*'s cargo most certainly saved many lives that would otherwise have been lost to IRA terrorist violence in Northern Ireland. However, had the IRA chosen to import a similar cargo three years earlier, the Irish Naval Service would have been unable to intercept them. Even the seizure of the *Claudia* required the Naval Service to use three of its four ships. The Service was still under-resourced, especially if it was expected to deter terrorist arms smugglers from landing weapons anywhere along the country's long coastline. The absence of a coastguard service and of maritime surveillance aircraft contributed greatly to the navy's problems.

On 1 January 1973 an event occurred which would have far reaching implications for the Naval Service; Ireland, together with Denmark and the United Kingdom, joined the European Economic Community. (Norway was also to have joined but this decision was reversed by a referendum.) Ireland's membership of the EEC did not oblige her to abandon or modify her traditional policy of military neutrality, but, eventually, the Community's fisheries policy would have an enormous impact on the Naval Service.

As the middle of the decade approached the Naval Service was still equipped with three ex-RN coastal minesweepers and one offshore patrol vessel. However, in December 1975 the government signed a contract with Verolme Cork Dockyard for the construction of a second *Deirdre* type patrol vessel. Some significant modifications were to be incorporated in this Mark 2 version. Some of these changes resulted from lessons which had been learnt from the recent Anglo-Icelandic "Cod War". The *Deirdre* was a prototype vessel and therefore the Naval Service wanted her performance to be fully evaluated before a second unit was built.

The modifications to new Mark 2 *Deirdre* class OPV were to include:

- increasing the length of the hull by 4 per cent
- improving seaworthiness by partially raising the foredeck and providing collapsible open rails
- raising slightly the wheelhouse, to improve all-round visibility
- accommodation was rearranged and improved in an attempt to reduce noise levels and vibrations
- improving the standard of watertight integrity
- upgrading vessel's main armament with the installation of a 40mm Bofors L70 gun in place of the *Deirdre*'s L60 version. The latter has a range of 1,500 metres compared to the L70's range of 2000 metres
- installing two single 20mm Oerlikon guns abaft of the bridge
- installing more powerful machinery.[11]

The new Mark 2 offshore patrol vessel would be 213 feet in length and have a displacement of 1004 tons.

Although the contract to build a new and improved patrol vessel was signed on 22 December 1975, it would not be until February 1977 that the vessel's keel would be laid down. In the interim period the Service had to deter foreign trawlers and terrorist gun-runners with four ships.

An unprecedented period of expansion, 1976-80

By the end of 1975 the Naval Service was poised for a period of unprecedented expansion which to most of its officers and men must have seemed unreal (see Table 7); memories of the near demise in 1970 were still vivid. However, the country's entry into the European Economic Community had transformed everything. There was a real prospect that the current 12-mile fishing limit would be extended to 200 miles. (Originally the British and Irish governments were only interested in a 50-mile fisheries limit, but at the Berlin Conference agreement was secured on a 200-mile limit.) The decision to introduce a Community-wide 200-mile exclusive economic zone (EEZ) was taken at an EEC fisheries

Table 7: Selected Force Levels in the Irish Naval Service, 1971-80

Year	*1971*	'72	'73	'74	'75	'76	'77	'78	'79	'80
Corvettes	1	0	0	0	0	0	0	0	0	0
Offshore patrol vessels	0	1	1	1	1	1	1	2	3	4
Coastal minesweepers	3	3	3	3	3	3	3	3	3	3
Sea-going auxiliaries	0	0	0	0	0	1	2	1	1	1

ministers' conference in West Berlin in 1976. At this important meeting, the Irish minister for agriculture and fisheries, Brian Lenihan, persuaded the other delegates of the need to assist Ireland in building up an adequate fishery protection force.[12] The argument being, that a force of modern Irish fishery protection vessels was necessary if the EEC's Atlantic waters were to be effectively monitored and policed. These two decisions—to introduce a 200-mile EEZ and to provide Ireland with financial assistance—were to transform the Irish Naval Service out of all recognition.

The continuing violence in Northern Ireland also obliged the navy to have the ability to aid the civil power (the police) in a marine environment. (Terrorist arms' smugglers were not the only lawless elements who provoked the Naval Service into resorting to force. In 1976 the minesweeper *Fola* had to fire warning shots from its 40mm and 20mm guns in order to arrest a Soviet trawler.) The successful interception of the *Claudia* was no guarantee that the IRA or other terrorist groups would not attempt to smuggle arms and explosives into Ireland again. The days of the Irish Naval Service being seen as the Cinderella branch of an already small and under-resourced national defence force were over.

In expectation of the expansion that would be required, the navy acquired an ex-lighthouse tender from the Commissioners of Irish Lights—the MV *Isolde*. This vessel was commissioned into service on 8 October 1976 as LE *Setanta*. The 1150 m/t vessel had been built in Dublin in 1953. With a top speed of 10 knots, she was too slow to act as a patrol vessel, yet she proved useful as the first sea-going training and supply ship—a type of vessel which the Naval Service had been hoping to acquire since the early 1950s. Her armament was limited to two single 20mm Oerlikon guns. Primarily, her duties consisted of training regular and reserve naval personnel, disposing of navigational hazards, and moving military stores. It is interesting to note that when the Naval Service was called upon to transport military supplies to Irish UN troops in south Lebanon in 1979, they did not use their only designated transport vessel. Instead, they employed LE *Emer*, the first of the new P21 class OPVs. The decision was made on the basis that the *Setanta*'s oil consumption would have made a long-range transport mission unduly expensive. However, the *Setanta* was sent on a goodwill visit to Iceland in 1977.

22 LE *Setanta* (ex-MV *Isolde*). Photo taken while the vessel was still in service with the Commissioners of Irish Lights.

In 1977 the Naval Service acquired a sixth vessel, albeit on a temporary basis. The prospect of having to police a 200-mile fishing limit obliged the government to expand the Naval Service. Therefore, while the keel of a second and modified version of the *Deirdre* class of OPV was about to be laid, a Danish trawler was leased for service. The *Helen Basse* was a 456 m/t stern trawler (built in 1965). She was chartered from her Danish owner, Mr Basse, for a 12-month period, with the option to purchase after satisfactory service.[13] On 17 January 1977 the *Helen Basse* was commissioned into Service as LE *Ferdia*. Her classification was A16. The *Ferdia's* armament was even more modest than that of the *Setanta*, as it consisted of a single 20mm Oerlikon gun.

Who in 1970 would thought it possible that such a reversal of fortune was possible? The *Claudia* incident had clearly vindicated those who argued that the Service had an important role to play in combating terrorism. With the promise of financial aid from Brussels to help build up Ireland's fishery protection force, the Naval Service had good reason to feel optimistic.

In 1978, with the expiry of the vessel's lease, the *Ferdia* was decommissioned and returned to her Danish owner. The government did not opt to purchase the vessel. Faced with the prospect of policing 130,000 square miles of sea, the Irish Naval Service was still under-resourced and undermanned for the task that lay ahead. In 1975 Ireland's sea-going fleet consisted of four vessels, of which only one, the OPV LE *Deirdre*, was capable of operating in offshore waters. The three ex-RN "Ton" class minesweepers were obliged to confine their patrols to inshore areas. Aerial surveillance was non-existent. It was only in 1977 that the Air Corps acquired its first maritime patrol aircraft since the days of the wartime Avro Ansons. Initially, as with the LE *Ferdia*, the first patrol aircraft was chartered. The type chosen was a Beechcraft Super King Air. By 1979 three of these twin-engined short range executive transport aircraft had been purchased.

The Service's fleet received a major boost in the years 1977–80, when in an unprecedented period of expansion in naval vessels and manpower, three new modernised *Deirdre* type OPVs were built and commissioned into service. The funding for this expansion came from Brussels: 50 per cent of the capital costs of the ships were paid for by the EEC. However, the Irish government had to pay for the cost of the vessels' defensive armaments. In March 1977 the Irish defence minister, Robert Molloy, stated that a total of eight *Deirdre*/P21 class OPVs would be constructed—one per year. In fact in the same year, the minister stated that in order for the 200-mile Exclusive Economic Zone to be effectively policed, a force of 15 offshore and ten coastal patrol vessels would be required.[14]

Such a programme of expansion would be very expensive. Although Ireland did receive a grant of approximately £32 million from the EEC, it was insufficient to finance such an ambitious programme of ship procurement.[15] In 1980 the Naval Service acquired its third and final P21 class offshore patrol vessel, LE *Aoife*. These upgraded *Deirdre* type OPVs were slightly better armed. However, according to Cdr. John Jordan the Naval Service's building officer for both the P21 and P31 class vessels, "the EEC's involvement meant a strong non-military influence on outfitting and costs." In addition to the standard open-sighted 40mm Bofors gun, the P21s were equipped with two (single) 20mm Oerlikon B.OI AA guns, two (single) 7.62mm GPMGs and two 57mm Wallop flare launchers.[16]

Naval manpower strengths in the 1970s increased from a low of 412 in 1970, to a doubling in size by 1980. Furthermore, the dignity of the Service was enhanced by two events: the creation of the new naval title of Flag Officer Commanding the Naval Service, with the rank of commodore, and the decision by the army to hand over Spike Island. Prior to 1980, all commanding officers of the Naval Service held the rank of captain, the naval equivalent of an army colonel. Even today, all corps in the Irish army (except the Air Corps) are commanded by officers holding the rank of colonel. With the creation of the rank of commodore, the Naval Service was elevated to a status above that of the army's corps.

The expansion of the Naval Service had caused difficulties in terms of overcrowding of personnel and storage of materials. This problem was exacerbated by the fact that Haulbowline Island is also shared by Irish Steel Ltd. In 1980 the Army's Southern Command handed over control of the fortifications and barrack accommodation on Spike Island to the Naval Service. Unfortunately, the Service's stay on the island was to be short. (After the formal disbandment of Coast Defence Artillery in 1979, the Army no longer needed Spike Island.) In 1985 the department of justice acquired the fortified island and converted it into a civilian prison. To this day, Spike Island continues to function as Fort Mitchel Prison.

The introduction of the 200-mile EEZ in 1977 imposed an onerous burden on the Irish Naval Service. In that year, the only ship which was capable of patrolling Ireland's offshore waters was the *Deirdre*. The *Coniston* class minesweepers were completely unsuited to such tasks and were therefore confined to inshore waters. The naval auxiliary, *Setanta*, was nearly 25 years old in 1977 and with a top speed of 10 knots, she was too slow to act as an effective patrol ship. The temporary lease of a Danish stern trawler improved the situation, but what the Naval Service urgently needed were more all-weather offshore patrol vessels. The addition of three P21 class OPVs provided the Naval Service with a creditable deterrent, but these vessels had their limitations. In order to patrol the outer limits of the 200-mile EEZ, the Naval Service needed a helicopter-

23 LE *Aoife*

carrying ocean-going patrol ship. Such a vessel would be capable of staying at sea for more than three weeks, thereby permitting the smaller OPVs to concentrate their patrol activity closer to the coastline. The initial requirement was for two large patrol ships. Unlike the numerous requirements for new ships set out by Naval Service in the 1950s and 1960s, on this occasion success was assured as the European Community was going to finance 50 per cent of the building costs.

The Eithne *class helicopter patrol vessel*

Planning for the construction of a second generation patrol ship began in 1979, when a Naval Board submitted an outline of the Navy's require-ments. Unlike the *Deirdre*/P21 class OPVs, the new patrol ship was to have a partial military role. The intended prototype vessel would have twice the tonnage of the *Deirdre* and would be equipped with an embarked helicopter. Shipborne aviation was something about which the Naval Service had no previous experience. The new patrol ship was to be built by Verolme Cork Dockyard (VCD), the company which had constructed the *Deirdre* and more recently the P21 class OPVs. (The decision to build in Ireland was to provoke some controversy later on.) The keel of the first helicopter patrol vessel was laid in December 1982. Nearly two years later, on 7 December 1984, the new patrol ship, LE *Eithne*, pennant number P31, was commissioned into service after intensive sea trials.

Regardless of the controversy surrounding the cost of building the *Eithne* at VCD, the Naval Service's new flagship was a remarkable vessel. Purpose-built, she was comparable in every respect to the most modern patrol ships then in service with the United States Coast Guard or the Royal Norwegian navy. Even the Royal Navy did not possess an OPV as advanced and capable as the *Eithne*. The vessel's outfitting was partly akin to that of a modern frigate. Her sonar was a hull-mounted Plessey PMS 26 active search and attack system—a type of anti-submarine sonar system currently in service with many European navies, for example, the Royal Netherlands navy. The vessel was also equipped with a sophisticated Signaal DA 05 Mk4 (air warning) radar system, which is linked to the *Eithne*'s equally sophisticated Signaal LIOD Optronic Fire Director. The *Eithne*'s armament was very modest in relation other frigate-sized naval vessels. This comprised one 57mm Bofors gun and two single 20mm AA guns. The former is capable of firing 235 rounds per minute, putting more high explosive into a target in 30 seconds than any other gun of less than 100mm calibre. No anti-submarine weapon system was incorporated, although such a system can be fitted at short notice.

The absence of an ASW equipped patrol vessel was highlighted during the 1980s when several Irish registered trawlers were accidentally sunk by submarines transitting the Irish Sea. Apparently, the fishing nets of the

24 LE *Emer*

unfortunate trawlers had become ensnarled in the propellors of patrolling submarines. In view of the highly secretive nature of Soviet and NATO submarine activity in this area, the relevant Naval powers were not anxious to acknowledge the presence of their boats. This was especially applicable to boats armed with nuclear weapons. Ireland was not the only European neutral power that was having difficulty deterring subsurface military traffic in the 1980s; Sweden was having similar problems with Soviet submarines along its long and exposed Baltic coastline.

Originally, it was thought that the new patrol ship would carry a Lynx helicopter, a type currently in service with many NATO and non-Western navies, for example, Nigeria. However, the more modern SA 365 F Dauphin 2 was chosen. Two navalised and three conventional Dauphins were delivered in 1986. All of them are unarmed, but as with the *Eithne*, the navalised Dauphins are capable of being modified at short notice to carry anti-submarine torpedoes or anti-shipping missiles. The *Eithne* does not carry the navalised version of the Swedish-made RBS 70 surface to air missile, a system currently in service with the Irish army. Although capable of incorporating this system into the vessel's defences, the Naval Service did not see the need for such an acquisition. The RBS 70 is a laser beam riding weapon and as such is largely dependent on good weather—no rain, squalls, mist etc. The vessel's 57mm gun can delivery a larger, more effective (pre-fragmented high explosive) projectile in all types of weather. In addition, the *Eithne* has an integrated operations room with remotes for helicopter control, gunnery action, command console with multi-radar selection, that is, surface or air.

Although the European Community had agreed to help Ireland build up a fishery protection force, it would not finance the cost of the weapon systems on board the new patrol ships. The cost of these weapon systems had to be borne by the Irish department of defence. Cdr. John Jordan has stated that, "the military side of the department of defence allowed a subvention for expenditure on a modern weapon system. This was at some sacrifice to current capital aquisitions at that time." Jordan went on to comment that, "I was personally grateful to the serving Chief of Staff of the Defence Forces, Lt.-Gen. Carl O'Sullivan, who found the money for the *Eithne*'s military outfit".[17]

The first of the P31 class helicopter patrol vessels entered service in December 1984. A second P31 type vessel was to have been built in 1984-5, but the decision to build was postponed. During the construction of the *Eithne*, serious delays and cost overruns had occurred. In this period Verolme Cork Dockyard experienced serious financial problems and the European Community refused to finance the construction of a second P31 class vessel. In the end Verolme went bankrupt and was closed down. In fact, the *Eithne* was the last ship to be built at this shipyard. With the closure of VCD, there was little prospect of the Naval Service acquiring a second P31 class vessel. The addition of an ocean-going patrol ship to the INS's fleet allowed Ireland to become a participating member of the North Atlantic Fisheries Organisation (NAFO). In 1990 LE *Eithne* spent part of her operational time patrolling a section of Canada's eastern seaboard. *Eithne*'s temporary home port was St Johns, Newfoundland.

AID TO THE CIVIL POWER

The success of the Naval Service's interception of the MV *Claudia* clearly illustrated its potential for combating terrorism. But the interdiction of terrorist gun-runners was not a specified role for the Service. Such operations were classified as "aid to the civil power". The Naval Service would only get involved in anti-terrorist operations at the request of the Garda, and would require a police officer to be on board during such operations.

The Naval Service's day-to-day priority was fishery protection. The interception of suspicious vessels within Irish territorial waters was not undertaken at random, but as a result of information derived from police and intelligence agencies within Ireland and from overseas. In all such operations the navy would act solely as an aid to the civil power—the Irish police. This was in contrast to the role of the Royal Navy in Northern Ireland, where British inshore patrol boats could stop and search any vessel within the territorial limit without recourse to a search warrant. No police officer was required when Royal Marines boarded and searched a fishing boat or coaster. To this day the Royal Navy maintains a small force of inshore patrol vessels and craft for service in Northern Ireland. In the 1970s and 1980s *Coniston* class minesweepers and *Loyal* class tenders were used. In recent years, these vessels have been phased out and replaced by 124-ton *Seal* class inshore patrol craft. Royal Marines personnel continue to use Rigid and Arctic Raider craft.

These forces operate from Warrenpoint and Belfast and patrol the coasts of Northern Ireland from Lough Foyle in the north-west to Carlingford Lough in the south-east. In addition, small numbers of Royal Marines patrol Lough Neagh and the lakes of Fermanagh in order to deter the movement of terrorist arms by boat across these waters. Upper Lough Erne is actually dissected by the Irish border. Therefore, the Royal Ulster Constabulary, supported by the British army, endeavours to prevent the IRA from smuggling weapons on board small craft across this part of the border. The policing of Northern Ireland's maritime border is also indirectly shared by the Irish defence forces.

Carlingford Lough and Anglo-Irish security cooperation

Northern Ireland is partly bordered by two legs of water—Lough Foyle and Carlingford Lough—both of which are dissected by the frontier between the Republic of Ireland and the United Kingdom. Irish naval vessels regularly enter both of these waterways in order to deter terrorist incidents and to represent the authority of the Irish State. In 1982 Lough Foyle was the scene of a rare example of maritime terrorism when the IRA planted a bomb on board the cargo ship *St Bedan*. Its crew were forced to abandon ship and the Naval Service was requested to enter Lough Foyle in order that the vessel could be secured.

Carlingford Lough, in the south-east of Northern Ireland, is over 17 miles long (25km) and two miles (4km) wide at its entrance. Commercial traffic from the shipping terminal at Warrenpoint has made it a busy waterway. Ever since 1971, the Royal Navy has maintained a presence in the Lough—their role being to deter the IRA from transporting men and warlike materials into Northern Ireland. In the early 1970s political controversey arose over alleged incursions across the maritime border by Royal Navy patrol boats stationed in the Lough. The Royal Navy maintained that searches of Irish registered trawlers and boats did take place, but only if they were within British, that is, Northern Ireland's territorial waters.[18] The Naval Service was unable to verify any of these claims, as they did not have any craft or personnel stationed on the Irish side of Carlingford.

Throughout the early and mid-seventies, the Irish army strengthened its presence along the 200-mile long border with Northern Ireland. By 1976 an infantry brigade comprising three 500-man infantry battalions and one cavalry squadron had been established. These troops were strung out along ten permanent military posts from Letterkenny in Co. Donegal to Dundalk in Co. Louth. These newly-established formations were given priority in the acquisition of modern light armoured vehicles; each battalion had an APC mounted company. However, unlike their British counterparts to the north, they did not have access to troop-carrying helicopters. The Irish army only had two Alouette III helicopters available for service along the entire length of the border. Both of these machines, which were based at Finner Camp in Co. Donegal and Monaghan barracks, were, for technical reasons, unable to fly at night-time.

The Naval Service's role in border security operations was understandably very limited, as the border is primarily a land frontier. But even during the height of the violence in the 1970s, the Naval Service did not maintain a presence in Carlingford. No shore personnel were deployed to this area, no patrol launches were purchased or leased, and no army troops were stationed on the Cooley peninsula, adjoining Carlingford. In fact, the nearest regular army formation was the 27th Infantry Battalion in Dundalk, a military unit which did not possess any marine craft, such as rigid raider boats.

In 1976 Carlingford was the scene of several attacks on Royal Navy patrol vessels. On 20 April of that year, HMS *Alert*, a 134-ton tender, which was being used as patrol craft, was fired on from the southern side of Carlingford. Two months later, HMS *Alert* was again fired on by an IRA unit operating from the southern side of Carlingford. The RN and Royal Marines personnel returned fire, but neither side claimed any hits. Less than three weeks later, HMS *Vigilant*, *Alert*'s sister ship, was machine-gunned as she left Warrenpoint dockside. Fire was returned, but without any hits being claimed on either side.[19] Three years later, another IRA attack mounted from across the border did inflict serious losses on the British army. At Narrow Water, at the northern tip of Carlingford, 18 British soldiers were killed when a military convoy was ambushed.

One senior British officer who was very familiar with this area is Brigadier Peter Morton (retd). During 1976 he was the commanding officer of the 3rd Battalion of the Parachute Regiment, which was based in south Armagh. According to Brigadier Morton, "there was no particular reason why the IRA should wish to move munitions across the Lough, but the presence of a RN vessel probably ensured that they did not consider it worth the risk." Morton went on to state that "we were always, through HQNI [Headquarters Northern Ireland], keen to encourage the Irish army and Garda to do more in the Carlingford Lough area but we were very well aware of their limited resources and, quite frankly, we were much more interested that they would do more in other parts of the South's border with south Armagh." In conclusion, Morton mentions, "that there was no call from us for the Irish Navy to do anything in Carlingford. It was vital, however, that they stopped and searched suspicious vessels in Irish territorial waters. Ninety per cent at least of all IRA weapons and explosives came into the Republic of Ireland by sea. So the Irish Navy had a very significant role to play—but their resources were very limited."[20]

Security cooperation between the two police forces on the island of Ireland, the Garda and the Royal Ulster Constabulary, has greatly improved since 1976. The signing of the Anglo-Irish Agreement in November 1985 has added substance to this improvement in relations. However, there is still no arrangement for direct army to army or navy to navy communications. Should a Royal Navy patrol boat stationed in Carlingford wish to communicate with a Naval Service vessel on the southern side of the Lough, the RN must communicate via the Royal

Ulster Constabulary, who then pass on the message to the Garda, who in turn inform the Naval Service of the contents of the RN's message. To those not familiar with the very sensitive role which the border plays in contemporary Irish history and politics, this situation must seem unreal. However, before the fall of the Berlin Wall in November 1989, a similar situation existed in former East Germany. When Allied personnel came into contact with East German police or military officials in East Berlin, they would only speak to them via a Soviet officer. To communicate directly with an East German official would be viewed as recognising the existence of the GDR State in what the Allies still saw as the occupied city of Berlin. According to Merlyn Rees, former secretary of state for Northern Ireland 1974-6, "the Irish were quite clear on the issue—there was to be no army-army cooperation. The Irish would only deal with the RUC."[21]

The seizure of the Marita Ann

Eleven years after the arrest of the IRA arms ship, *Claudia*, the Naval Service made another significant contribution to the struggle against terrorism. In late September 1984 the American FBI warned the Garda that they should expect a shipment of arms bound for the IRA to arrive somewhere along the coast of south-west Ireland. In expectation of another *Claudia* type operation, the Garda assembled 30 highly experienced officers for an interception at sea. These officers were drawn from the Special Branch and the Garda's Special Task Force, a heavily armed anti-terrorist unit. The 30-strong group was ordered to assemble in an atmosphere of complete secrecy at Haulbowline Island. At the naval base, the anti-terrorist unit was joined by the arresting officer for the operation, Inspector Eric Ryan. It was only when they were at sea, that these police officers were informed of the nature of the operation.

Three naval vessels were made available for the interception and were placed on maximum alert. They were LE *Deirdre*, which had participated in the *Claudia* operation, and two P21 class OPVs—LE *Emer* and LE *Aisling*. The *Deirdre* was designated as a reserve unit in the operation, while the OPVs were to intercept and seize the arms ship. The Garda was informed by the FBI that an American "mothership", outward bound from New York, would rendezvous with an Irish trawler off the south-west coast of Ireland and transfer the arms at sea. This was to be done in international waters and thereby beyond the jurisdiction of the Irish State. The Garda also knew from their surveillance operations that the actual arms ship was a Fenit based trawler, *Marita Ann*. This vessel had left Fenit on Wednesday 26 September. At the same time, the Naval Service interception force patrolled the coast of Kerry. Late on Thursday night, the *Marita Ann*, met up with the American supply ship, *Valhalla*, at an area of shallow sea known as Porcupine Bank, located 120 miles off the

25 The IRA gun-runner, MV *Marita Ann*

south-west coast of Ireland. After the arms were transferred, the *Marita Ann* proceeded towards the Irish coastline. However, the Naval Service had no accurate intelligence as to the *Marita Ann*'s course and ultimate destination. The very rugged coast of south-west Ireland is characterised by many sheltered bays, inlets and natural harbours. Such an environment affords a smuggler of arms or drugs adequate cover.

During the course of their patrol duties off Co. Kerry, the OPVs were blacked out and strict radio silence was maintained. All communication between the patrol vessels was made by flag signals. Late on the evening of Friday 28 September, LE *Emer*'s captain, Lt.-Cdr. Brian Farrell, received a message from Naval Headquarters in Dublin. This information allowed Lt.-Cdr. Farrell to plot the course of the *Marita Ann* and to estimate the precise time she would arrive within the three-mile territorial limit. According to the *Irish Times*, the information, without which no interception could have been made, was provided by British intelligence. However, the provision of such valuable intelligence does not in itself guarantee a successful arrest. The orders were clear—intercept, arrest and seize.

The *Emer* was now designated as the pursuit ship, with the remaining two OPVs staying in reserve. The intelligence provided by Naval HQ had allowed the *Emer* and and the two OPVs to close in on the arms ship. In the period before interception, the *Emer* had to use the massive, jagged outcrops known as the Skelligs as radar cover. This tactic required all of Lt.-Cdr. Farrell's experience and skill as a ship's captain, as he had to negotiate a path for the *Emer* through these rocks in very heavy seas.

At 12.15 a.m. on Saturday 29 September, the *Marita Ann* was intercepted 2.8 miles off the coast of Co. Kerry. The Garda had expected the IRA to resist arrest, and even if capture was inevitable, they did not want the IRA to have the pleasure of scuttling their ship and its cargo at sea. In order for the terrorists to be disarmed and arrested, and for their vessel and its cargo to be taken intact, the Naval Service devised an ingenious method of interception. While the *Marita Ann* was approaching the Irish coastline, LE *Emer* suddenly slipped away from the Skelligs and came into view. The *Emer*'s commander challenged the *Marita Ann*, but not on the grounds of transporting terrorist arms. To the relief of the *Marita Ann*'s crew, the *Emer* simply wanted to know if they were engaged in salmon fishing. Such an inquiry by a patrol vessel in these waters was not unusual. The *Marita Ann*'s crew had good reason to co-operate, assuring the *Emer*'s captain that they had not been engaged in inshore salmon fishing. While this conversation was taking place, two high-speed Gemini craft, with armed Garda and naval boarding personnel, approached from the stern and amidships on the blind side of the trawler. As this was happening the *Marita Ann* attempted to escape but tracer

26 LE *Eithne*

shells were fired across her bows, forcing the trawler to stop. Immediately, naval boarding personnel overwhelmed the crew of five and they were promptly arrested by Inspector Ryan.

The circumstances of the boarding operation were apparently quite frightening for Inspector Ryan and his naval escort. All of them had been warned that armed resistance could be expected. As they approached the trawler in appalling weather conditions, it must have been apparent that they were very vulnerable to attack from the *Marita Ann*'s crew of armed IRA men. It was only possible to board the trawler once the waves had forced the Gemini craft up against the side of the *Marita Ann*. The Garda's concern about the possibility of armed resistance was confirmed when the naval boarding party discovered loaded rifles in the trawler's wheelhouse. However, thanks to the professionalism of the Naval Service's boarding parties, a major sucess was achieved without any loss of life or injury being sustained.

After the trawler had been seized, the vessel's skipper was allowed to remain on board under Garda and Naval Service supervision. The other four crewmen were transferred to the *Emer* and *Aisling*. During the 20-hour voyage back to Haulbowline, the *Marita* Ann experienced engine problems and had to be towed by one of the patrol vessels. At Haulbowline, the trawler's contents were collated and displayed, before being transported by road to Dublin. The cargo consisted of seven tons of arms and explosives, including:

- one 12.7mm Browning heavy machine-gun with 1000 rounds of ammunition
- 300 American-made Ruger, M16 and M15 (Armalite) assault rifles
- an unspecified number of pump-action shotguns, 5.56mm rifles, FN self-loading rifles and Heckler & Koch 7.62mm sub-machine-guns
- 50,000 rounds of mixed ammunition
- unspecified quantity of handguns and Korean-made grenades.

In addition, the *Marita·Ann*'s cargo comprised flakjackets, radio equipment, military training manuals and medicines.

Clearly the success of the seizure was a product of the Naval Service's ability to secure and detain a rogue vessel at sea. However, all of this would not have been possible without the information which was supplied by the FBI and British intelligence. In the wake of the *Marita Ann*'s arrest, it was revealed that the movements of the IRA's American supply ship, *Valhalla*, had been monitored by an American KH II-spy satellite orbiting the earth. Apparently, this was the same type of "keyhole" surveillance system which had given the Royal Navy so much assistance during the 1982 Falklands War.[22]

The Eksund *incident*

The seizure of the *Marita Ann* apparently did not dissuade the IRA from smuggling arms and explosives into Ireland by sea. Over three years later, the IRA nearly received a consignment of arms some twenty times larger than that seized on the *Marita Ann*. On 30 October 1987 the French Customs Service, acting on intelligence, intercepted a Panamanian-registered coaster off the island of Batz, six miles north-west of Brest, France. The vessel was the *Eksund* and its cargo consisted of over 150 tons of arms and ammunition, including Soviet-made man-portable surface-to-air missile launchers, anti-tank rockets, mortars, assault rifles, machine-guns, ammunition for all of these weapon systems, and explosives. The source of this vast array of weaponry, which had an estimated value of £15 million, was Libya.[23] Apparently, Libya's "generosity" towards the IRA was motivated by a desire to exact revenge on Britain for its part in the American bombing of Tripoli in 1986. The United Kingdom was the only country in Europe which allowed American aircraft based on its soil to attack targets in Libya. The *Eksund*'s cargo did not reach Ireland, but it is widely assumed that other similar-sized cargoes did.

By the mid-1980s the Naval Service's programme of expansion had come to a halt. Once again it seemed as if the Service was going to have to endure another period of contraction. In 1985 the department of defence handed Spike Island over to the department of justice. From then on, continuation training would be conducted at the old British cavalry barracks at Ballincollig. In 1984 the Naval Service lost its only training and supply ship when the *Setanta* was de-commissioned and scrapped. In the same year the minesweeper *Banba* was de-commissioned and scrapped. By 1985 the fleet comprised one helicopter patrol ship, four OPVs and two coastal minesweepers. The second of the P31 class helicopter patrol vessels never materialised. The continuing absence of a second *Eithne*-type vessel was confirmed when the Verolme Cork Dockyard was finally closed. Throughout most of 1986, the minesweepers were confined to port as harbour training vessels. The following year both were de-commissioned and sold for scrap.

In 1987 the Naval Service had only five ships in commission—the same number that were in service in 1976, that is, before the introduction of a 200-mile Exclusive Economic Zone. Admittedly, the capabilities of the *Eithne* compensated for much of the Naval Service's difficulties. However, there was still an urgent need for more surface units, especially for coastal patrol craft. In the intervening period, while suitable replacements were sought, the Naval Service attempted to police the 130,000 square miles of sea which it was responsible for.

Anglo-Irish naval relations in the 1980s

In 1988 Dublin celebrated its millenium and naval visitors came to Ireland and its capital city from all over the world. These included ships from Latin America, the USA, Europe and the Soviet Union. One prominent navy which was conspicuous by its absence was Britain's Royal Navy. In fact, the last time a British naval vessel paid a visit to Ireland was in 1968. In contrast, Irish naval vessels occasionally make goodwill visits to British ports, and in 1991 the Naval Service's flagship, LE *Eithne*, with the then FOCNS on board, paid a formal visit to London. According to the British ministry of defence, the reason for this situation is as follows:

> There are obvious difficulties in the present situation attached to a visit to the Republic of Ireland by a Royal Naval vessel, not least that the freedom of the crew to circulate freely ashore would of necessity have to be curtailed. That we have not visited in recent years is therefore no reflection on our relationship.[24]

Sadly, this assessment of the risk posed by the IRA to a visiting RN vessel and its crew is also shared by Irish naval officers. However, such a visit need not take place in Dublin. A RN vessel could pay a short visit to Haulbowline Island, where its security could be guaranteed by a combination of Garda, Naval Service and Army Rangers' personnel. A suitable candidate for such a visit would be a patrol ship from the Royal Navy's fishery protection squadron at Rosyth or one of the Royal Navy's hydrographic survey vessels. Such vessels could not be classified as warships and, therefore, would be more suited to an initial trial visit. The successful outcome of such a visit would be another small stepping stone towards Anglo-Irish relations.

It is interesting to note that while acknowledging the risk posed by terrorism, some senior Irish politicians now welcome the prospect of a RN vessel coming to Ireland. Such a political standpoint would have been untenable in the 1970s, a period when Anglo-Irish relations were considerably strained. Brian Lenihan TD, the elder statesman of Ireland's Fianna Fáil Party, has stated that he would be "all in favour of a Royal Naval vessel paying a goodwill visit to an Irish port". Mr Lenihan went on to say: "One must remember that Anglo-Irish relations have been transformed since the 1970s."[25] Similarly, Dr Fitzgerald has said that he would be in favour of a RN vessel paying a goodwill visit to Ireland. Indeed, he has mentioned that he would have been "very happy if it had been possible for the British Head of State, Queen Elizabeth II, to visit Ireland during his period as Taoiseach."[26]

Since the signing of the Anglo-Irish Treaty in 1921, no British Head of State has paid a goodwill visit to Ireland. Indeed, it was only in 1972 that a British prime minister (Edward Heath) agreed to visit Ireland. On that occasion, his stay was restricted to the officers' mess at Baldonnel aerodrome, where he met with the Taoiseach, Jack Lynch.

Historically, the Royal Navy and the Irish Naval Service have always enjoyed good relations. Founded in 1946, the Naval Service's first commander was an ex-RN officer, Capt. Jerome. The Irish Navy's first warships were ex-RN *Flower* class corvettes. These were replaced by ex-RN *Coniston* class minesweepers, which in turn were replaced in 1988 by ex-RN *Peacock* class patrol vessels. Since 1946 all Irish naval officers have undertaken part of their training at the Britannia Royal Naval College, Dartmouth, and at the Royal Naval Engineering College, Manadon. From time to time senior Irish naval officers go on to attend the Royal Naval Staff College at Greenwich. Furthermore, many specialist training courses—such as, radar, sonar, gunnery and underwater ordnance disposal—are conducted at Royal Naval establishments.

However, despite the close association between the two navies, the relationship is not codified or formally set out in any defence or foreign relations treaty. Britain is a fully integrated member of NATO, while Ireland, in contrast, is the only European Community member state which pursues a policy of military neutrality. (In 1991 Ireland agreed to attend meetings, on an observer basis, of the security organisation—the Western European Union.) Therefore, in view of Ireland's ongoing policy of neutrality, the Royal Navy and the Irish Naval Service do not participate in any joint military exercises. However, both navies are responsible for significant areas of sea which adjoin both the UK and Ireland—the Irish Sea, the Celtic Sea/St Georges Channel and the northwest Atlantic sea area between Donegal and the Scottish Hebridean Islands. In these waters, the Royal Navy and the Naval Service are jointly responsible for policing the European Community's EEZ and providing, when possible, for pollution control and marine search and rescue. The latter is a role which has brought both navies together in joint humanitarian operations. Examples of major joint SAR operations are Operation Tuskar in 1968, the Fastnet Race rescue in 1979 and the Air India disaster in 1985. On that occasion long-range helicopters from the Royal Air Force and the Royal Navy's Fleet Air Arm assisted the Air Corps and Naval Service in rescue operations. Similarly, the RAF and Fleet Air Arm rendered invaluable assistance in joint Irish-British rescue operations in Galway Bay and Dublin Bay in 1990 and 1991.

The level of co-operation between Irish and British search and rescue units has increased in recent years. This has been characterised by a series of exchange visits between SAR helicopter crews from Baldonnel and RAF Brawdy in north Wales. Most recently, an Air Corps Dauphin 2 helicopter visited the Royal Navy's main SAR air station at Yeovilton. In addition, in a joint SAR exercise, the Naval Service's flagship, *Eithne*, proved the feasibility of refuelling a RAF Sea King helicopter while it hovered over the vessel's heli-deck. Such joint Anglo-Irish SAR exercises are essential if lives are to be saved in future marine accident situations.

The Peacock *class patrol vessel*

In 1987 the Naval Service scrapped the last of its *Coniston* class minesweepers LE *Fola* and LE *Grainne*. This left the Navy with only five ships in commission, of which none were designed for inshore patrols. In the interim period, possible replacements were sought. The French P400 class inshore patrol craft was identified as a possible candidate. The French navy used this type of vessel as a general purpose patrol craft, which included EEZ protection duties. However, in view of their size and displacement, it was not certain if they could operate effectively in all weathers off all of Ireland's coasts. Fortunately for the Naval Service, suitable replacements were located in Britain.

In 1988 the British ministry of defence decided to sell two of the Royal Navy's new *Peacock* class patrol craft. These vessels had been built in 1984-5 by Hall Brothers in Aberdeen for service in Hong Kong. Prior to 1985, the Crown Colony's seaborne security was the responsibility of five *Coniston* class minesweepers. The Royal Navy's specifications for inshore patrol craft were remarkably similar to those of the Irish Naval Service. These were:

1. the ability to conduct close quarter operations with other vessels at sea.

2. a SAR capability out to 400 miles offshore.

3. the ability to operate at sea for at least ten days, including open typhoon conditions.

4. an endurance of 2500 nautical miles at economical speed.

5. the ability to operate at low speeds (0-5 knots).

6. a damage control capability of being able to stay afloat despite the flooding of two adjacent compartments.

7. the ability to take aboard 100 passengers.[27]

These vessels exceeded the needs of the Irish Naval Service, most notably in damage control and fighting capability. Their only drawback was that they were not designed for Atlantic gales and do not have good open-ocean abilities. However, they are fast enough to escape bad weather conditions. On 21 November 1988 Ireland purchased two *Peacock* class patrol vessels from Britain: HMS *Swift* and HMS *Swallow*. The two

Table 8: Selected Force Levels in the Irish Naval Service, 1981-90

Year	1981	'82	'83	'84	'85	'86	'87	'88	'89	'90
Helicopter patrol vessels	0	0	0	1	1	1	1	1	1	1
Offshore patrol vessels	4	4	4	4	4	4	4	4	4	4
Coastal minesweepers	3	3	3	3	2	2	2	0	0	0
Coastal patrol vessels	0	0	0	0	0	0	0	0	2	2
Sea-going auxiliaries	1	1	1	1	0	0	0	0	0	0
Shipborne aircraft	0	0	0	0	0	2	2	2	2	2
Land-based maritime aircraft*	2	2	2	2	2	5	5	5	5	5

* These figures comprise the two dedicated Beechcraft maritime patrol aircraft and the three Dauphin SAR/maritime reconnaissance helicopters.

vessels cost £4 million each; however, the total cost rose to £10 million, as this included spare parts, travel, accommodation and training of the transfer crew. The purchase of the *Peacocks* was an undoubted bargain, as each vessel had originally cost £11 million to build.[28] Part of the funding for this purchase came from the European Community.

The *Peacocks* were handed over to the Naval Service at Rosyth in eastern Scotland. The Irish naval crews that were to take over the new vessels travelled overland to Scotland by coach from Haulbowline Island via Rosslare/Milford Haven. After an intensive week-long period of harbour and sea acceptance trials, the Naval Service took delivery of LE *Orla* and LE *Ciara* (P41 and P42 respectively). Ireland's newest and most heavily armed warships made their way home to Cork via Scotland's north and west coasts; *en route* they were met by the *Eithne* and *Aisling*. In January 1989 the *Orla* and *Ciara* were formally commissioned into service at Dun Laoghaire by the Taoiseach, Charles Haughey.

Unlike the *Eithne* and *Deirdre*, these vessels were purpose-built warships. The *Deirdre* and P21s were clever adaptations of ocean-going trawler designs and their defensive armaments comprised unsophisticated Bofors and Oerlikon guns. The *Eithne*, although a well-equipped and air capable patrol vessel, was, however, not a conventional warship. The *Peacock* class with its 76mm Oto Melara gun has true small warship capability. Although the computerised gun (Sea Archer fire control system) is optical, and thus relatively ineffective against aircraft, it does provide a degree of close-in support. The *Peacock* class was also armed with four single 7.62mm general purpose machine-guns (GPMGs). When the *Peacocks* entered Irish service, their defensive armament was upgraded with the addition of two single 12.7mm heavy machine-guns. With a maximum (sprint) speed of 30 knots, these vessels are fast and flexible. Being designed to British warship standards, the damage control capability is excellent for a small ship. There is redundancy and cross-connect

27 LE *Orla*

capability between engineroom spaces.[29] The *Peacocks* also have the capability to replenish, that is, refuel at sea. In essence, for the first time since the 1950s, the Naval Service had a class of small warship which allowed it to briefly challenge control of the seas against an aggressor on the surface.

By the end of the 1980s, the Naval Service had been transformed out of all recognition (see above table 8). The fleet was now responsible for patrolling over 130,000 square miles of the European Community's EEZ; Irish naval vessels now paid goodwill visits to ports in Europe, North America and the Middle East; and the Naval Service also performed a whole range of other duties from SAR, pollution control, UN re-supply voyages to the interdiction of terrorist arms at sea. However, even with the delivery of the two ex-RN *Peacock* class vessels, the Naval Service was still undermanned and understrength in terms of sea-going ships. The provision of maritime aviation was restricted, as the Beechcraft Super King Airs were nearing the end of their employability. It would not be until 1994 that the two maritime patrol variants of the Casa 235 would enter service.

6

THE IRISH NAVAL SERVICE TODAY

ORGANISATION AND ESTABLISHMENT

The Irish Defence Forces (IDF) are an integrated national defence force comprising regular and reserve land, sea and air components. The Naval Service has the special status of an independent command area similar to the Air Corps. The IDF is sub-divided into two components:

The Permament Defence Force: includes the regular army, the Air Corps and the Naval Service.

The Reserve Defence Force: which comprises the Army's First Line Reserve (the members of which have formerly served in the Permanent Defence Force); An Forsa Cosanta Aitiuil (FCA), the Second Line Territorial Army Reserve, and An Slua Muiri, the Second Line Naval Reserve. There is no second line reserve component of the Irish Air Corps.

The Republic of Ireland which constitutes over four-fifths of the territory of the island of Ireland is sub-divided into military districts. These are known as Commands, of which there are four: Western Command, with its headquarters at Athlone; Eastern Command, with its headquarters at Collins barracks, Dublin; Curragh Command, with its headquarters in the Curragh; and Southern Command with its headquarters in Collins barracks, Cork.

The Naval Service is regarded as a maritime or offshore Command. However, it is interesting to note that no provision has been made to sub-divide the country into naval districts, although such a suggestion was made by Capt. Jerome in the early 1950s, and by his successor Capt. McKenna in his Naval Policy memorandum of 1961. At that time, Capt. McKenna recommended that the Republic of Ireland be sub-divided into three geographic naval districts—Western, Eastern and Southern. Capt. McKenna also suggested that in addition to the existing naval base in Cork, two sub-depots should be established: one in Dublin and the other either at Killybegs or at Rathmullan, both in Co. Donegal. However, in the words of Capt. McKenna, his recommendations "came to naught".

Establishment and defence expenditure

The Republic of Ireland has a population of 3,500,000, of which there are 440,000 young men aged between 18-32. Yet even with this limited pool of manpower, Ireland's defence forces are very modest in size. The establishment provides for a Permanent Defence Force of approximately 18,000 all ranks and 23,000 in the Reserve Defence Force. The Naval Service's establishment is 1281 persons (160 officers, 578 NCOs and 543 seaman), with 675 in the Second Line Naval Reserve. At present there are approximately 130 officers and 865 men in the regular navy, 21 officers and 155 men in the First Line Naval Reserve, and 432 all ranks in the Second Line Naval Reserve. The overall active strength of the Permanent Defence Force is approximately 12,700, which includes 110 women.

Ireland's GDP in 1992 was £28.06 billion.[1] The defence vote in 1992 was £328.5 million, of which less than five per cent went on the procurement of new equipment. The absence of conscription has meant that retaining an all-volunteer professional army, navy and Air Corps is very expensive.

Command structure

The supreme commander of Ireland's defence forces is the President, who is elected for a term of seven years. The present incumbent is the distinguished lawyer and academic, Mary Robinson. Under the President's direction (acting on the advice of the government), military command is exercised by the government through the minister for defence. Command of the defence forces has been delegated by the minister to the four general officers commanding the commands, to the flag officer commanding the Naval Service and to the general officer commanding the Air Corps. A body entitled the Council of Defence stands established whose function is to aid and counsel the minister on all matters in relation to the business of the department of defence on which the minister may consult the Council. It meets whenever summoned by the minister.

The Council of Defence

The Council of Defence is composed of:

a) The minister of state for the department of defence and the secretary of the department of defence. Both of these individuals are of course civilians.

b) Other members are: the chief of staff, the adjutant-general and the quartermaster-general. The former is a lieutenant-general and the remain-

ORGANISATION OF THE IRISH DEFENCE FORCES

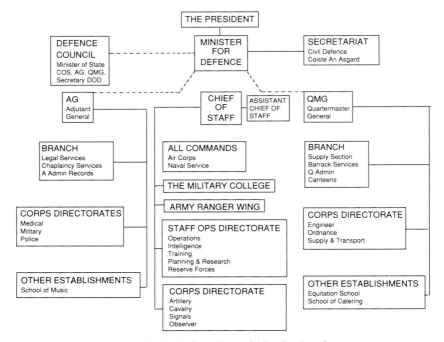

Source: Irish Defence Forces' Handbook 1987

der hold the rank of major-general. At present all three officers are from the army. However, in recognition of the Naval Service's increase in size and responsibilities over the past two decades, this arrangement may be modified. Brian Lenihan, a former defence minister and deputy prime minister of Ireland, has stated that he would be in favour of making the Flag Officer Commanding the Naval Service a member of the Council of Defence.[2]

THE ORGANISATION OF THE NAVAL SERVICE

The Irish Naval Service, although firmly integrated within Ireland's army-dominated defence force, does have its own unique character and organisation. The Headquarters of the INS is located at the department of defence in Dublin. It is from here that Ireland's most senior naval officer, the Flag Officer Commanding the Naval Service (FOCNS), commands the country's navy. The present FOCNS is Cmdr. John Kavanagh. In the course of his service with the INS, Cmdr. Kavanagh has attended the Irish Military College in the Curragh, the Royal Naval Staff College, Greenwich and the United States Naval War College, Rhode Island.

Naval Headquarters comprises the FOCNS and his supporting staff. With the exception of Naval Headquarters in Dublin, most regular naval personnel are located on Haulbowline Island in Cork harbour. A small detachment of naval personnel is also attached to the *ad hoc* naval training centre at Murphy Barracks, Ballincollig, Co. Cork. In addition, a very small number of regular naval personnel are attached to the four Slua Muiri (Second Line Naval Reserve) training centres at Waterford, Dublin, Limerick and in Cork.

Naval operations section

It is from Naval Headquarters that the chain of command flows from the FOCNS to the naval base and dockyard on Haulbowline Island, to the operational units of the Fleet, to the Naval School, and to other shoreside units of the regular and reserve Naval Service. A naval operations section is divided between Naval Headquarters in Dublin and the naval base on Haulbowline. The scope and intensity of naval operations under its direct control has expanded considerably since the late 1970s. An Irish patrol vessel spends a minimum of 180 days a year at sea, with 200 days per year not uncommon. This can mean that each of these ships will travel an average of 2000 miles per month on patrol. Therefore, constant monitoring is required. In addition, the Naval Operations Section at Haulbowline contains the National (Fishery) Supervisory Centre (NSC) for Ireland. This is linked to the Naval Computer Centre (NCC) where the Lirsat

ORGANISATION OF THE IRISH NAVAL SERVICE

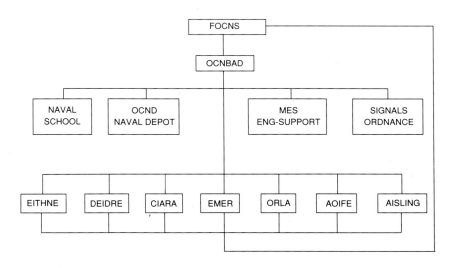

Source: Naval Headquarters, Dublin

Project is currently in operation. This is a pilot project which has been undertaken by the Naval Service to investigate the feasibility of using position-finding equipment and satellite communications to track the positions of vessels at sea and report these back to the naval computer centre. The project involves the placing of tamper-proof electronic equipment on board two fishing vessels. This box includes satellite communication (INMARSAT) and position finding equipment (GPS), in addition to controller hardware and software.

This technology could be used to implement a comprehensive coastal surveillance system, similar to an air traffic control system for all sea areas under Irish jurisdiction, The system could also support pollution control functions, as well as SAR and possibly covert operations.

NAVAL BASE AND DOCKYARD

The Irish Naval Service's only base and main training centre is located on Haulbowline Island, in Cork harbour. More than half of the island is owned by Irish Steel Ltd, and the encroachment of the steel plant has posed problems for the Naval Service in the past. The island is simply to small to accommodate an operational naval base, dockyard, training centre, as well as a commerical steel producer. The island's physical isolation was ended in 1965 when a bridge was built connecting it with the mainland. Prior to this, cargo boats and passenger launches had to be used to keep the island supplied.

Accommodation on the island consists of buildings and barracks left over from the British period, but there is also a modern purpose-built accommodation block for 100 personnel. The older barrack buildings have been refurbished and brought up to standard in recent years. In addition, there are a limited number of buildings on the island which are designated as married quarters. Recreational facilities on the base consist of a multi-purpose gym, small theatre, squash courts and a football pitch. The latter is also used as a helicopter landing site. The base does not possess a swimming pool, as local public baths are utilised for training.

Haulbowline Island is also home to the Naval Service Pipe Band (NSPB). Formed in the late 1980s, the NSPB has attracted well-deserved publicity in Ireland and overseas. Unlike the Army's Central and Command bands, the personnel in the NSPB are not full-time musicians, yet in their very short history they have performed throughout Ireland, as well as in France, Denmark and Britain. All of the NSPB's musicians receive their training at the Army School of Music in Dublin. The present Officer Commanding the Naval Base and Dockyard is Capt. McElhinney, NS.

28 NSPB drummers perform on LE *Eithne*'s heli–deck during an official goodwill visit to London

The Naval dockyard

The Naval dockyard and shore support unit, though small by any international standard, have acquired a cross section of technical expertise far in excess of its size. As well as their responsibility for routine maintenance of all Naval Service ships and auxiliary vessels, in 1985 they completed a half-life refit on LE *Deirdre*. This is the first time an operation of this magnitude has been undertaken.

The Naval School

The Naval school is located on Haulbowline Island, but also maintains a naval detachment at Murphy barracks, Ballincollig. All petty officers and senior ratings are also sent to Southern Command's NCOs' training centre in Collins barracks, Cork. The Naval School is responsible for running all military as well as professional courses for the Executive and Engineering branch. The Naval School is not formally sub-divided into a cadet school and a ratings' school, but training is carried out separately for young officers, cadets, NCOs and ratings. These are partly conducted at the four training bays—technical, sail training, seamanship training, and gunnery.

Naval Diving Unit

The Naval Diving Unit (NDU) has responsibility for mine warfare, underwater explosive ordnance disposal, search and rescue diving, aircraft recovery, ship maintenance and salvage, as well as all service diving to a maximum depth of 55 metres. In 1981 the NDU was able to carry out its own training when a four-man decompression chamber was acquired. Prior to this, all naval divers were trained by the Royal Navy. The unit ran its first course in 1982. In the period 1982-7 over 30 ship's divers and ship diving officers have been completed the very demanding six-week long courses which are conducted by the NDU. The introduction of such training courses has enabled the Naval Service to maintain a fully operational ship's diving team on each patrol vessel.

Naval Museum

At present Ireland does not have a designated national army or naval museum. There is a National Maritime Museum in Dun Laoghaire; however, it does not contain a permanent exhibition dedicated to the Naval Service. Similarly, the achievements of the Irish Defence Forces are not recorded at the National Museum in Dublin. There are private military museums housed within army barracks, for example, Collins barracks, Cork, and Mullingar barracks. In addition, there is the dedicated coast defence museum at Fort Dunree in north Donegal. Ireland is still without a national army museum.

The Naval Service does maintain a small naval museum on Haulbowline Island. It is housed within the island's Martello tower and consists of an unrivalled collection of photographs, badges, uniforms and medals. It is open to arranged tours and information is available on request.

THE FLEET

The Irish Naval Service's sea-going force of helicopter patrol, offshore patrol and coastal patrol vessels is informally known as the 'Fleet'. This small force of seven vessels is not designated as a squadron or a patrol flotilla. However, such designations were used in the late 1940s, when the embryonic Irish navy operated a motor torpedo boat squadron and a corvette flotilla. With the expansion of the Irish Naval Service in the late 1970s and early 1980s, it became feasible to have an annual fleet review. This can take place in any Irish port at anytime of the year.

In October 1993 the Irish Naval Service's sea-going fleet comprised:

- one Corvette (helicopter patrol vessel) LE *Eithne*

- four offshore patrol vessels: LE *Deirdre*, LE *Emer*, LE *Aoife*, LE *Aisling*

- two coastal patrol vessels: LE *Orla*, LE *Ciara*.

The Naval Service also operates one harbour launch (*Colleen II*), which is based in Haulbowline, and a small sail training yacht, *Tailte*. The latter is used by naval cadets and other members of the Naval Service for seamanship training. The Second Line Naval Reserve also operate two elderly sail training yachts, *Nancy Bet* and *Creidne*.

The department of defence Fleet

The Irish Naval Service does not operate an equivalent of Britain's Royal Maritime Auxiliary Service or the Royal Fleet Auxiliary Service. There is no immediate need for sea-going oilers, or replenishment ships, although in 1954 Capt. Jerome NS did identify the need for a dual-purpose ocean-going cargo/training ship, which could be employed as a minelayer in wartime.

The only time the Irish Naval Service has ever operated a naval auxiliary was between 1976–84, when LE *Setanta* was in service as a training and supply ship. However, the Irish department of defence does maintain a small fleet of civilian-manned harbour auxiliaries. This maritime service operates a number of small craft for military personnel and cargo transportation at various locations, in particular around the naval dockyard in Cork harbour. This service became operational in October

1938, when the British withdrew from Spike Island and the coastal forts which guard the entrance to Cork harbour. Originally, all of the motor launches and cargo vessels employed by the department were former British craft, but by the mid-1970s most of these had been scrapped. It is only in Cork harbour that the department operates such a maritime transportation service.

In October 1993 the department of defence's fleet comprised:

- one cargo and passenger transport vessel: MV *David F*

- two harbour transport craft: ML *Fainleog* and ML *Faichdubh*

- one harbour tug: *Seabhac*.

MARITIME AVIATION

Air Corps/Naval Service operations

Unlike the Royal Navy, the Irish Naval Service does not operate its own naval aviation branch. With the introduction of the 200-mile Exclusive Economic Zone in 1977 and the advent of the P31 class helicopter-carrying patrol vessel, the need for maritime aviation was recognised. In view of the integrated nature of Ireland's defence forces, the Irish Naval Service did not develop its own autonomous naval air arm, but chose to rely on the expertise of the the Irish Air Corps. The practice of utilising air force personnel and aircraft for naval usage is very common. The navies of Norway, New Zealand, Belgium, and Portugal all employ air force helicopters and patrol aircraft for ship and land based maritime operations.

The Irish Air Corps (IAC) is a small but highly efficient and flexible air arm numbering no more than 800 officers and enlisted personnel. Although very distinctive in character and organisation, the Air Corps is still integrated within the Irish army. In terms of uniform, the Irish ground and air crews are indistinguishable from infantry, artillery or signals' personnel. They wear the same olive green No. 2 uniforms and combat dress, and can only be identified by their metallic Corps badge and blue shoulder flash. Admittedly, flying crews do wear very distinctive gold embroidered wings.

At present the IAC operates 15 helicopters and 24 fixed-winged jet and turbo prop aircraft. These aircraft are organised into seven nominal air squadrons, of which all but one have their headquarters at the main air base at Baldonnel, outside Dublin. The other air station is at Gormanston in Co. Meath. In addition three helicopters are permanently attached to the following locations: the Naval Service flagship LE

29 LE *Eithne*'s Dauphin 2 helicopter embarks on a maritime reconnaissance patrol.

Eithne; Finner Camp, Co. Donegal and Monaghan barracks, both of which are very close to the border with Northern Ireland.

Maritime Squadron

Following the introduction of a 200-mile EEZ in 1977, the Air Corps leased two Beechcraft Super King Airs before purchasing them outright in 1979. A third aircraft was bought in May 1980. These aircraft had to fly fishery patrols at very low levels in inclement weather. In 1990 the Beechcrafts were retired and an order for three Spanish-built Airtech Casa CN 235 maritime patrol planes was placed. The first of these high performance aircraft (a transport variant) was delivered in May 1991. In October 1993 this aircraft is still the only operational unit in the Maritime Squadron. The remaining two maritime surveillance variants of the Casa 235 series will not enter service until 1994.

Naval Support Squadron

The Naval Support Squadron was established in 1986 when the Air Corps took delivery of two navalised Dauphin 2 helicopters. This variant of the Dauphin 2 was equipped with crash-proof fuel tanks and a harpoon hook. One of these Dauphins was seconded to the navy's flagship, LE *Eithne*. The remaining helicopter, which should have been allocated to the second but cancelled P31 class vessel, was earmarked as a reserve unit. Since 1986, the Air Corps has detached a small number of pilots and support personnel to serve aboard *Eithne*. In total, this normally consists of eight Air Corps officers and men.

Search and Rescue (SAR) Squadron

In 1986 the Search and Rescue Squadron was established when three Dauphin 2 helicopters were delivered. Contrary to popular perception these very expensive high performance helicopters are classified as inshore SAR units. They have a maximum range of 410 miles and can carry five passengers. The responsibility for medium/long-range SAR operations currently rests with a private company, Irish Helicopters Ltd. They operate two Sikorsky S-69 helicopters from their base at Shannon airport, in south-west Ireland. In 1981-2, the Irish Air Corps did operate a comparable machine when they leased a single Puma troop carrying helicopter from the French aircraft company Aerospatiale. However, the need for urgent economies, obliged the Irish department of defence to terminate the lease after one year.[3]

The Irish Air Corps may acquire dual purpose troop carrying/SAR helicopters in the future, but this of course will be dictated by the condition of the Irish economy. The possibility of purchasing cheaper helicopters from the aircraft companies such as Kamov in the former

Soviet Union is unlikely. Although physically robust and very price competitive, the department of defence may be intimidated by the current political uncertainty in Russia and the threat this could pose to a regular supply of spare parts.

Irish military airfields

Baldonnel The Irish Air Corps' headquarters is located in the department of defence in Dublin, and the main base and the centre for all basic and advanced flying training is located at Casement aerodrome, Baldonnel. In 1965 the aerodrome adopted its present name when the then British government agreed to release the remains of Sir Roger Casement, who was executed for treason in 1916. His remains were disinterred from Pentonville prison and flown back to Ireland aboard an Aer Lingus aircraft.

Baldonnel is also home to six air squadrons: Light Strike, Maritime, Naval Support, Army Support, Search and Rescue; and Transport and Training.

Gormanston The IAC's second airfield is located at Gormanston, 25 miles north of Dublin, on the site of a former Royal Flying Corps station during World War I. Gormanston has one tarmac runway and is home to the seven Cessna 172 aircraft comprising the Army Cooperation Squadron. Although primarily employed in an internal security role, the Cessnas are also used for target towing, for both army and navy anti-aircraft gunnery practice. The Defence Forces' air firing ranges are located out to sea from Gormanston airfield.

Finner The Air Corps has been present at Finner Camp, Bundoran, Co. Donegal since 1972, when a single Alouette III was detached from Baldonnel to assist the Garda (Irish police) and the resident army battalion at Finner (28th Infantry) with internal security work.[4] This battalion was not formally established until 1973. Prior to this date, an *ad hoc* infantry group aided the civil power in this border area.

In 1978 a 450-metre-long tarmac airstrip was constructed, which allowed Cessna 172 aircraft from the Army Co-op Squadron to operate from Finner. In addition a spacious heated hangar was built for the helicopter. In 1989 an all-weather Dauphin 2 helicopter was relocated from Shannon to Finner. For the first time the people of the north west of Ireland were provided with 24-hour SAR cover.

THE ROLE OF THE NAVAL SERVICE IN PEACE AND WAR

The roles which the Irish Naval Service have to undertake are subdivided into primary and secondary, the former being those which would be allocated priority in time of war. The latter are those roles which take up most of the navy's activity in peacetime.

Primary or wartime roles of the Naval Service would be:

- deter and resist aggression

- uphold neutrality by patrolling the territorial waters. This would involve air, surface and subsurface surveillance

- seaward defence of the country's main ports (this encompasses harbour defence and port control)

- minesweeping of designated channels and estuaries.

Secondary or peacetime roles of the Naval Service are:

- offshore fishery protection and surveillance of the Exclusive Economic Zone

- aid to the civil power

- search and rescue (SAR)

- support of Irish UN contingents

- pollution control

- salmon fishery patrols (inshore fishing)

- army and Air Corps cooperation

- hydrographic survey

- conduct diving operations.

Primary or wartime roles

At present the Naval Service would be unable to perform most of these primary roles, as this would require a fleet equipped with modern anti-submarine frigates, mine warfare vessels and seaward defence boats. To equip the INS with such vessels would prove to be prohibitively expensive. In 1961, during the height of the Cold War, the then commanding officer of the Naval Service, Capt. T. McKenna advised on the type of fleet that would be required to carry out the navy's primary roles. In the memorandum, Capt. McKenna recommended that a force of 37 ships and inshore craft would be required to provide the country with the means to protect Irish neutrality.[5] The then requirement was subdivided into four categories—eight fast anti-submarine frigates, six coastal minesweepers, 11 inshore minesweepers and 12 seaward defence boats. At the time, Ireland's navy consisted of three corvettes, of which only one was in commission. No action was taken to pursue these recommendations, as this would have involved enormous financial expenditure.

In Ireland it is widely felt that expenditure on defence which is not related to internal security, fishery protection and SAR is a waste of money. The country has no enemies and is not subject to any perceived external threat. This view has been given enormous credence since the demise of the Soviet Union and the Warsaw Pact. The apparent absence of what was formerly East/West naval rivalry in the Atlantic waters off Ireland has undermined the need to equip the Naval Service with appropriate anti-submarine vessels, minesweepers and seaward defence boats. All the vessels which are currently in service have been built or procured for the Naval Service's main peactime role, that is, fishery protection. Of the seven vessels currently in commission only two can be classified as naval warships—the ex-RN Peacock class vessels LE *Orla* and LE *Ciara*. These vessels are fast; they have an average speed 20 knots, with a capability to reach a 'sprint' speed of 30 knots. Their main armament (one 76mm Oto Melara Automatic gun) has the capability to inflict significant damage on other small warships. Both the Flagship *Eithne* and the four *Deirdre*/P21 class OPVs are more akin to the medium-grade cutters currently in service with the United States Coast Guard.

The *Eithne* is, of course, much more capable than the P21 type OPVs, as she has a range of 7000 miles and is equipped with an embarked helicopter, an anti-submarine sonar system and a 57mm Bofors gun which is capable of firing 235 rounds a minute. The latter is linked to a sophisticated fire control system (LIOD) However, although capable of detecting subsurface intruders, at present she is not equipped with an ASW system. The reason for this is of course dictated by the need to prioritise defence procurement. And anti-submarine weapon systems are not a priority at present, although the *Eithne* is capable of being retrofitted with an appropriate system.

Secondary or peacetime roles

The Naval Service's current sea-going fleet is well equipped to perform the majority of the prescribed secondary roles. Fishery protection is the prime peacetime function of the Irish Naval Service, and this role takes up ninety per cent of the navy's duties. The current mixture of coastal, offshore and helicopter carrying patrol vessels compare very favourably with the OPVs of other navies and seaborne coastguard services. However, the current fleet of seven ships is too small to effectively patrol the 200-mile EEZ, in addition to performing other necessary roles. Unlike the Royal Navy's Fishery Protection Squadron at Rosyth, the Irish Naval Service does not have a reserve of minesweepers and frigates to fall back on. In addition, the Royal Navy is very fortunate in that

Scotland has its own seaborne fishery protection service, namely the Scottish Fishery Protection Agency (SFPA). The SFPA currently operates a modern fleet of four unarmed patrol ships, two fast inshore patrol craft and two patrol launches. This maritime force is backed up by two Cessna Caravan II fisheries patrol aircraft which are equipped with the Seaspray 2000 maritime surveillance radar system. Similarly, the Norwegian coastguard (Kystvakt) which was established in 1977 (the year the 200-mile EEZ was introduced in Europe) has a very significant fleet of 13 patrol ships ranging in size from 3450 m/t to 650 m/t, supported by Royal Norwegian air force helicopters and Orion long-range maritime patrol aircraft.

Ireland's designated fishery protection vessels enjoy no such benefits. The Irish patrol vessels which police the EEZ are also required to perform a whole range of other duties. According to *Jane's Fighting Ships*, in order to patrol Ireland's EEZ, a force of 12 patrol vessels is required consisting of two of 2000 tons (each with an embarked helicopter), six of 1000 tons and four of 500 tons.

Non-fishery protection duties

Aid to the Civil Power   The Naval Service is also required to carry out numerous other duties, which are unrelated to fishery protection. Aid to the Civil Power is the expression used when the Naval Service is required to help the Garda (police) or any other branch of State in a marine environment. The most notable examples of such aid being given occurred in 1973 and 1984, when the Service intercepted the IRA arms ships MV *Claudia* and MV *Marita Ann*. On both occasions, the Naval Service was acting in support of the police. In July 1993, the Naval Service illustrated its ability to help the police and customs service against the criminal gangs who try to smuggle drugs into Ireland. On this occasion, LE *Orla* intercepted a yacht with a multi-million dollar cargo of cannibis aboard. It was a very skilful operation, which gave credence to those who advocate that the interdiction of drug smugglers at sea is a role which should be permanently assigned to the Naval Service. Of course, to provide for such an interdiction service would require significant additional funding.

Search and rescue   Ever since the foundation of the Naval Service in 1946, Irish naval vessels have always been made available to assist in search and rescue operations in coastal and offshore waters. In 1958, LE *Macha* assisted in the search for the wreckage of a KLM Constellation aircraft which had crashed into the Atlantic after taking off from Shannon airport. On that occasion, the *Macha* was assisted by an Air Corps Anson from Baldonnel. From 1960 to 1972, the Naval Service manned the country's Marine Rescue and Coordination Centre. In 1968, the corvettes *Macha* and *Cliona* assisted in the search for the wreckage of a crashed Aer Lingus Viscount off Tuskar Point. In 1979, the Naval Service was heavily involved in the Fastnet Race rescue operation. Six years later, the Service was called upon to provide vessels to search for the wreckage of the Air India 747 jetliner blown up by Sikh terrorists over the western Atlantic. On this occasion, one officer, one petty officer and two ratings were decorated with the Distinguished Service Medal in recognition of their courage and devotion to duty.

In view of the increased volume of civil air traffic over the Irish Sea, and the already heavy volume of commercial shipping, fishing vessels and pleasure craft off Ireland's coasts, the importance of search and rescue has never been more prominent. As in Britain, inshore rescue is still primarily the responsibility of the Royal National Lifeboat Institution, assisted by the local coastal and cliff rescue units located around Ireland's coastline. The Naval Service will despatch one of its vessels to an incident if so requested by the Marine Rescue and Coordination Centre in Dublin. (The MRCC is now based at the department of marine in Lesson Lane, Dublin; all coast radio stations are remoted to this HQ.) The MRCC also has close links with the Air Corps, the RNLI, the RAF, the Royal Navy and HM Coastguard.

Army and Air Corps co-operation The Naval Service as an integrated branch of the Defence Forces is available to carry out various tasks on behalf of the Army and the Air Corps. Traditionally, this comprised four functions—supplying the coastal forts; ammunition transport from England and occasionally continental Europe; target towing for coast defence batteries and Air Corps aircraft; and ensuring range clearance for the Air Corps during live firing exercises. With the formal disbandment of Coast Defence Artillery in 1979, there was no longer a need for CDA-related target towing and supply voyages. However, the other functions have not only remained, but have expanded with the Air Corps' involvement in fishery protection duties, maritime SAR operations and the interdiction of terrorist arms and drug shipments. There is still a requirement for a naval vessel to provide range clearance at the Air Corps' air firing ranges off Gormanston. The aircraft which are involved in these exercises come from the Light Strike Squadron (Fouga Magister armed jet trainers) and the Transport and Training Squadron (Siai Marchetti armed turbo-prop basic trainers). A Cessna 172 from the Army Cooperation Squadron is also used to tow targets for anti-aircraft practice for both army and naval gunners. The Army's AA gun batteries normally conduct their live firing at Gormanston.

Although heavily involved in range clearance and target towing, the Naval Service's own annual fleet exercises are normally conducted elsewhere, for example, off Galley Head, Co. Cork. The need to transport arms and ammunition from Britain and continental Europe is still an occasional requirement. However, when this duty was carried out in 1961, the corvette *Cliona* was obilged to empty her magazines. The reason being that the *Flower* class corvette was not designed to carry cargo and ammunition is an extremely hazardous cargo; if there is a fire, at least a magazine can be flooded.

Support of UN contingents The Naval Service's only direct involvement with United Nations peacekeeping operations is centred around the bi-annual resupply voyages to the Lebanon. Since 1979, a *Deirdre*/P21 class patrol vessel has carried stores and re-fitted armoured cars to an Irish infantry battalion serving with UNIFIL. The patrol vessel which is normally required to carry out this task, can carry two Panhard AML 90 armoured cars.[6] A small number of Naval Service personnel have also been assigned to the Irish UNIFIL battalion as administrative staff. Naval officers also serve on the staff of UN headquarters at Naquora in south Lebanon. In addition, Naval Service petty officers have served in Cyprus, and a naval officer has just completed a tour with the UN in Central America.[7]

Hydrographic survey The need for a hydrograhic survey was recognised as "a must" back in the 1950s and again in Capt. McKenna's memorandum in 1960. However, although funding was promised, nothing came of the plan to purchase and convert an ex-RN inshore minesweeper for such duties. In 1977 the Naval Service leased a Danish Stern trawler, which prior to entering Irish service was employed as a seismic survey vessel. At the time it was thought possible to convert this trawler into a dual purpose patrol/survey vessel. However, as Capt. McKenna pointed out in his memorandum, Ireland would require a survey vessel more akin to that of an inshore minesweeper, that is, with a very shallow draft and capable of manoeuvring in tight confines. The Naval Service does not operate any hydrographic survey vessels and never have. This function is now carried out by the department of marine's oceanographic survey vessel, *Lough Beltra*, which is manned by civilians.

Pollution control and diving operations In view of Ireland's geographic position lying astride the main shipping (including tanker) routes, leading to and from Europe, the risk of seaborne chemical pollution is ever present. Therefore, all Naval Service vessels carry out pollution control drill during the annual fleet exercises. Chemical dispersants are not carried on board patrol vessels, but are held in storage at Haulbowline in the event of a pollution incident. The dispersant is only used offshore, as the department of marine are not in favour of their use in coastal waters, because of the damage they may cause to the environment.

The requirement for such training and awareness was demonstrated in 1978 by the Whiddy Island disaster in Bantry Bay oil terminal. On that occasion, Naval Service vessels were involved as control ships in the aftermath of the huge oil spillage. Again in 1991, there was the risk of oil pollution when an accident occurred involving a coastal freighter and a cross-channel ferry, the *Kilkenny*. The accident occurred in Dublin Bay and the Naval Service patrol vessel *Aoife* was called upon to act as a control ship. Fortunately, the risk of significant oil pollution on this occasion was not realised.

The Naval Service is also called upon to carry out diving operations in order to dispose of wartime sea mines which occasionally become ensnarled in the nets of trawlers. This is a very hazardous duty which requires great skill and physical courage, as the mines are often in a highly volatile state.

RECRUITMENT AND TRAINING

All service in the Irish Defence Forces is voluntary. In fact obligatory military service or conscription has never been applied in Ireland, even during the height of the Emergency. Prior to 1994, service in the INS was still restricted to men, but in 1994 the first female cadets for the Naval Service will be inducted. This will be the first step in opening up the service, in all its aspects, to women.

All males between the ages of 17 and 27 years may enlist in the Naval Service as seamen for a minimum period of five years, with a commitment to serve a further seven years in the reserve. The minimum period of service in the army or Air Corps is three years. Naval cadets are selected on the basis of two interviews in addition to aptitude, psychological and technical assessments. They must be aged between 18 and 24. All candidates must possess an honours leaving certificate, as well as pass a strict medical examination. Graduate entrants must possess a degree from a recognised college or university. In general the quality of most officer candidates exceeds these requirements. All general recruits, that is, ratings, must have completed a basic education; they are selected on the basis of an interview.

In the past, most Irish naval recruits came from Dublin, Cork and Waterford. This is no longer the case. Recruits are drawn from all over Ireland, both from coastal and inland districts. In addition, a small percentage (less than five per cent) of naval personnel come from outside the State, for example, Northern Ireland and Great Britain. The latter are second- or third-generation Irish. Most recently, applications to serve in the INS have been received from former and serving Royal Navy personnel and even from interested candidates of Irish extraction living in the United States. In 1992, 400 applications were received for cadetships in the INS.[8] Recruitment is not continuous: for example since 1990 there has been a selective moratorium on further recruitment within the IDF. However, in 1992 50 recruits were taken on for general service in the INS.

Officer training

All officer candidates spend three months undergoing basic military training in the Curragh, before being sent to the Naval Cadet School on Haulbowline Island. The period of training from cadet entry until the naval officer in the Executive Branch passes his watchkeeping examinations lasts four years. For an officer candidate in the Engineering Branch, his training will last six years. For both officer candidates in the Executive Branch and Engineering Branch his training is subdivided as follows:

	Military	Sea Training	Academic	Overseas	Miscellaneous
Executive Branch	20%	40%	13%	20%	7%
Engineering Branch	18%	17%	45%	14%	6%

Sea training is conducted aboard the training yacht *Tailte* and operational naval vessels; military and academic training is undertaken in Cork and at the Military College in the Curragh. The Naval Service has its own small cadet school, which is part of the much larger Naval School on Haulbowline Island. Engineering cadets are trained at Cork Regional Technical College and the Royal Naval Engineering College at HMS *Manadon*. The Army's training centres in Southern Command are also available for use. After nearly one year and nine months of academic, military and seamanship training, the cadet will be commissioned into the Irish Naval Service as an ensign. This takes place in July. The following year, the newly-commissioned ensign will receive further seamanship and academic training (in the United Kingdom) before being promoted to the rank of sub-lieutenant. In the fourth year of his training, the newly-promoted junior officer will be sent to attend the International Sub-Lieutenants Course (ISLC) at the Britannia Royal Naval College (BRNC), Dartmouth, in the United Kingdom.

The ISLC consists of nine weeks of academic training at BRNC before officers move on to HMS *Dryad* for eighteen weeks of specialist warfare training. Subjects covered at BRNC include radar and telecommunications, ship technology, marine environment, computing and navigation. Other nations attending the ISLC course have included officers from Singapore, Oman, Guyana, Pakistan, United Arab Emirates, Ghana,

Nigeria, Thailand, Malaysia, Fiji, Sri Lanka, Yemen, Trinidad and Tobago, Barbados, and Jamaica.

In the period 1984–93, 18 Irish naval officers have completed the International Sub-Lieutenant's Course at BRNC, Dartmouth (see table 9).

After returning from Dartmouth, the sub-lieutenant undergoes a further three months' sea training before sitting his final watchkeeping examinations in May–June. In July, and after nearly four years of training, the fully qualified sub-lieutenant will receive his first posting.

Follow-up courses

The training facilities available to the INS are limited; therefore, officers, NCOs and senior ratings have to receive additional training elsewhere either within the Irish military system, or abroad. In Ireland, training can be conducted at the various Corps workshops and schools which belong to the Army, as well as the Military College (for officers). The latter contains an infantry school, a cadet school and a command and staff school.

Specialist naval training is normally undertaken in the United Kingdom. This takes place at the following locations:

Royal Naval Engineering College, HMS *Manadon*, Plymouth;

Portland (Helicopter Control Officer/Flight Direction Officer);

HMS *Phoenix* (Damage control/Firefighting);

HMS *Cambridge* (Gunnery);

HMS *Vernon* (Diving);

HMS *Dryad* (Sonar);

various RN vessels (ISLC and Midshipman).

Source: Naval Headquarters, Dublin

All middle-grade officers attend command and staff courses at the Irish Military College. Some senior naval officers, above the rank of lieutenant commander, attend courses at the Royal Naval Staff College, Greenwich in England. However, this is dependent upon the availability of funds from the department of defence. Although most overseas training is undertaken in the United Kingdom, two Irish naval officers (Capt. McElhinney OCNBAD and Cmdr. Kavanagh FOCNS) have also attended a staff course at the United States Naval War College, Rhode Island.

Other courses which are in constant demand are diving, mine disposal and gunnery. With the commissioning of the *Eithne* in 1984 and the two ex-RN *Peacock* class vessels in 1988, the Naval Service had now acquired vessels that were no longer armed with the standard open sighted 40mm Bofors gun. The *Eithne*'s 57mm Bofors gun and the ex-RN vessels' 76mm Oto Melara compact guns require a higher degree of gunnery skill.

Table No. 9: Attendance of Irish Naval Service officers
at Britannia Royal Naval College, Dartmouth

May 1984	5 students
May 1985	5 students
Jan 1986	2 students
Sept 1989	1 student
Sept 1991	3 students
Jan 1993	2 students

Source: BRNC, Dartmouth

One of the most demanding courses is the Royal Navy's Long Diving Course, which is conducted at Portsmouth. The former FOCNS, Cmdr. J. Deasy, was the first Irish naval officer to undergo this physically arduous diving course back in 1964, thus becoming the Naval Service's first trained diver.

Most overseas technical and staff training courses are undertaken in the United Kingdom, but some naval personnel do attend specialist courses in Europe and in the USA.

Exchange programmes

At present an officer exchange programme operates with the navies of Denmark, Germany and, to a limited extent, the United Kingdom. The relationship with the Royal Navy has always been close, but since the introduction of the 200-mile EEZ contact with the Royal Danish navy has increased significantly. The latter is responsible for policing a vast area off the coasts of Greenland, the Faeroes Islands, as well as the Danish homeland. Danish warships frequently visit Ireland.

Ratings

All recruits to the "lower deck" are inducted at the naval base on Haulbowline Island. Their training lasts 16 weeks and covers naval and general military skills. From 1980 to 1985, all naval ratings were trained on Spike Island, but in 1985 the Naval Service was obliged to vacate the island. From then onwards all naval ratings receive part of their basic and continuation training at Murphy barracks, Ballincollig. To this date this "unsatisfactory situation" prevails. However, a decision is eagerly awaited regarding the construction of a new and purpose-built training establishment at Ringaskiddy.

After basic training at the Naval School on Haulbowline and at Ballincollig barracks, ratings are normally attached to a patrol vessel, where they will undergo "on the job training". The use of young trainees on operational patrol vessels has provoked some criticism, a practice which senior naval officers admit is unsatisfactory.[9] Their use is partly a result of the high turnover in recruits and the absence of any sea-going training vessels. The last non-sail training ship, LE *Setanta*, was scrapped in 1984. Quite simply, the INS does not have any other vessels on which to train junior ratings. Other navies have the luxury of possessing designated training ships or sea-going auxiliaries, but Ireland's entire fleet is solely composed of seven patrol ships. As with naval officers, senior ratings and NCOs attend courses within the Irish military system or overseas. The latter normally take place in the United Kingdom.

SUPPORT SERVICES

Naval Infantry / Special Forces

Regardless of the utility of seaborne troops which was clearly illustrated during the Irish Civil War, the IDF does not possess a naval infantry or marine component. The Naval Service is only equipped with general-purpose patrol vessels, and does not possess any landing craft or transport vessels capable of carrying military supplies and infantry formations by sea. However, the IDF does possess a special forces unit which is capable of operating from naval patrol vessels and mounting small seaborne landings.

The Army Ranger Wing was established in 1980 in response to the need for a specially equipped and trained anti-terrorist unit within the defence forces. They are modelled on the United States Army Ranger battalions. During the late 1960s, several Irish army officers were sent to the USA to train with these specialist units, and their experience was built upon to create Ireland's own Ranger unit.

The Army Ranger Wing is based in the Curragh and consists of a training cadre and an operational company (120 men). They may be used in either a military or an unconventional role. The latter may consist of dealing with embassy sieges, aircraft hijackings and protecting visiting heads of governments, for example, the visit by the British prime minister John Major to Dublin in 1991.

All Rangers are qualified marksmen, trained military parachutists and experienced swimmers. They have access to specialist equipment and train to a peak of physical fitness. They can operate from naval vessels and mount seaborne landings from sea rider craft. All naval vessels have surplus accommodation for additional boarding personnel, and the use of such specialist army troops from a naval platform is an attractive option. This is especially pertinent when countering terrorists or armed drug smugglers: the length of Ireland's coastline and the limited nature of coastal road communications argues in favour of such seaborne operations.

Naval Provost

The Irish Naval Service does not operate a Shore Patrol as in the United States Navy or an equivalent of the Royal Navy's force of Naval Regulators. The enforcement of order and the maintenance of discipline in the naval base and at shore training establishments is the responsibility of the army's Military Police Corps. Since 1939 a detachment of military police has been based on Haulbowline Island. Historically, they have been responsible for maintaining order on the passenger transports which carried naval and army personnel from Haulbowline Island, Cork and Cobh to Spike Island and the coastal forts defending the entrance to Cork harbour. Today, most of these services are no longer required; Spike Island is a civilian prison, and the coastal forts have long since been deactivated. However, department of defence passenger and cargo transport craft still carry civilian, naval and army personnel to and from Haulbowline Island to Cobh and Cork. The military police still maintain a presence on these DoD vessels.

Discipline aboard a Naval Service patrol vessel is the responsibility of the ship's commander. If an offence is committed which requires investigation, the military police will be called in. If the crime is proven and the sailor is convicted by a joint army/navy court martial, the sailor may be sentenced to any one of a range of punishments as prescribed in the Defence Act (1954).

Naval officers who are subject to a court martial will face a joint army/navy board. Normally, the prosecuting officer will be an army lieutenant-colonel. In essence, this ensures impartiality, as the defendant will be tried outside the small community of Ireland's Naval Service.

Medical services

The Naval Service does not possess its own autonomous medical service comprising a naval hospital with surgeons, doctors, dentists and nursing staff. The INS is simply too small to justify a medical service, separate from the Defence Forces' Army Medical Corps. However, there is a small medical clinic on Haulbowline Island, and while at sea, each patrol vessel has a naval Sick Berth Attendant (SBA) aboard. This individual has a level of medical competence comparable to that of a fully trained paramedic/ambulance crewman. His level of training is sufficient to treat relatively minor injuries, but anything more serious would result in the injured crewman or naval officer being taken ashore either aboard his patrol vessel or in one of the Air Corps' Dauphin helicopters.

Treatment for serious injuries would be given in one of Ireland's three military hospitals—Cork Military Hospital; the General Military Hospital, Curragh; and St Bricin's Hospital, Dublin. If suitable treatment cannot be given in any of these medical centres, the sick or injured member of the Naval Service would be sent to the nearest civilian hospital.

One of the most hazardous aspects of Naval duty is deep sea diving. During such operations, a doctor from the Army Medical Corps is always in attendance. Similarly, when disposing of rogue sea mines or any other explosive devices, a military doctor must be aboard the vessel. The Army Medical Corps in Southern Command has a close working relationship with the Naval Service. At Haulbowline, where the Service have installed a decompression chamber, an army medical officer (doctor) has completed studies in certain aspects of naval medicine and is qualified to care for deep sea divers.

Chaplains

The religious and spiritual welfare of Irish naval personnel is the responsibility of the chaplain. Until 1990 attendance at religious services was regulated, that is, Mass (Church) parades were compulsory in the Irish Naval Service. However, the religious affiliations of non-Roman Catholics have always been respected, especially as this is guaranteed under the Constitution. The Naval Service has one full-time designated naval chaplain. The present incumbent is Fr Campion, who ministers to an overwhelmingly Catholic populace on Haulbowline Island. In addition to his formal duties as a Roman Catholic priest, Fr Campion acts as a counsellor to those officers and men who are experiencing problems and difficulties in their private and professional lives. The nature of naval life is unlike that of any other branch of the defence forces. Men may be at sea for more that 180 days a year, and this inevitably places an enormous strain on those who are not accustomed to long periods of separation from family, girlfriends and wives. The naval chaplain is there to act as a counsellor, independent of the naval system. In addition to his pastoral duties on the naval base, the chaplain occasionally joins the crews of naval vessels on two week-long EEZ patrols. This enables him to familiarise himself with the harsh demands of sea-going life aboard the Naval Service's relatively small patrol vessels.

For a long time the Church of Ireland has had contact with the Irish Naval Service and has provided a chaplain engaged in pastoral care and ministry to non-Roman Catholics. According to the present Protestant chaplain to the Naval Service, Revd Norman McCausland, the religious affiliation of members has always been recognised and respected. Revd McCausland went on to state: "My own experience in the past two years has been very positive and I have been afforded full courtesy and the privileges of access etc. at all times. I am invited to attend all formal events." Furthermore, Revd McCausland states that, in the past, the formal blessings of newly-commissioned warships have been ecumenical in nature and Irish Protestant ministers have participated in full, for example, at the commissioning of LE *Orla* and LE *Ciara* in January 1989. In addition, when the present Church of Ireland primate, Archbishop Eames, was bishop of Derry and Raphoe, he visited Irish Naval vessels when they were at Rathmullan in Co. Donegal. Finally, during the general pastoral visitation to Cobh, the present Church of Ireland bishop of Cork visits the Naval Base.

OVERSEAS PORT VISITS

Prior to the late 1960s an overseas port visit was a rare event in the INS. In the early 1950s the corvettes *Macha* and *Cliona* did pay goodwill visits to ports in France, Spain, Denmark, Sweden and the UK. However, after 1954 this policy lapsed as the number of ships in permanent commission shrunk from three to two. In 1961 the corvette *Cliona* was sent to Antwerp to collect a consignment of new FN rifles. This was to be the last foreign visit by a Naval Service vessel until 1975. The reasons for this were quite obvious. From 1946 to 1971, Ireland's navy consisted solely of three corvettes, which by the early 1960s were showing signs of severe strain. Once the Naval Service began to cautiously expand in mid-seventies, it was once again possible to send vessels abroad.

Port visits fall into three identifiable categories—the official, or diplomatic visit; the goodwill visit; and the operational visit. The official or diplomatic visit is primarily a foreign policy operation which receives widespread media coverage in Ireland and the host country. Senior Irish politicians, diplomats and military officials will probably be in attendance in the host port. Such important visits are normally assigned to Ireland's flagship LE *Eithne* (the *Eithne* also paid a goodwill visit to Spain during EXPO 92). This vessel is the largest and most sophisticated warship in the Naval Service fleet. Unlike the equally-modern and well-armed *Peacock* class patrol vessels, *Eithne* is not a second-hand warship; she is Irish designed and built and the Naval Service is justifiably proud of her. One of the first high-profile visits performed by LE *Eithne* was to Boston in 1986, the first by an Irish warship to North America. In 1991 *Eithne* paid an official visit to London, with the then FOCNS Cmdr. J. Deasy aboard. During the course of the *Eithne*'s three-day visit, the then First Sea Lord and Chief of Britain's Naval Staff, Admiral Sir Julian Oswald, was warmly welcomed aboard the Naval Service's flagship. Later on Cmdr. Deasy paid courtesy calls on the Admiralty and the Royal Naval College, Greenwich, where he had attended a senior naval officers' staff course in 1978.

Goodwill visits are important for image projection, but also cater for the needs of crew rest and recreation. With the expansion of the fleet in the 1980s, goodwill visits to ports in France, West Germany, the Low Countries, Iceland and Scandinavia became more frequent. The attendance of the INS's first Irish-built OPV, LE *Deirdre*, at Hamburg and Kiel for the annual Kiel Week was an event which was looked upon with great interest by other navies concerned with fishery protection. Foreign visits enhance morale and break the tedium of fishery patrols.

Operational visits meet the needs of the vessel, for example, for bunkering or refuelling. Every six months since 1979, the Naval Service has sent the *Deirdre* or one of P21 class patrol vessels on a re-supply voyage, either to the port of Haifa in northern Israel or the Lebanese capital, Beirut, the objective being to transport dry stores, ammunition and sometimes Panhard AML 90 armoured cars to the 800 Irish UN troops in south Lebanon. On the outward and return journeys, the patrol vessel is normally required to refuel at two ports. In the past this has taken place in Portugal, Spain (including the Balearic Islands), Malta and Italy. Gibraltar is no longer used as a bunkering port. More recently, the Cypriot port of Limassol has been a regular port of call. In addition, in 1991 and 1993 Irish patrol vessels have stopped over in Alexandria, Egypt.

No Irish warship has yet availed of the opportunity presented by such a regular passage to pay an operational/goodwill visit on any of the other coastal states in North Africa or in the eastern Mediterranean. The reasons for this are of course dictated by government policy in Dublin. It would be inconceivable to send an Irish warship on a goodwill visit to Libya, a country which in the past has supplied weapons to the IRA. The ongoing political instability in Algeria would rule out a visit to Algiers or Oran. However, there seems no reason why a Naval Service vessel could not visit Morocco or Tunisia. Throughout most of the 1980s, the Naval Service supplied the Irish battalion attached to UNIFIL, through Haifa in Israel. On these occasions, the port visit was treated purely as an operational affair. Since the end of the Lebanese civil war in 1990, the Naval Service has been able to resume its re-supply voyages to Beirut. However, regardless of the official end to hostilities, the visiting Irish naval crews have to take precautions which were not required in Haifa, for example, wearing steel helmets and flak jackets while in port.

Although the Irish navy has been sailing to the eastern Mediterranean since 1979, not one of their vessels has ever paid a formal goodwill visit to Israel. The reasons for this are political. Although Ireland granted Israel *de jure* recognition in 1964, successive Israeli governments had been refused permission to establish an embassy in Dublin. However, Irish-Israeli relations are improving: in 1991 the President of Israel, Chaim Herzog (who was born in Belfast and educated in Dublin), visited Ireland, and in

30 Musicians from the Naval Pipe Band perform on the heli–deck as LE *Eithne* departs the Port of London.

December 1993 the government agreed to the establishment of a resident embassy in Dublin. The main source of disagreement between the two countries is over the role of the UN forces in southern Lebanon. Since the Israeli invasion of southern Lebanon in 1978, Ireland has contributed a reinforced infantry battalion to the United Nations Interim Force In Lebanon (UNIFIL). In this period, 26 Irish soldiers have been killed while on operational service with UNIFIL.

Another politically-sensitive location for potential port visits is Northern Ireland. In many ways, the Irish Naval Service is faced with the same problems that one would associate with a Royal Naval vessel visiting Dublin or Cork. This was not always the case. During the 1930s, the Irish Free State's fishery protector, *Murichu*, used to patrol the waters off Northern Ireland and frequently anchored in such northern ports as Donaghadee, Ballycastle and Bangor.[10] At no time was the vessel or its crew molested by any irate unionists. In addition, the sea-going lighthouse tenders of the Dublin-based Commissioners of Irish Lights frequently visit ports in Northern Ireland. This all-Ireland body is responsible for the maintenance of lighthouses and navigational buoys around the coasts of both Northern Ireland and the Republic of Ireland. The CIL's two tenders, *Atlanta* and *Granuiale*, fly the Irish tricolour, yet they are never molested while in port. However, according to Dr Garret Fitzgerald, "sending an Irish warship into a northern port would be unduly provocative to the Unionist population of Northern Ireland."[11]

THE RESERVES

The size of Ireland's naval reserve is very modest, especially when one appreciates the length of the country's coastline. The Reserve is comprised of two branches—First Line Reserve and An Slua Muiri (Second Line Reserve).

First Line Reserve

The First Line Reserve is composed of former regular naval personnel. On joining the Naval Service, a recruit signs on for a minimum of five years in the regular navy, with an obligation to stay on the reserve list for an additional seven years. Reservists may be obliged to attend refresher training courses and must be available for call up. As of October 1993 there are 21 officers and 151 men in the First Line Naval Reserve.

An Slua Muiri (Second Line Reserve)

An Slua Muiri is the navy's equivalent of the Army's Second Line reserve, An Forsa Cosanta Aitiúil (FCA). Although there is an equivalence in roles, there is a great disparity in size: in 1993 there were 15,200 men and 636 women in the FCA, yet the number in the country's naval reserve was only 432 officers and men. The latter is a very low figure for an island state with over 1900 miles of coastline. The official establishment of An Slua Muiri is 675, but even this figure is very modest.

The main role of the Second Line Reserve is seaward defence, port control, and harbour defence. At present not one of the Slua Muiri units is equipped to carry out this function. Coastal monitoring is carried out with the aid of lorry-mounted radar modules; unlike the wartime Coastwatching Service, Ireland does not have any system of shore-based coastal surveillance.

Slua Muiri personnel also train in a number of other areas. These include fire-fighting, engineering, first aid, survival at sea, etc. Additionally, they are trained to assist civil defence units in both radiation monitoring and in coastal casualty situations.

At present Slua Muiri covers only a small part of the coastal territory of the Republic of Ireland. There are no Slua Muiri units along the rugged coast of Co. Kerry in the south-west, or along the entire coast of the province of Connaught, that is, from Galway to Sligo. Similarly, Slua Muiri is absent from Ireland's main fishing ports in Co. Donegal and from Co. Louth—the maritime frontier areas of Carlingford and Lough Foyle.

Slua Muiri is composed of five shore companies—two in Dublin and one each in Cork, Waterford and Limerick. The three shore companies in Dublin and Waterford comprise Eastern Group, and the personnel in Cork and Limerick comprise Southern Group. Slua Muiri's two Dublin companies conduct most of their drill and weapons' training in Cathal Brugha barracks, Rathmines. However, seamanship training and weekend camps are held at the old coast guard station in Dun Laoghaire. The latter is a permanent Slua Muiri training facility. A similar situation applies in the other three port cities. In Limerick, drill and weapons' training is conducted in Sarsfield barracks, while seamanship training is conducted at Kilrush Marina. In Waterford, the city's military barracks is used for weapons' training, while seamanship skills are acquired at Dunmore East. In Cork, in addition to the naval base, the former coast defence installation at Fort Templebreedy is regularly used as a training centre.

Each shore company has an establishment of 135 officers and men. A regular Naval Service officer, normally a lieutenant, is attached to each shore company. Training is conducted once a week in a drill hall. All reservists are obilged to attend an annual week-long camp. This involves either attendance at a local army camp, or a week's sea duty aboard a naval patrol vessel. Unlike Britain's Royal Naval Volunteer Reserve, Slua Muiri is not regarded as a conventional naval reserve; this decision was taken in

1958, when it was realised that it would not be feasible to integrate Slua Muiri reservists within operational warships. Lt.-Gen. S. MacEoin stated that "An Slua Muiri personnel were untrained for sea duties and cannot be regarded as material for a ship's crew, that is unless they enlist as recruits in the regular Naval Service. To date only two have done so in the past 20 years."[12] Irish Second Line naval reservists are primarily dedicated to port control and harbour defence; they are not seen as a pool of trained personnel able to augment the manpower needs of the regular sea-going navy in time of war. In addition, unlike the RNVR, An Slua Muiri does have access to any sea-going naval craft. As of October 1993, the only boats available to Ireland's naval reserve are four Gemini craft, seven BP 18 dinghys and two elderly sail training yachts (the *Nancy Bet* and *Creidne* are berthed at Dun Laoghaire and Crosshaven respectively). Slua Muiri's small collection of whaler boats were boarded in 1985 and the training craft *Kathleen Roma* was disposed off in 1989. The need for inshore patrol craft and port control launches has been officially acknowledged, but so far funds have not been made available for this purpose.

THE 1990s AND BEYOND

The new decade which the Naval Service entered was characterised by dramatic and far-reaching international developments which would make an important impact on Ireland. The collapse of the Communist system in Eastern Europe and the former Soviet Union transformed the global, and, in particular, the European military balance. The old scenarios of how Ireland would try to survive an East-West conflict fought out in the North Atlantic are now redundant. The Ireland of 1993 is firmly integrated within a European Community (to be known as the European Union from January 1994) which may move towards eventual political and economic union. In such circumstances, it is difficult to visualise the continuance of Irish military neutrality. Such a policy may become as obsolete as the Berlin Wall. In light of these transformed circumstances, the Irish Naval Service may be required to extend its role beyond fishery protection, SAR and coastal patrol. At present, the coasts of west and south-west Ireland are seen as a window of opportunity for criminal organisations, their intention being to smuggle large quantities of drugs into the European Community via Ireland. In such circumstances, the Naval Service would be Europe's first line of defence against this insidous threat. Eventually, the role of drug interdiction may come to rival that of fishery protection; another service which is partly funded by and carried out on behalf of the European Community.

The Naval Service's immediate targets for the remainder of the 1990s concern the preservation and possible expansion of the fleet; the acquisition of a much needed purpose-built training centre; and the adoption by the European Community of the Irish designed fishery/maritime surveillance system. Most of these are primarily dependent on external funding.

The Fleet

The Naval Service's current sea-going fleet of seven vessels is too small to adequately patrol Ireland's 200-mile EEZ, in addition to performing other necessary tasks. A decision regarding the procurement of another *Eithne*

31 LE *Aisling*

type helicopter carrying patrol vessel (HPV) is still pending. (Officially the prospect of acquiring it is still only regarded "as a possibility"[1]). The latter is of course dependent on the European Community providing at least 50 per cent funding for such an acquisition.

In 1990/91 it was mentioned that there was official interest in acquiring more RN *Peacock* class inshore patrol vessels. However, the remaining three *Peacock* class vessels are still in service with the Royal Navy in Hong Kong and there is little prospect of these vessels being sold prior to British withdrawal from the colony in 1997. (Another possible interested party is Brunei, which showed an interest in buying one of the two *Peacocks* in 1988.) The *Deirdre* and P21 Class OPVs are likely to remain in service well into the first decade of the next century, although they will require necessary refits and upgrading of equipment.

Unlike other small maritime countries, Ireland has not taken advantage of the availability of cheap surplus naval craft in abundance since the end of the Cold War. Indonesia and Algeria acted decisively and bought up an impressive array of minor warships and naval craft which had formally belonged to the East German navy. In these particular cases, the choice was logical as both of these countries have in the past acquired much of their weapons from the former Soviet Bloc. Integrating such naval vessels into their navies would not have posed any serious problems. However, the East German navy also possessed patrol craft and trawler type auxiliaries which might have met some of Ireland's needs. Some of these vessels are still in service with the *Bundesmarine*.

With the exception of possibly acquiring another *Eithne*-type patrol vessel, the Irish department of defence has no immediate plans to purchase or lease any additional ships, inshore craft or harbour launches.

Maritime aviation

Although the Naval Service is unlikely to receive any additional ships or small craft in the near future, the Air Corps' circumstances are much more fortunate. In 1994 the Maritime Squadron will take delivery of two high performance Casa 235 maritime surveillance aircraft. Unlike the sole transport variant which is currently in service, these two aircraft are equipped with sophisticated FLIR (forward looking infra-red) and 360-degree Litton V5 radars.

No definite decisions have been made regarding the possible procurement or lease of long-range SAR helicopters. At present, of the four shore based SA 345F Dauphin 2 helicopters in service, only one is on 24-hour standby for SAR duty. This machine is located at Finner Camp in Co. Donegal. Therefore, SAR coverage for the rest of Ireland's coastal and offshore sea areas is the responsibility of the civilian operator, Irish Helicopters Ltd. The practice of employing civilian operators for SAR

32 Sub-Lt. John Kavanagh (the current FOCNS)

coverage is not unusual. In the United Kingdom, the helicopter operator Bristows provide much of the SAR coverage in the North Sea.

Since the disposal of the Beechcraft Super King Airs in 1991, the Irish Air Corps' maritime surveillance force has consisted of a single Casa 235 tactical transport aircraft. In the words of Capt. John E. Moore (editor of *Jane's Fighting Ships* 1972-87), "the most important criticism I have heard of Ireland's maritime surveillance is that it is a wide mesh colander." Capt. Moore went on to comment that "with the growing lawlessness of the Spanish fishermen, I reckon that they need more and more surveillance aircraft—nothing flashy."[2]

Certainly, if Ireland is to cope with the demands of policing the EEZ, interdicting drugs and terrorist arms, and being able to participate in SAR and pollution control operations, more aircraft will be needed.

Manpower

In 1993 there were 130 officers and 865 men in the regular Naval Service. At present there are no immediate plans to recruit substantial numbers of additional personnel and certainly none to raise the regular Service's establishment above its present level. However, if the INS is to acquire a new *Eithne*-type patrol ship in the mid-1990s, then additional personnel will be required. Should the INS be required to act as the maritime arm of a European-funded drug enforcement agency, then manpower levels will have to be increased. In Ireland, manpower is a very expensive commodity. It is estimated that in order to recruit an additional 100 men, the defence budget must be increased by £1 million annually.

Historically, in Ireland defence has always been regarded as a low priority for government expenditure. Most recently, this has been exasercbated by the urgent need to curtail government spending. An Irish government which has to service a debt of £27 billion, cannot afford to raise defence expenditure above its current level. The net result of such monetary restraint is a high turnover in personnel. "Although their personnel are exceptionally well-trained and motivated, particularly in the context of a consistent policy of official neglect, morale is rapidly being eroded": this observation, made in 1987, is still applicable to conditions in the 1990s. The high turnover of personnel is a problem which is officially acknowledged. Personnel wastage in the Naval Service is twice that experienced by other branches of the defence forces.[3] With restricted finances, promotional opportunities are limited. Junior officers in the INS will stay in their junior rank for three times longer than their counterparts in other Western navies. "The turnover of personnel appears to be a symptom of the failure of the state, so far, to create a Naval Service with the national appeal that it ought to have."[4]

Naval defence in the 1990s

The question of what type of Naval defence Ireland would require to defend itself was addressed both in 1936 by the Irish Army's G2 (Intelligence branch) and Capt. McKenna in 1961. The comments made by the CONS in 1961 are as valid today as they were over 30 years ago. To provide Ireland with an adequate naval defence would require a layered fleet of fast all-weather anti-submarine frigates, minesweepers and seaward defence boats. These vessels would require sophisticated ASW, SAM and SSM systems backed up by modern sonar and early warning radar systems. An elaborate system of fixed coastal surveillance posts, port defence units and maritime aviation aircraft would be required to provide Ireland with defence against seaborne attack. Such a programme would bankrupt the Irish exchequer.

Ireland's circumstances are not unique. Canada too has a small population, a democratic system of government and one of the longest coastlines in the world. The Canadian Armed Forces are simply too small to effectively monitor and secure all the Canadian territories which border the Atlantic, Pacific and Arctic Oceans. In the past, Canada's security against attack from its Arctic neighbour, the former Soviet Union, rested on its geo-strategic value to the USA. An attack on Canada would have been seen as an attack on the security interests of the USA. Australia's predicament is similar to Canada, although it does not enjoy the benefits of sharing a land border with the USA. The 16 million inhabitants of the world's largest island rely on a relatively small all-volunteer navy to defend their coastline. The threat which Australia faces is not from a former superpower but from 165 million Indonesians.

In parliamentary democracies, it is always difficult to persuade the electorate of the need for increases in defence expenditure. In the absence of any perceived external threat, it is virtually impossible to secure electoral backing for such programmes of expenditure. However, some countries with parliamentary systems of government do maintain large military establishments with the consent of the electorate. The most notable examples are Israel and Greece. The latter is of most interest, because since 1945 Greece has not been the victim of external aggression, yet in the wake of Greece's humiliating climbdown over the Turkish invasion of Cyprus in 1974, the Greek electorate have been willing to shoulder the burden of one of the world's highest rates of defence expenditure. Similarly, the rise in Irish defence expenditure in the 1970s was not queried, as all parties in the Irish parliament acknowledged the need to secure the border against a possible overspill of terrorist violence.

A time to redefine the primary and secondary roles of the INS?

In September 1993 the Irish government formally recognised that Ireland's defence forces perform roles which are unlike those carried out by the armed forces of other small European countries. In the statement issued by the minister for defence on 27 September 1993, the newly defined role is:

1. To defend the State against armed aggression; this being a contingency, preparations for its implementation will depend on an ongoing assessment of threats;

2. to aid the Civil Power: meaning in practice to assist, when requested, the Garda Síochána, who have the primary responsibility for law and order including the protection of the internal security of the State;

3. to participate in United Nations missions in the cause of international peace;

4. to provide a fishery protection service in accordance with the State's obligations as a member of the European Community;

5. to carry out such other duties as may be assigned to them from time to time, such as search and rescue; air ambulance service; ministerial air transport service; to assist on occasion of natural or other disasters and to assist in connection with maintenance of essential services; and deal with oil pollution at sea.[5]

The need to deter and resist external attack is recognised. However, in reality it is acknowledged that since the fall of the Berlin Wall and the demise of the Soviet Empire, the security situation in Europe has been transformed. Ireland may no longer face the prospect of being dragged into an East-West war, but this does not diminish previous ongoing threats to Ireland's security, or exclude new ones.

Fishery protection is still the Naval Service's primary peacetime function. It is very unlikely that this situation will be reversed or altered. In protecting Ireland's EEZ, the Naval Service is also protecting these waters on behalf of the European Community.

Interdiction of terrorist arms and drugs

The interdiction of terrorist arms is still a requirement which the Naval Service must be able to undertake. At present, this role is encompassed within the requirement to aid the civil power. Interdicting terrorist arms' ships at sea is primarily a reactive role. The Naval Service act in support of the Garda, who act on intelligence obtained from Irish police sources or from overseas agencies, for example, the American FBI, British police agencies (including the RUC) or Interpol. The Naval Service is therefore not involved in proactive interdiction, periodically searching coastal fishing, commercial and pleasure craft. The interdiction of terrorist arms

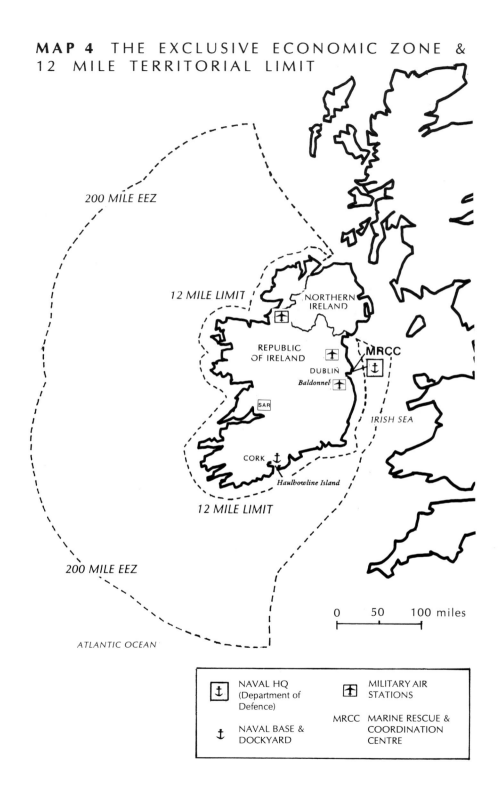

MAP 4 THE EXCLUSIVE ECONOMIC ZONE &
12 MILE TERRITORIAL LIMIT

200 MILE EEZ

12 MILE LIMIT

NORTHERN
IRELAND

REPUBLIC
OF IRELAND

MRCC

DUBLIN

Baldonnel

SAR

IRISH SEA

CORK

Haulbowline Island

12 MILE LIMIT

200 MILE EEZ

ATLANTIC OCEAN

0   50   100 miles

| | NAVAL HQ (Department of Defence) | | MILITARY AIR STATIONS |
| | NAVAL BASE & DOCKYARD | MRCC | MARINE RESCUE & COORDINATION CENTRE |

is dependent on two crucial factors: possessing accurate intelligence, and having the means to intercept, board and secure an arms ship at sea. The Naval Service is certainly in possession of suitable vessels and highly-trained boarding personnel.

Although Libya has stated that it no longer supplies arms and explosives to Irish terrorist groups, this does not mean that these same organisations will not seek to obtain arms from other sources. Since the demise of Soviet bloc, it has become much easier for cash buyers to procure arms from illegal sources in Eastern Europe and the former Soviet Union. In addition, the ongoing civil war and anarchy in parts of former Yugoslavia is an ideal area for unconventional arms buyers. In many ways, Yugoslavia may come to rival that of Lebanon as an area of opportunity for arms and drugs' smugglers. With the countries and territories of the Balkans, Central Europe and the former Soviet Union still in a state of flux, there is ample opportunity for organisations such as the IRA to purchase additional quantities of arms. Should such a scenario take place, then it is very likely that they would choose to transport the weapons by sea to Ireland and smuggle them ashore.

Drugs

The interdiction of drugs at sea is encompassed with the Naval Service's requirement to aid the civil power. At present the interception of drugs at sea is the joint responsibility of the Garda and the Customs Service; Ireland does not have a national drug enforcement agency. In view of the potential threat posed by criminal organisations in Europe, Latin America and the USA, it is widely felt that a properly thought out response is required to safeguard Ireland from an influx of smuggled drugs. Mr Brian Lenihan TD has stated that "the Naval Service is the obvious agency to be chosen to monitor and intercept seaborne drug smugglers". Lenihan went on to say: "Naturally, this would require external funding from Brussels."[6]

According to Capt. John Moore RN, the key to successful drugs interdiction is knowing the point of shipment and reception. The means of transport normally comprise airlines, private aircraft, merchant ships, fishing vessels after transhipment and private vessels or trans-border motor vehicles

Only the last three should concern the Naval Service (with the possible exception of motor vehicles). Merchant ships are the concern of customs once they are alongside in port. The prolonged searches required would be inappropriate at sea. Therefore, this leaves the INS to deal with fishing vessels (which might include coasters) and private vessels. For both of these means of entry, opportunities are present to allow for successful interception. However, they are also inherent difficulties in identifying the vessel's ultimate destination. Targeting the vessel is a product of intelligence obtained from international police cooperation and surveillance forces. The latter may be obtained from subsurface, surface and airborne units.

To deal with such a situation requires the following:

- a total integration of the various Irish forces with the relevant international organisations.

- an ability to conduct aerial surveillance of any likely approach routes.

- a group of effective craft (not necessarily heavily armed) to be available to act on the aircraft sighting reports.

- a local force of incorruptible citizens to keep eyes and ears open for local gossip. With a certain amount of goodwill and explanation, this could be harnessed for the benefit of all.

According to Capt. Moore, what Ireland needs to deal with this problem are more maritime reconnaissance aircraft, good communications between all Irish anti-drugs agencies, and all-weather fast patrol craft.

The essential components of such a system of coastal surveillance are mobility and communications. The coastwatchers of the 1990s would be equipped with cars and mobile phones. With coast roads available round most of Ireland, a single coastwatcher could be responsible for every 25 or even 35 miles of coast. He or she would then be able to react to a report and phone back his/her findings to a central station. Aircraft are the key for long-range sightings.

How such a drug enforcement role should be organised is still uncertain. However, the experience of the United States Coast Guard is an invaluable guide. In 1982 the federal government made the interdiction of drugs a multi-agency effort, with the USCG at the helm in many areas. Every year the USCG averages 200 boat seizures. Possible solutions include the establishment of a Coastwatching Service, along the lines of Ireland's highly-effective wartime service. This could be encompassed within a larger Naval coastguard service. This would require part-time volunteers to man fixed coastal observation posts. These would be equipped with the necessary radio and telephone communications. In view of Ireland not possessing a coastguard, this seems a logical step towards effectively monitoring the country's inshore waters, bays and natural harbours. The obvious candidates to man such a service would be local fishermen and residents in coastal areas who are intimately familiar with their localities. Such a service would have benefical by-products, for example, enhanced SAR coverage, especially for small pleasure craft in remote coastal waters.

Coastal surveillance from fixed posts is a necessary component, but in order to intercept drug smugglers before they can scuttle their vessel and cargo, suitable pursuit craft would be required. In order to operate off Ireland's west and south-west coasts, such patrol craft would have to be fast, robust and capable of operating in all weathers. Their defensive armament could be restricted to 0.50 calibre (12.7mm) heavy machine-guns, which are currently in service aboard the *Peacock* class vessels and LE *Deirdre*. To equip the Naval Service with such craft, as well as recruiting additional regular and part-time personnel would be very expensive. But, as Mr Lenihan has stated, "One must understand that when the Irish Naval Service engages in drug interdiction, it is acting in the interests of the entire European Community. Therefore, in order to perform this role, it is necessary that financial assistance should be provided from the Community's funds. After all, we will be the European Community's first line of defence against this deadly menace."

NEUTRALITY

Prior to the collapse of the Warsaw Pact, one of the main areas of concern for NATO naval planners was the North Atlantic. Ireland's geographic position, lying astride of the Western Approaches, highlighted the country's geo-strategic importance. In the 1950s Ireland's decision to stay outside of NATO and to maintain its wartime policy of military neutrality was not seen as a major obstacle to NATO. The navies of the USA, Canada, France and the UK dominated the North Atlantic, while the Soviet navy was primarily a coast defence force. Furthermore, technological advances since the mid-1940s, for example, very long-range aircraft, had offset the need for Irish air bases. However, in the wake of the Cuban Missile Crisis in 1962, Ireland's geo-strategic value was to come under greater scrutiny. (The Rt. Hon. Enoch Powell, MBE has stated that the Cuban Crisis was a watershed event for Ireland. After this confrontation, various American governmental agencies showed a growing interest in involving Ireland in the maritime defence of the western Atlantic.[7]) In the period 1963-76, the Soviet navy, under its highly regarded commander, Admiral Gorshkov, expanded until it was the world's second largest "blue water" navy. Soviet long-range submarines, operating from their bases in the Soviet Far North, threatened to sever the mercantile lifeline between North America and Europe. Therefore, the naval and maritime value of Ireland was to come under closer focus.

Much of this standard appreciation of Ireland and its position in East-West rivalry has thankfully been made redundant by the events of 1989-91 in Eastern Europe and the former Soviet Union. The Soviet navy no longer exists, and its successor, the much reduced Russian navy, is not viewed as a comparable menace. In such altered circumstances, where does this leave Ireland's traditional policy of neutrality?

Ireland is not a member of NATO, or any other military or political security alliance. There are no foreign troops on the territory of the Irish State; no foreign warships or military aircraft utilise Irish port or airfield facilities; no foreign-owned weapon systems, munitions, warlike stores or nuclear weapons are kept in Ireland. In this sense, Ireland is strictly neutral. However, Ireland's neutrality does differ from that of the traditional European neutrals of Switzerland and Sweden. Both of these countries maintain a policy of "armed neutrality", that is, they can claim with a significant degree of confidence that any potential invader would be obliged to pay a high entry price for infringing their sovereignty. Ireland is certainly not in this category.

Militarily, Ireland's defence forces are not equipped to perform their primary role, which is to deter and resist aggression. The Naval aspect of Irish defence policy was properly appraised in 1961, when Capt. McKenna CONS submitted his famous memorandum. However, 25 years earlier, Irish military intelligence had come to similar conclusions regarding the impossibility of defending Ireland against seaborne invasion. In 1936 the G2 Branch (Intelligence) of the Irish army produced a remarkable paper entitled "Fundamental Factors Affecting Saorstat Defence Problem". The army officers who produced this paper stated that in order to defend Ireland, the country would require a navy comparable in size to that of Sweden or the Netherlands. Such a programme of expenditure would have been untenable in a civilian-run democracy where, according to the authors of the 1936 defence paper, "the Irish were sovereignty but not security conscious". In 1936 the maritime defence of Ireland was both in theory and practice, the responsibility of the Royal Navy. Even after the Irish State took over responsibility for the security of her own ports and coastal waters, in reality it was the Royal Navy that held sway in Ireland's offshore waters. There is no doubt that, but for the Royal Navy, Nazi Germany would have invaded Ireland.

The onset of Northern Ireland's "troubles" may have boosted expenditure on the already under-resourced Irish Defence Forces, but this funding went on internal security related expenditure. Unlike the armies of the traditional neutrals, the Irish army is primarily an infantry and internal security orientated force. The army is presently comprised of eleven 500-man infantry battalions, of which only four have a single APC (Panhard M3) mounted company; the rest of Ireland's regular troops rely exclusively on lorried transport. Armoured support is restricted to 14 Scorpion light tanks and 51 Panhard AML 90/60 light armoured cars. The only modern artillery in service is the excellent British-built 105mm light gun, of which 12 are in service. The remaining regular and FCA field artillery batteries are equipped with World War II vintage 25 pounders and 1950s-era 120mm mortars. The only anti-tank missile system in service is the man portable Milan ATGW, of which there are 24 in service. Air defence is the responsibility of one regular and three reservist AA gun batteries, which are equipped with L60/L70 40mm Bofors guns. The regular AA battery also contains a missile section comprising seven Swedish-made short-range RBS 70 SAM launchers. The latter are linked to a Giraffe radar/air defence system. The Air Corps is not equipped for an air defence role, as its only combat aircraft are subsonic trainers armed with rocket pods and machine-guns.

In essence, the Irish army is not equipped for its primary role which is to deter external aggression. To do so would impose an enormous burden on the Irish exchequer. Therefore, in view of the ever real threat of Republican or Loyalist terrorist violence spilling over the border, scarce resources are concentrated on securing the 200-mile long border with Northern Ireland. In addition, because of the IRA's constant requirement for funds, Irish troops are obliged to escort deliveries of large sums of cash within the Republic. They also escort terrorists to court and guard prisons where terrorists are being held.

To alter this situation would require enormous capital expenditure. The Irish are justifiably proud of their low defence expenditure, preferring to focus scarce resources on the construction of hospitals, roads and educational institutes, rather than on anti–submarine patrol ships. No one questions the reasoning behind such a defence posture, especially in view of the absence of any publicily perceived external threats. Unlike in Sweden, where the traditional enemy Russia dominated the Baltic, many Irish people felt comfortably isolated from the machinations of the Cold War. This partly explains why defence in Ireland is restricted to a small number of regular and reservist personnel who are carefully vetted in order to ensure that "subversives" do not gain access to military training.

Unlike in Sweden and Switzerland, the general populace are not schooled in guerrilla warfare—a factor which has been heavily influenced by an understandable reticence to inadvertently act as tutor to terrorist groups. One other factor which illustrates the difference between Irish and Swiss or Swedish defence policy is an unwillingness to engage in a policy of scorched earth. The Swiss have never concealed their intention of destroying the high alpine tunnels and strategic industrial centres rather than surrender them to an invader. In contrast, Ireland has not adopted such strategies of denial. No one doubts the strategic importance of Shannon airport to a potential invader, yet it appears that the IDF does not possess any runway demolition mines. The IDF may not may be able to deter a major Atlantic power such as the USA from seizing this strategically important airport, but they could destroy its runways and vital facilities before an invader had time to occupy the surrounding area.

The importance of this wideswept airport on the edge of Europe was highlighted during the recent Gulf War in 1991, when the United States Air Force airlifted tens of thousands of troops direct from continental USA to the Arabian Gulf area via Shannon. Ireland granted America access to the airport because Operation Desert Storm had been authorised by the United Nations Security Council.

The collapse of the former Soviet Union and of its security organisation in Europe, the Warsaw Pact, has not significantly altered the geo-strategic importance of Ireland. This is especially true in a era of growing conventional (non-nuclear) conflict in Europe and in the non-First World. In fact the 1990s are proving to be most violent decade in European history since 1945. There is no indication that the ethnic conflicts and territorial disputes which currently disturb parts of Eastern Europe and the former Soviet Union will dissipate. It is unclear what relevance neutrality will have in the coming years, especially as the European Community may evolve into cohesive political union. Indeed, in such circumstances, Irish political and military neutrality may have to be sacrificed in the interests of European solidarity. (The government has given an undertaking that if any question arises, in the context of European Community membership of Ireland joining a military alliance, there would be a referendum, and the people will decide on the matter.)

WOMEN

The involvement of women in Ireland's defence forces is a very recent event. It was only in 1979 that the ban on women entering the Army was rescinded. (On 17 July 1979 legislation was introduced in the Irish parliament which enabled women to enter the IDF. The first four females were sworn in on 10 March 1980.) During the height of the Emergency in 1940, de Valera refused to allow women to enlist in the country's defence forces. The only possible exception to this prohibition on female military volunteers was the Army Nursing Service, which was founded in 1934.

Initially, it was suggested that a separate Women's Army Service Corps should be established along the lines of the Women's Royal Army Corps (WRAC) in the United Kingdom. However, this was discounted on financial and practical grounds. Establishing a separate Corps is very expensive, as it would require its own depot, training school and administrative back-up. In addition, all Corps in the Irish Army are commanded by officers holding the rank of colonel (with the exception of the Air Corps, which is commanded by a brigadier-general). Therefore, a separate Women's Corps would have required the department of defence to allocate funds to cover the cost of recruiting at least one suitably qualified women officer, who would hold the rank of colonel. Possible candidates (of Irish extraction) could have been recruited from Britain's WRAC, in the same way as Capt. Jerome NS was recruited from the Royal Navy in 1946. However, in view of the modest size of Ireland's defence forces, it was decided that a separate Women's Corps was not required. Therefore, women were to be recruited directly into the Army's non-combatant Corps and support arms. In fact the IDF's approach to the recruitment and employment of women was very enlightened. The British Army adopted a similar scheme in the late 1980s and formally disbanded the all-female WRAC in 1991-2.

Two relatively recent developments have occurred since 1980. In 1990 it was decided that women would be accepted for training in the Army and Air Corps Apprentice schools and would be allowed to join the FCA. The first female trainee pilot joined the Air Corps in 1993. These reforms have proved to be very successful, as the Army, the Air Corps and the FCA are now receiving high-calibre female recruits. Unlike their British counterparts, women in the IDF have never been required to leave the service because of pregnancy. Irish female military personnel are eligible for maternity leave on the same basis as other public service employees. Since the early 1980s women have served as dentists, doctors, signals' personnel and adminstrative support staff with the permanent Irish UN contingent in Lebanon.

According to the Defence Forces' press office (January 1993), the status of women in the IDF is as follows: "a recent Chief of Staffs' Board recommended that females be fully integrated into all aspects of Defence Forces' service. This policy has been accepted by the government and is at present being implemented." The statement went on to mention that 'the service of females in the Naval Service is currently under investigation as to how they will be integrated into the organisation'.[8] The investigation into the problems that would be encountered when integrating women into the Naval Service has now been completed. One of its authors was a female army officer, who was temporarily attached to the Naval Board set up to investigate this matter. Their report has since been submitted to the IDF's chief of staff. The findings of the report have yet to be made public.

In Ireland, attitudes to the role of women in business, public life and government service have changed significantly in recent years. Ireland's head of state is a woman, as is the the country's minister for justice. With regard to the employment of women in the INS, Brian Lenihan has stated that: "I am all in favour of women being firmly integrated within the Naval Service, and that they should be permitted to serve on an equal basis with men, that is, at sea and ashore." Furthermore, Lenihan went on to state that the argument of having women aboard a naval vessel would somehow undermine the vessel's efficiency was "pure nonsense".[9]

The most commonly voiced arguments against women recruits have been that it would require an expensive programme of modification to shipborne and shoreside accommodation. In addition, some officers and NCOs believe that it is not practical to have women sailors aboard a small patrol vessel for up three weeks. They maintain that discipline and the ship's operational efficiency would suffer. Some privately express the view that these decisions are made by politicians, yet it is the INS that will have to live with their repercussions. However, the argument that the INS is too small to absorb women volunteers is not valid. This has been accepted by the government, which decided in 1993 to open service in the INS to women. The first female entrants will be appointed in 1994. The Icelandic Coast Guard, with which the INS has much in common, is less than one-fifth the size of Ireland's navy, yet it has female personnel serving ashore and at sea. Similarly, the Scottish Fishery Protection Agency which operates a fleet of eight patrol ships and inshore craft employs female shoreside and sea-going personnel. Ironically, one of their sea fisheries officers is a female university graduate from Ireland.

THE EXPERIENCE OF OTHER NAVIES

Europe

Britain has had a Women's Royal Naval Service since 1917. Although this organisation was disbanded in 1919, it was quickly reformed at the outbreak of war in 1939. Since then the WRNS have been a permanent feature of the Royal Navy. However, in 1993 it was decided to disband the WRNS and intergrate women completely into the Royal Navy. Prior to the mid-1980s, women were barred from service aboard naval warships and auxiliaries. This ban was eventually rescinded in 1990, and today women serve on most types of naval aircraft and surface ships, including the smaller offshore patrol vessels of the Royal Navy's Fishery Protection Squadron based at Rosyth in Scotland. However, service on submarines is still restricted to men.

The navies and seaborne coast guard services of Belgium, Norway, Sweden, Denmark, and Holland all permit women to serve at sea. In the Spanish navy, women enjoy the same privileges and duties as men, both at sea and ashore. The French navy took women aboard warships on an experimental basis in the years 1986-7, and in December 1992 the navy formally adopted the principle of employing female personnel aboard all surface vessels. Since 1992, female officers, petty officers and ratings are allowed to join any of the General Service Branches. However, they cannot be employed as naval aviation pilots, Marines or aboard submarines. In 1993, women serve aboard France's two aircraft carriers and their support ships as administrative and medical staff. Twenty-one women are currently embarked on board the frigates *Montcalm* (in Toulon) and *Latouche Treville* (in Brest). Finally, since June 1993, the tender *Athos* with an exclusive male crew has a female commanding officer. The French navy is committed to allowing more women to serve at sea once the problem of modifying shipboard accommodation has been resolved.

The *Bundesmarine* or German Federal navy does not allow women to serve aboard any of their warships or coastal craft. According to the German naval attache in London, "women are only allowed on board ships of the *Bundesmarine* during their basic training and up to now only from the medical service. There are no female entries to other branches."[10] In the former German Democratic Republic (GDR), women were permitted to volunteer for service in the *Volksmarine* or People's navy.* East German female naval personnel were primarily employed in the following shoreside areas—medical service, communications, administration, military courts, finance, construction, metrology, cartography, printing, storage and care of rations. In the GDR armed forces women could attain officer rank, and many became instructors at naval and military schools and academies. Although no formal restrictions were placed upon women, in reality service on board the GDR's fleet of corvettes, minesweepers, missile boats and patrol craft was confined to men.[11]

North America, Latin America and Asia

Women are now well integrated within the United States Navy and US Coast Guard (USCG). In fact the USCG, with which the Irish Naval Service has much in common, have women officers in command of several cutters (armed patrol ships). Women also serve at sea in the navies of Australia, New Zealand, and Canada (including coast guard and department of fisheries and oceans). However, the Royal Australian navy does restrict service aboard submarines to men. This is a rule which is applied by every navy in the world. In view of the cramped and communual life aboard most submarines, it would be impossible to retain the necessary level of discipline and operational efficiency if women sailors were serving on board.

---

*In the wake of German reunification in October 1990, the GDR's armed forces were disbanded. According to the new All-German Federal government in Bonn, "all women who had served as sailors and officers in the *Nationale Volksmarine* were dismissed. Only a few of them work as civil secretaries in the Bundeswehr (Federal Defence Forces) now".

In Latin America, women are permitted to serve at sea in the navies of Venezuela, Colombia, Ecuador, and Brazil. In Peru women are allowed to join the navy as administrative and medical personnel, but are not permitted to serve at sea. In Chile a similar situation exists. Argentina also allows women to serve in its navy, and at present there are women officers and petty officers in the Argentine navy, but they are not permitted to serve on board warships.

In Asia, Vietnam is one of the very few countries to allow women to serve at sea on board warships. Thailand allows women to enlist, but only as shoreside administrative and medical staff. In Malaysia, women can join the navy; however, they are restricted to shore establishments and may only go to sea aboard sail training vessels. In the Indian navy women are not permitted to serve at sea in any capacity. The Republic of Korea (South) is currently investigating the possibility of integrating women into their navy.

One of the very few countries in the world to apply conscription to its female citizens is Israel. It was the first Middle Eastern country to grant Arab women the vote, and within her formidable armed forces women are active in most branches. Yet in the navy, women are confined to shoreside duties and may only serve on harbour tugs. In the aftermath of the Yom Kippur war of October 1973 the Israeli military had a significant re-think on the utility of female service personnel.

Overseas service in the 1990s

Since the INS's first direct involvement in United Nations operations in 1979, opportunities for overseas service have increased. In the past fifteen years, the INS has mounted over 30 re-supply voyages to the Irish UN battalion in south Lebanon; and Naval Service personnel have served in an administrative capacity with UN formations in Cyprus, Lebanon and Central America. In addition, Ireland's decision to become a participating member of the North Atlantic Fisheries Organisation (NAFO) may result in the *Eithne* being required to patrol off Newfoundland again. With the increasing involvement of the United Nations in many of the world's areas of conflict, it seems likely that more INS personnel will be called upon to serve overseas. However, it is unlikely that in the immediate future, the Naval Service will be able to detach one of its seven patrol vessels for overseas service with the United Nations.

The INS is currently understrength in terms of ships and manpower, and it would be unrealistic to exacerbate this situation by denuding the fleet of a valuable patrol ship. During the 1991 Gulf War, other countries with much larger navies found it difficult to contribute more than a token unit to the UN-endorsed blockade patrols in the Red Sea and Arabian Gulf. Denmark sent a corvette and Poland sent a hospital ship. Even if

Ireland had agreed to send a warship, it is likely that the *Deirdre*/P21 type patrol vessels (PVs) would have been kept far away from the fighting, as they are not suited to employment in a war zone. Should Ireland agree to contribute a naval unit to the current blockade patrols in the Adriatic Sea, it is likely that the most suitable vessel for such operations would be the *Peacock* class PVs. These vessels have true "small warship capability", as they are fast and well armed. However, such prolonged operations are very expensive and require significant logistical back-up.

It seems likely that in the foreseeable future, Irish Naval involvement in United Nations operations will be confined to the provision of personnel. In the words of Brian Lenihan TD, "one of the country's greatest assets are the skills and experience of its Defence Forces' personnel". Irish military experience of United Nations' peacekeeping operations is far in excess of those in the armed forces of the USA, Germany and even the United Kingdom. Similarly, the Naval Service's expertise in marine SAR, coastal patrol, fishery protection, drugs and arms interdiction could be harnessed for the benefit of poorer countries. Such a programme of training would have to part-financed through the European Community or the United Nations.

THE RESERVES IN THE 1990s

In the coming years the roles currently undertaken by Ireland's naval reserves may be redefined, although the role of the First Line Reserve is unlikely to change. They will continue to function as a pool of former regular personnel who are liable to be called up in time of war or crisis. However, the role of An Slua Muiri (Second Line Naval Reserve) is capable of being redefined.

Ever since the foundation of An Slua Muiri in 1947, it has been responsible for the seaward and harbour defence of Ireland's four main ports: Dublin, Cork, Waterford and Limerick. In practice, at no time during the past four and half decades has it been equipped to carry out this role. Indeed it has not been equipped with any sea-going craft, let alone specially designed seaward defence boats, or port control launches. In view of the department of defence's recent decision to review the role of the Irish Defence Forces, it seems only reasonable that An Slua Muiri should be included in this review. This is especially valid when one considers that Ireland is not subject to any external threat, and that the need for seaward defence is rather academic. However, the need for motivated and trained naval reservists is not disputed. The question which must be asked is how should such experienced and motivated individuals be utilised for the country's good?

At present, Ireland's Second Line naval reserve consists of 432 officers and men. Their designated role continues to be seaward defence and port control. However, it would seem more appropriate if this very small organisation could act as a nucleus for a much larger naval coastguard service. If Ireland is to counter the threat of seaborne drug smugglers, the country will require a coastwatching-type service. An Slua Muiri could make an enormous contribution to such a service. This would inevitably result in such a navalised coastguard service gaining access to greater funding and resoures than currently available. At present Ireland's volunteer naval reserve is less than the size of an infantry battalion, yet the FCA can muster over 16,000 personnel. The disparity in size and distribution between the FCA and An Slua Muiri is quite startling. FCA units are located in nearly every county of the state, and be found in some of Ireland's most remote locations, for example, Cardonagh in the far north of Co. Donegal. Yet, there seems to be a palpable aversion to do anything about expanding the country's naval reserve. In addition, it seems odd that a country with such a long coastline should oblige its naval reservists to train for seaward defence without any suitable craft or equipment. At the same time, Ireland does not have a coastguard service or any means of effectively monitoring its coastal waters and shoreline.

If An Slua Muiri was to be transformed into a naval coastguard it would require additional training centres. Regardless of any plans to redefine its role or organisation, Mr Brian Lenihan has stated that "I would be all in favour of expanding the number of An Slua Muiri training centres and increasing the overall size of the naval reserve. The obvious choice for a new training centre is Galway. But other ports are worthy of investigation as well." Galway is certainly an obvious choice; an important port city and regional capital of the west of Ireland, the city has a regular army barracks, where weapons training and drill could be conducted. This permanent military post could be used to house the headquarters and sub-depot for a newly established Western Group of naval reservists. The fact that Naval Service patrol vessels frequently call in on Galway, would no doubt prove to be of great interest to naval reservists in the city. Finally, Galway is also home to one of Ireland's finest universities. The recruitment of students into naval reserve units in other countries such as the United Kingdom has proved particularly beneficial. Not only does it help to enhance the navy's image in the wider community, but it may encourage university graduates to consider the Naval Service as a possible career option.

In order for such a scheme to work in Galway, it seems only logical that the role of such a naval reserve unit should seem relevant and worthwhile. Training for seaward defence without the requisite equipment and a realistic threat perception is not conducive to successful and effective recruitment. Furthermore, a naval reserve unit in Galway would have to be capable of going to sea. Gemini craft are useful for harbour training, but they would not be capable of visiting the Aran Islands. In view of Galway's location, a very strong case could be made for the lease or purchase of a small trawler-type boat. Such a boat could take reservists on training cruises to the Aran Islands and even as far north as Westport or Killybegs in Co. Donegal. Mr Brian Lenihan, a former defence minister, has stated that "An Slua Muiri urgently needs sea-going craft."

If the naval reservists in Galway were trained to act as part of a nationwide coastguard service, then the unit's *raison d'être* would be indisputable. The existence of such a naval coastguard service in the coastal areas of the west of Ireland would make a significant contribution to both local and national life. Other possible centres for an expanded An Slua Muiri or coastguard are Drogheda, Wexford, Bantry and Tralee. Should such a scheme prove successful, a Naval coastguard could be extended west and north of Galway to Westport, Sligo, Killybegs and Lough Swilly.

An expanded naval reserve, either in its present form or as new Naval coastguard service would make a significant contribution to Ireland. Not only would it help to deter criminal gangs from smuggling forbidden substances ashore, but it would act as an eyes and ears of the country's SAR units.

The Naval Service and the IDF

When the Naval Service was founded in 1946, it was established within the army-dominated Permanent Defence Force. Although accorded the status of an independent command area, the new service was still subordinate to a tier of senior officers drawn exclusively from the Army. In the period 1946-76, the relationship between Ireland's navy and army was certainly not one of equals. In terms of manpower, the Irish Naval Service was actually smaller than infantry battalion. The effect of such a system of subordination had its notable side effects, for example, when in 1957 the IDF's chief of staff vetoed an Argentine offer to allow two Irish naval officers to study in Buenos Aires. Ireland's entry into the EEC transformed this situation; the Naval Service was thrust into national and international prominence. From 1977, the INS was responsible for policing over 130,000 square miles of sea. In addition, the threat posed by terrorist gun-runners highlighted the need for a viable sea-going navy.

While the Naval Service acquired modern patrol ships and tripled its manpower size, it was understandable that some discussion might arise over the continuing utility of the integrated structure of the IDF. Unofficially the question was voiced: should the Naval Service become an independent navy? The answer to such speculation is best summed up by

Brian Lenihan: "The present integrated structure of Ireland's defence forces works well. But due recognition should be accorded to the significantly increased importance of the Naval Service. Today the IDF is a partnership."[12] This assessment of the Naval Service's relationship within the IDF structure is valid. Separating the Naval Service from the rest of the IDF would be very expensive. Such a navy would have to establish its own medical, transport, aviation, police and legal services. However, this doesn't mean that the present structure is not in need of reform. As Mr Lenihan has already stated, one way in which the Naval Service's greatly increased importance could be recognised would be to appoint the FOCNS to the Council of Defence. Thereby, officially according due recognition to the importance of the country's maritime defence forces.

The Naval Service and Ireland

The past two and a half decades have witnessed a remarkable change of fortunes for the Irish Naval Service. In 1965 there were less than 285 officers and men in the regular service; the sea-going fleet comprised three obsolete second-hand corvettes, of which only two were in commission; and maritime aviation was non-existent. Today, the Irish Naval Service possesses one of the most modern fleets of patrol ships in Europe. Maritime aviation is now a reality in the form of shipborne Dauphin 2 helicopters and land-based Casa 235 maritime surveillance aircraft. The INS's flagship, LE *Eithne*, is a source of much interest among Far Eastern navies. In terms of sophistication and performance she is equal to any warship in service with the United States Coast Guard or the EEZ patrol services of Denmark, Norway and the United Kingdom. Naval Service officers are among the best educated individuals in the whole of the IDF; all of them are graduates of one of the world's greatest naval academies— the *Britannia* Royal Naval College, Dartmouth. Many go on to attend specialist training courses in Ireland, United Kingdom, Europe and the USA. Yet, it is a regrettable fact of life that most Irish people are quite unaware of the very high calibre of individuals who presently comprise their country's navy and of the tremendous contribution they make to Ireland.

Some have attributed this unfortunate situation to the reputed indifference and even hostility of the Irish people to all things maritime. The absence of a memorial in the form of a plaque or a street named in honour of Commander S. O'Muiris, founder of Ireland's wartime navy, is an indication of this indifference. Sadly, during the course of his research in Ireland, the author can testify to encountering on numerous occasions, a wilful indifference among the general population towards Irish naval and maritime achievements. Many Irish people prefer to content themselves

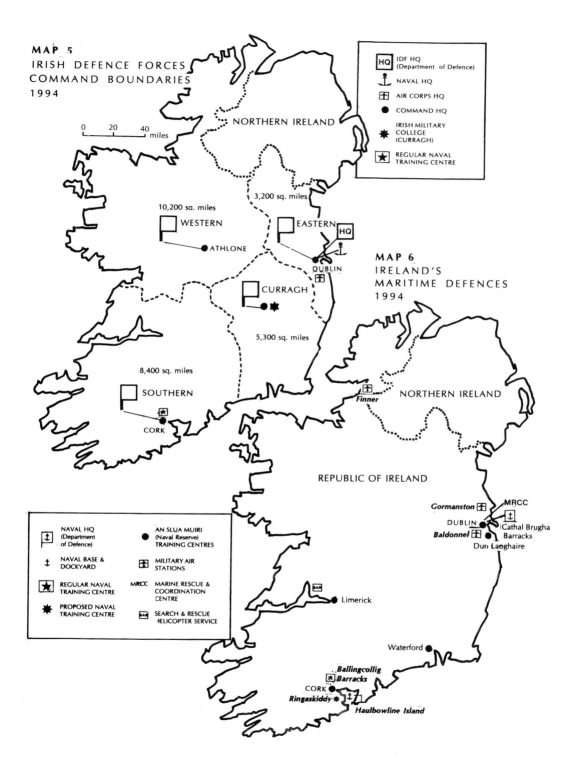

MAP 5
IRISH DEFENCE FORCES
COMMAND BOUNDARIES
1994

HQ	IDF HQ (Department of Defence)
	NAVAL HQ
	AIR CORPS HQ
●	COMMAND HQ
✸	IRISH MILITARY COLLEGE (CURRAGH)
★	REGULAR NAVAL TRAINING CENTRE

0   20   40
miles

NORTHERN IRELAND

3,200 sq. miles

10,200 sq. miles
WESTERN
● ATHLONE

EASTERN
HQ
● DUBLIN

MAP 6
IRELAND'S
MARITIME DEFENCES
1994

CURRAGH
● ✸

5,300 sq. miles

8,400 sq. miles

SOUTHERN
★ CORK

Finner

NORTHERN IRELAND

REPUBLIC OF IRELAND

Gormanston   MRCC
DUBLIN ●   Cathal Brugha
Baldonnel   Barracks
Dun Laoghaire

	NAVAL HQ (Department of Defence)	●	AN SLUA MUIRI (Naval Reserve) TRAINING CENTRES
	NAVAL BASE & DOCKYARD		MILITARY AIR STATIONS
★	REGULAR NAVAL TRAINING CENTRE	MRCC	MARINE RESCUE & COORDINATION CENTRE
✸	PROPOSED NAVAL TRAINING CENTRE		SEARCH & RESCUE HELICOPTER SERVICE

● Limerick

Waterford ●

Ballingcollig
★ *Barracks*
CORK ●
Ringaskiddy ✸
Haulbowline Island

with an image of the Irish Naval Service, as portrayed in the mid-1960s by the renowned folk group, the Dubliners ("When the captain blows his whistle, the ship goes home for tea"). One of the obvious reasons why so few Irish people have an opportunity to update their perception of their country's navy by at least 30 years, is that the INS rarely comes into contact with the wider population. The patrol ships are nearly always "out of sight and out of mind", that is, they are at sea for 180 days a year. When not on patrol, they are normally tied up alongside in the country's only naval base, Haulbowline Island. For those who do not live in any of the country's main ports or near a sheltered deep water natural harbour, it is unlikely that they will come into contact with the Naval Service.

This problem is exacerbated by the draft restrictions imposed by the *Eithne* and *Deirdre*/P21 class patrol vessels. These ships are simply too large to come into many of the country's smaller harbours. This sense of isolation from the wider populace is not helped by an official unwillingness to expand the naval reserve to other ports and towns. In contrast, most Irish people will have an opportunity to come into contact with army units. Nearly every town in Ireland has an FCA training centre, or is close to one. All of Ireland's cities have regular army barracks and the sight of military vehicles and uniformed army personnel is not unusual. The Army's role in support of the civil power at home or overseas with the United Nations, receives regular coverage in national newspapers. Most Irish people are well informed about Ireland's contribution to the United Nations' forces in Lebanon and most recently in Somalia. The Irish army is held in high regard among most Irish people. It is seen as a manifestation of sovereignty, especially as the army claims an unbroken link with the insurrectionists of 1916. Unfortunately, the Naval Service enjoys no such legacy, founded in 1946, its first commanding officer was from the Royal Navy.

The future of the Naval Service

The Irish Naval Service has come a long way since the country's first maritime force, the Coastal Patrol Service, was established in 1923 and disbanded in the following year. Although Ireland's naval significance may not have been noticed by many Irish people, the country's former rulers never underestimated it. Ireland's historical predicament, that is, being subservient to Britain, was rooted in its geography. It was this geographic reality which determined the substance of Ireland's independence. When Ireland achieved freedom in 1921, the naval dimension of this geo-strategic reality obliged the new Irish Free State to allow the Royal Navy to maintain naval bases on its territory. Even after Britain withdrew from the Treaty ports and formally handed over control of Ireland's coastal waters to the Irish State, the dominance of the Royal Navy in the offshore waters mitigated against any serious effort to establish a viable Irish navy. To build up such a navy would have required enormous financial expenditure, something which was felt to be unnecessary in view of the implicit protection provided by the Royal Navy. When in 1946, a regular Irish navy was created out of the wartime Marine Service, its main role was that of fishery protection. All attempts to procure the some of the vessels needed for an adequate naval defence, for example, anti-submarine vessels, minesweepers and seaward defence craft, were directly or indirectly vetoed by the department of finance.

During this period of extreme penury, there were times when the Naval Service only had one ship in commission; foreign training cruises had petered out in the 1950s, and pay and conditions had fallen significantly behind those of other navies. Yet despite the starvation of funds, the Naval Service retained a core of highly trained and dedicated officers and men who kept the navy alive. It was thanks to their loyalty and unstinting efforts that it was possible to embark on a programme of expansion after the introduction of the EEZ in 1977. Sadly most Irish people are unaware that the officers and men who "chase the Spanish trawlers" are regarded in private as the most professional branch of the IDF. While some of the Army's regular units are still equipped with 30-year-old armoured cars and 45-year-old artillery pieces, the weapons and communications' systems on board naval patrol ships are a quantum leap ahead of anything possessed by the land-based IDF units. Today the INS is one of the most sophisticated branches of the IDF.

The future of the Naval Service, like that of Ireland, is linked to the European Community. At present the Naval Service's primary peacetime role is to police over 130,000 square miles of the European Community's EEZ, a herculean task for a navy comprising seven ships. In fact, the Naval Service's ability to keep all of its fleet in commission has been noted with much admiration by overseas navies. Should the European Community decide to establish a pan-European maritime drug enforcement agency, then the Naval Service will be able to make a significant contribution to such a service. The past successes against seaborne gun-runners and drug smugglers have shown that the Irish Naval Service is well qualified to undertake such a role. Should such a policy decision be taken by the European Commission, then additional funding would have to be provided to finance the procurement of suitable inshore craft, the recruitment and training of personnel, and the possible establishment of a Naval Coastguard. The latter could be built on the the structure of the Slua Muiri shore companies. What ever happens in the near future, the Naval Service will continue to render loyal and efficent service to Ireland and the United Nations.

SHIP LIST*

VESSELS AND CRAFT OF THE COASTAL AND MARINE SERVICE 1923-4

Deep sea tug/patrol sloop

Name: DAINTY
Pennant number: -
Dimensions: length 141' 9", beam 30' 3", draft 15'
Displacement: 468 tons
Speed: 11.5 knots
Armament: one 12-pounder gun

Former Admiralty deep sea tug. During her brief service with the CMS, SS *Dainty* was the designated leader of coastal patrol.

Patrol vessel

Name: MURICHU (ex-HMY *Helga*)
Pennant number: -
Built: Dublin Liffey Dockyard, 1908
Dimensions: length 156', beam 13', draft 4' 6"
Displacement: 323 tons gross
Machinery: triple expansion, 1 Scotch boiler 140N4P, 1000 SHP. Twin screw
Speed: 16 knots max. (30 mins), 10 knots cruising
Complement: 23
Armament: one 12-pounder gun

Former fishery protection vessel, pressed into war service as an armed yacht in 1915. Shelled republican positions in central Dublin during the 1916 revolt. In 1918, HMY *Helga* sank a German submarine with gunfire off the Isle of Man. Handed over to Irish Free State authorities on 7 August 1923, and renamed *Murichu* on same date. In 1923-4 employed by the CMS as a patrol vessel; from 1924 to 1939 served as Ireland's only fishery protection vessel.

---

* Sources: *An Cosantóir*, Naval Headquarters, Dublin and *Jane's Fighting Ships*.

Mersey class armed trawlers (steel)

Names: JOHN DUNN, WILLIAM HONNER, CHRISTOPHER DIXON,
ROBERT MURRAY, THOMAS THRESHER
Pennant number: -
Dimensions: length 138' 4", beam 23' 9", draft 14' 6"
Displacement, tons: 250
Speed: 11 knots
Complement: 19
Armament: one 12-pounder gun

Purchased from Admiralty through Ross Street Foundry and Engineering Co.
Ltd, Aberdeen

Canadian Castle class armed trawlers (steel)

Names: TR24, TR25, TR27, TR29, TR30, TR31
Dimensions: length 125', beam 23' 6", draft 13' 6"
Displacement, tons: 200
Speed: 11 knots
Complement: 19
Armament: one 12-pounder gun
Purchased from Admiralty through Ross Street Foundry and Engineering Co.

Drifters (wooden)

Names: INISHERER, JOHN S. SOMERS
Pennant number: -
Dimensions: length 65' 5", beam 17' 7", draft 8'
Displacement, tons: 36
Machinery: 270 HP engines
Speed: 7/8 knots
Armed with light machine-guns

Motor launches (wooden)

Names: ML1, ML2, ML3
Length: length 80', beam 19', draft 5' 6"
Machinery: 2 American standard engines, capable of 440 HP
Speed: 22 knots max

Built in New York. Ex-US Navy sub-chasers. Armed with light machine-guns.

Steam launches (wooden)

Names: "190" – Length 52' 7", beam 12' 4", draft 5' 1"
"199" – Length 69' 2", beam 14', draft 4' 10"
Speed: 9 knots ("190"), 10.3 knots ("199")
Ex-Naval pinnaces. Reportedly armed with light machine-guns.

River patrol boats (chartered)

Five river patrol boats. Two were stationed on the Shannon, one in Waterford, one on the River Lee and one was held in reserve.

VESSELS AND CRAFT OF THE MARINE SERVICE 1939-46

Fishery protection/patrol vessels

Name: MURICHU (ex HMY *Helga*)
Pennant number: -
Armament: one 3-pounder (solid shot), later replaced by one 12-pdr.
For additional details see vessels and craft of the coastal and marine service.

On 19 December 1939 *Murichu* was handed over by department of fisheries to department of defence. Commissioned by Lt. F.A. White on 15 January 1940. Sold to Hammond Lane in January 1947. Sank off Saltees on 8 May 1947, on passage to breakers.

Name: FORT RANNOCK
Pennant Number: -
Built: John Lewis & Son Ltd, Aberdeen, in 1936
Dimensions: 135 x 23.2 x 12.6 feet
Displacement, tons: 258 gross, 113 net
Machinery: single 3-cyl triple expansion
Fuel: coal
Speed: 11 knots
Complement: 23
Armament: one 12-pounder gun

Chartered by department of agriculture and fisheries from John Lewis Ltd in 1938. Handed over to department of defence on 10 November 1939, and purchased outright. Commissioned on 15 January 1940 by Lt. A. Thompson. Sold to Dublin Steam Trawling Co. on 8 July 1947.

Motor torpedo boats

6 Thornycroft type: M1, M2, M3, M4, M5, M6 (Pennant numbers)
Length: 72' (M1, M2, M3); 73' 9" (M4, M5, M6)
Beam: 16' 7" (M1, M2, M3); 16' (M4, M5, M6)
Draft: 5' 3" (M1, M2, M3,); 5' 6" (M4, M5, M6)
Displacement, tons: 40 (M1, M2, M3,) 74 (M4, M5, M6)
Machinery: 4 Thornycroft Rolls Royce 12 Cylinders in tandem of 650 HP each.
   2 propellors, 2 rudders each (M1, M2, M3). 4 Thornycroft RY/12 coupled in tandem to 2 SLM reduction gear boxes with 2 Thornycroft Ford V8's as auxiliaries. Coupled to main shafts by chain drives with disconnecting clutches. Twin screw, twin rudder 2400 HP.
Fuel: Petrol (1500-2000 gallons)
Speed: 35 knots (max) (M1, M2, M3,); 27 knots (M4, M5, M6)

Complement: 2 officers, 9 ratings

Armament: 2 x 18-inch (476mm) torpedoes; 1 x 20mm Madsen AA gun (on M4, M5, M6); 1 x .303-inch (7.62mm) Hotchiss machine-gun on M1, M2, M3; 4 depth-charges on M1, M4, M5, M6; 2 depth-charges on M2, M3.

MTB M1 Originally built for Estonia, was handed over to Marine Service at Hampton, 18 January 1940. Icebound till 30 January. Commissioned by Lt. Carey on 29 January; sailed 31 January 1940. Sold on 15 September 1948, to Col. Fitzmaurice.

MTB M2 Originally built for Latvia, was handed over at Hampton on 5 July 1940. Commissioned by Lt. A. Thompson, 6 July 1940. Sold to Col. Fitzmaurice, 15 September 1948.

MTB M3 Handed over on 25 July 1940 at Hampton. Commissioned on 26 July 1940 by Lt. J. Flynn. Arrived at Haulbowline on 1 August 1940. *En route* bombed by German aircraft off Isle of Wight. Assisted by RN MTBs. Fired on by Irish coastal batteries when the MTB's flag was mistaken. Sold to Col. Fitzmaurice, 15 September 1948.

MTB M4 Built 1940 Thornycroft at Hampton. Completed, December 1942. Handed over at Hampton, 2 December 1942 and commissioned by Lt. H. Austin, 3 December 1942. Sold to Col. Fitzmaurice, 3 July 1950.

MTB M5 (sister ship to MTB M4) Handed over to Sub-Lt. McKenna, 23 December 1942, and commissioned by him on same date at Tilbury. Sailed for Cobh on 26 December 1942. Arrived Cobh, 4 January 1943. Sold to Col. Fitzmaurice, 3 July 1950.

MTB M6 (sister ship to MTB M4 and M5) Handed over, 24 January 1943. Commissioned by Lt. T.A. Hamilton on same date. Sold to Col. Fitzmaurice, 15 September 1948.

Minelayer/stores ship

Name: SHARK
Pennant number: -
Built: 1891, by Grimsby Trawling Company (of iron construction)
Dimensions: 110' x 20' 7" x 10' 8"
Displacement, tons: 163 gross, 62 net
Machinery: Single. Triple expansion. 45 HP
Speed: 8-9 knots
Armament: unarmed
Other equipment: 5-ton derrick

Registered in Cork in 1926. Owned by Palmer Bros., Ringaskiddy. Used extensively in the salvage of material from the *Celtic*, which was wrecked off Roche's Point on 9 December 1928. Purchased by the Marine Service on 8 October 1940. Commissioned by Lt. D. Carroll on the same date. Sold to Haulbowline Industries on 9 September 1952 and scrapped.

Training schooner

Name: ISAALT
Pennant number: -
Built: Portmadoc, 1909. Wooden hull.
Dimensions: 94 x 23 x 10 feet
Displacement, tons: 134 gross, 84 net
Auxiliary engine: 2 Skandia Hot Bulb 55 BHP
Speed: 6 knots

This fore and aft 3-masted schooner was bought by the Marine Service from Mr Cadogan, Skibbereen, in December 1940. Sold to Messrs Kaar & O'Reilly, in May 1945. Foundered off Wicklow Head on the night of 4/5 December 1947.

Miscellaneous craft, 1939-50

GEATA BAWN
Half-deck fishing boat. Purchased from D. Fitzpatrick, Cobh, 1940. Used as liberty boat for the naval base. Sold to D. Fitzpatrick, Cobh, 18 December 1946.

"190"
Ex-Naval pinnace (52' in length). Served as a patrol craft in the former Coastal and Marine Service. Purchased from D. Fitzpatrick in 1940. Used as liberty boat. Resold to D. Fitzpatrick in 1946.

FAITH
Passenger launch (30' in length). Bought from D. Fitzpatrick, Cobh, in 1940. Used as a liberty boat. Sold to Mr Jeffries, Cork, on 9 July 1947.

COLLEEN
Originally *Noreen* (31' in length). Purchased from P. Devitt, Bray, in 1940. Served as examination launch in Waterford. Transferred to Garda Siochana on 16 December 1946 for use on salmon fisheries patrol.

SHEILA
Examination launch used by Cork Competent Port Authority (40' in length). Based at Haulbowline. Sold to B. Murphy, Berehaven, on 18 December 1947.

NORAY
Diesel tug. Built in Germany. Purchased from Dublin Port and Docks Board, 15 April 1941. Resold to them, 19 February 1946.

TONY
Purchased from Mr Gaynor, Dun Laoghaire on 3 July 1940. Used by Dublin Port Control for ferrying. Transferred to Haulbowline in 1945. Converted to dockyard workboat. Transferred to Office of Public Works in 1958.

EILEEN
Formerly *Lupin* (40' in length). Built 1932. 16.3-ton examination launch used by the Port Control Service on Lough Swilly. Sold to Mr Farren, 1945.

SYLVIA
Yacht (45' in length). Bought from Dr Roberts of Limerick, 1940. Used as an examination launch in Limerick. Sold to M. Whyte of Monkstown, 9 July 1947.

INISHOWEN
Examination launch used in Waterford. Burnt out in Waterford in 1943.

EXAMINATION BOAT No. 1
Converted RNLI Lifeboat. Used by the Port Control Service based at Fort Camden in Cork Harbour. Wrecked on Camden Point when engine broke down in heavy seas in 1942. No casualties.

EXAMINATION BOAT No. 3
Motor cruiser twin screw, built in 1927. Used as an examination launch in Cork Harbour. Replaced Examination Boat No. 1. Sank in Cork Harbour on 12 December 1942 with the loss of 4 lives.

LANDING CRAFT
Allied landing craft (49 feet in length). Salvaged off Aran Islands in 1941. Transferred from Receiver of Wrecks. Used for stores and transportation of cattle to Spike Island. Sold to Hammond Lane on 27 March 1947.

18 SHIPS' LIFEBOATS
Purchased from Receiver of Wrecks for use by Maritime Inscription. Sold in 1947.

CARGO BARGE
Converted water barge (55' in length). Purchased from Office of Public Works, Haulbowline, 1940. Sold to B. Rogers, Cobh, 13 April 1948.

SEAPLANE TENDER
High speed tender, equipped with 2 Power Meadoms 100 HP each. Transferred from Air Corps in 1940. Used as port control craft in Dublin 1939/40. Used as seaplane direction launch in Cork Harbour. Transferred to department of industry and commerce at Foynes in the same year.

POWER DINGHY
High speed skimmer (13' in length). Transferred from Air Corps in 1940. Sold to D.J. Purcell, Dublin on 7 March 1947.

REFUELLING DINGHY
2 Power Meadoms 100 HP each. Transferred from Air Corps, 1940. Returned to Air Corps, 1942.

TARGET BOAT
Armour plated launch (40' in length). 3 Power Meadoms 100 HP each. Transferred from Air Corps in 1940. Used practically continuously from then until 1945 as patrol launch on Lough Derg. Returned to Cobh in 1945, but en route was badly damaged by a fire. Sold on 16 January 1950 to Hammond Lane.

Chartered Vessels

SS OWENACURRA
Steam bucket dredger in service with Cork Harbour Commissioners. From 1940 to 1944 chartered as a blockship and held at Passage West ready for sinking.

MFV PRIDE OF GLANDORE
Chartered from J. Higgins, Cobh, from 1940 to 1941. Used as an examination vessel in Cork Harbour.

MV GULBAR
Bucket dredger. Chartered from Wexford Harbour Board from 1944 to 1945, to dredge the entrance to Haulbowline Basin.

VESSELS AND CRAFT OF THE NAVAL SERVICE, 1946-94

Corvettes

Name: MACHA (ex-HMS *Borage* K120)
Pennant number: 01
Built: By George Brown of Greenock. Laid down, 21 November 1940; launched, 6 November 1941; completed, 29 April 1942.
Dimensions: 205 x 33 x 14 feet
Displacement, tons: 1020 standard (1280 full load)
Machinery: Single reciprocating vertical 4-cylinder triple expansion by John Kincaid, Greenock. 2759 IHP. 2 cylindrical Scotch single-ended boilers. Single shaft.
Oil fuel, tons: 230
Speed: Max. 16 knots, 12 knots cruising
Complement: 5 officers, 74 ratings
Armament - Guns: one 4-inch (102mm) BL gun, one 2-pdr., two (single) 20mm mm A.A. guns
ASW Weapons: 1 x Hedgehog mortar, four depth-charge throwers, 2 depth-charge racks

Handed over to the Naval Service at Devonport on 15 November 1946 and commissioned by Lt. W. Reidy on the same date. Sold to Haulbowline Industries on 2 November 1970 and scrapped at Passage West.

Name: LE MAEV (ex-HMS *Oxlip* K123)
Pennant number: 02
Built: By H. & J. Inglis Ltd, Glasgow. Laid down, 9 December 1940. Launched, 28 August 1941. Completed, 28 December 1941. Engined by Kincaids as for *Macha*.

Handed over to the Naval Service on 20 December 1946 at Devonport and commissioned by Lt. W. Reidy on the same date. Sold to Haulbowline Industries on 23 March 1972 and removed on the same date to Passage West and scrapped.

Name: LE CLIONA (ex-HMS *Bellwort* K114) Sister ship to LE *Macha* and LE *Maev*

Pennant number: 03

Built: By George Brown & Co., Greenock. Laid down, 17 September 1940. Launched, 11 August 1941. Completed, 26 November 1941. Engined by Kincaid as for *Macha* and *Maev*.

Handed over to the Naval Service on 3 February 1947 at Devonport and commissioned by Lt. W. Reidy on same date. Sold to Haulbowline Industries on 2 November 1970. Removed to Passage West on 4 November 1970 and scrapped. *Macha* (03) was fitted as Leader and was markedly different from the other two corvettes with a longer upper deck and one of the mess decks converted into a suite of cabins for the senior officer of the flotilla. The lattice mast on all three corvettes was stepped in 1953.

Coastal minesweepers

Names: GRAINNE (ex-HMS *Oulston*, M1129) CM10
   BANBA (ex-HMS *Alverton*, M1104) CM11
   FOLA (ex-HMS *Blaxton*, M1132) CM12

Dimensions: 140 x 28 x 8 feet
Displacement: tons, 360 standard; 425 full load
Machinery: 2 diesels; 2 shafts; 3000 bhp
Oil fuel, tons: 45
Speed: 15 knots max
Range: 2300 miles at 13 knots
Complement: 30
Armament: single 40mm L40/60 Bofors gun on power-operated mounting twin 20mm Oerlikon gun mounting

Former British "Coniston" class minesweepers, purchased in 1970. LE *Grainne* was taken over on 8 December 1970 in Hythe, near Southampton and commissioned on 30 January 1971. *Fola* and *Banba* were taken over in Gibraltar on 22 February 1971 and commissioned on the following day. In 1984 *Banba* was taken out of service and sold to a Spanish company for scrap. Three years later, *Grainne* and *Fola* were also taken out of service and sold to the same Spanish concern for scrap.

Deirdre/P21 Class offshore patrol vessels

Name	Pennant No.	Builders	Launched	Commissioned
DEIRDRE	P20	Verolme, Cork	21-01-72	19-06-72
EMER	P21	Verolme, Cork	12-09-77	16-01-78
AOIFE	P22	Verolme, Cork	25-05-79	29-11-79
AISLING	P23	Verolme, Cork	27-07-79	21-05-80

Dimensions, feet (metres): 184 x 34 x 14 feet (56.2 x 10.4 x 4.4) (*Deirdre*) 213' 7" x 34' 4" x 14' (65.2 x 10.5 x 4.4) (remainder)
Machinery: 2 British Polar SF112 VS-F diesels; 4200 hp (3.13 MW); 1 shaft (*Deirdre*); 2 SEMT-Pielstick 6 PA6L - 280 diesels 4800 hp (3.53 MW);1 shaft (remainder)

Displacements, tons: 972 (*Deirdre*); 1020 (remainder)
Oil fuel, tons: 173.91
Speed: 17 knots
Range, miles: 4000 at 17 knots; 6750 at 12 knots
Complement: 43 all ranks (*Deirdre*); 5 officers, 41 other ranks and 9 trainees
Armament: single 40mm Bofors L40/60 gun on power operated mounting (120
   rounds a minute) and two single 12.7mm heavy machine-guns on LE *Deirdre*;
   single 40mm Bofors L40/70 gun (180 rounds a minutes); two single 20mm
   GAMB-01 A.A. guns 60-degree elevation; 900 rounds/minute to 2km.
Radar: Surface search; Selesmar/Selescan 1024; 1 band
Navigation: Racal Decca RM 1229; 1 band
Sonars: Simrad Marine; hull-mounted; active search; 34 khz

Deirdre was the first vessel ever built for the Naval Service in Ireland. All P20/
P21 Class are of Nevesbu design, stabilisers fitted. *Aoife* and *Aisling* are of similar
construction to *Emer* with the addition of a bow thruster and KaMeWa four
bladed skewed propellor, satellite navigation and communications (Decca MK 53
Navigator and SATNAV).

Training and supply ship

Name: SETANTA
Pennant number: A15
Built: Liffey Dockyard, Dublin in 1953
Dimensions feet (metres): 208 x 38 x 13 (63.5 x 11.6 x 4)
Displacement, tons: 1173
Main engines: Steam reciprocation: 1500 hp; 2 shafts
Oil fuel, tons: 276
Speed: 11.5 knots
Range, miles: 3500 at 10 knots
Complement: 44
Armament: two single 20mm Oerlikon A.A. guns

The *Setanta* was acquired from the Commissioners of Irish Lights in 1976. It
remained in service as a naval auxiliary until 1984, when she was sold for scrap to
Haulbowline Industries Ltd.

Patrol vessel (chartered)

Name: FERDIA (ex-*Helen Basse*)
Pennant number: A16
Built: Denmark (1965)
Dimensions, metres: 64 x 4.3 x 9.6
Displacement, tons: 651 gross, 231 net
Main engines: 1 x Deutz 1500 hp
Oil fuel, tons: 206.8
Speed: Max. 15 knots
Complement: 40
Armament: One single 20mm Oerlikon A.A. gun

The LE *Ferdia* was formerly a Danish stern trawler, *Helen Basse*, which was originally used as seismic survey vessel before being leased for twelve months to the Irish Naval Service in 1977.

Helicopter patrol vessel

Name: EITHNE
Pennant number: P31
Built: Verolme Cork Dockyard
Dimensions, feet (metres): 265 x 39.4 x 14.1 (80.8 x 12 x 4.3)
Displacement, tons: 1760 standard, 1910 full load
Main engines: 2 Ruston Paxman 12 RKC diesels; 6800 hp (5.07 MW) sustained; 2 shafts.
Oil fuel, tons: 308.12
Speed: 20 + ; 19 normal
Range: 7000 miles at 15 knots
Complement: 85 (9 officers)
Armament: 1 single Bofors 57mm/70 Mk 1; 75 degree elevation; 200 rounds/ minute to 17 km (9.3 nautical miles); weight of shell 2.4 kg; 2 (single) x Rheinmettal 20mm/20 A.A. guns; 2 Wallop 57mm launchers for illuminants
Fire Control: Signal LIOD system
Radar: Air/surface search; Signal DA 05 Mk 4; E/F band; range 137km (75 nautical miles) for 2 m2 target.
Navigation: Two Racal Decca; 1 band
Tacan: MEL RPB Transponder
Sonars: Plessey PMS 26; hull-mounted; lightweight; active search and attack; 10 khz
Helicopters: 1 SA 365F Dauphin 2

The *Eithne* was laid down on 15 December 1982; launched on 19 December 1983, and commissioned on 7 December 1984. She was the last vessel to be built at the Verolme shipyard in Cork.

Coastal patrol vessels

Names: ORLA (ex-HMS *Swift*) P41
       CIARA (ex-HMS *Swallow*) P42
Dimensions, feet (metres): 204.1 x 32.8 x 8.9 (62.6 x 10 x 2.7)
Displacement, tons: 712 full load
Main Engines: 2 Crossley SEMT-Pielstick 18 PA6V 280 diesels; 14400 hp (10.58 MW) sustained; 2 shafts; auxiliary drive; Schottel prop; 181 hp (m) (133 kw)
Oil fuel, tons: 54.5
Speed: 25 knots (sprint speed 30 knots)
Range: 2500 miles at 17 knots
Complement: 39 (6 officers) augmented by boarding party personnel
Armament: 1 single 76mm OTO Melara compact; 85-degree evelation; 85 rounds/minute to 16km (8.6 nautical miles); weight of shell 6 kg. 2 (single) x 12.7mm heavy machine-guns and four (single) x 7.62mm machine-guns

Fire Control: BAe Sea Archer (for 76mm gun)
Radar: Surface search: Kelvin Hughes Type 1006; 1 band
Structure: Can carry Sea Rider craft; have loiter drive. Displacement increased
  by the addition of more electronic equipment, including satellite and navigation communications.

Orla and *Ciara* were launched on 11 September 1984 and 31 March 1984
respectively. Both were commissioned into service with the Royal Navy (on 3
May and 17 October 1984), and served in Hong Kong from mid-1985 until early
1988. They were towed backed to the United Kingdom and sold to Ireland on 21
November 1988.

Miscellaneous craft

Harbour Launch

Name: COLLEEN II
The *Colleen II* was built in Arklow in 1972. She was acquired in 1974 and re-
engined in 1989 with a Perkins engine from the old ML *Raven*. *Colleen II* is the
only Naval Service-manned auxiliary.

Training craft

Name: KATHLEEN ROMA
The *Kathleen Roma* was operated by An Slua Muiri on the River Shannon during
the 1980s. She was taken on charter in 1981 and in purchased by the department
of defence in 1985. Sold in 1989.

Sail training yachts

Name: TAILTE
Dimensions, metres: 11.4 x 3.48 x 3.38
Displacement: 6.1 GRT
Complement: 8

The *Tailte* is a French-built Dufour yacht which was bought in 1979 for use by
the regular Naval Service.

Name: NANCY BET
Dimensions, feet: 44 x 13 x 7
Displacement: 21.5 GRT
Complement: 10

Handed over to An Slua Muiri in June 1979 for use as a sail training vessel. She
is held on a nominal long lease (£1.00 per annum). Berthed at Crosshaven, Co. Cork.

Name: CREIDNE
Dimensions, feet: 52 x 13 x 7.5
Displacement: -
Complement: 10

Handed over to An Slua Muiri in 1981 for use as a sail training vessel. Moored at
Dun Laoghaire.

33 LE *Ciara*

DEPARTMENT OF DEFENCE FLEET

Tenders

Name: JOHN ADAMS
Dimensions, feet (metres): 85 x 18 x 7 (25.9 x 5.6 x 2.1)
Displacement, tons: 94 gross, 34 net
Machinery: Diesel 216 bhp
Speed: 10 knots
Passenger certificate: 70 fine, 40 moderate weather

Built by Richard Dunston, Thorne, Yorks in 1934. Handed over by the British on 11 July 1938 in Cobh, the *John Adams* was used primarily as a cargo transport. The *John Adams* supplied Haulbowline and Spike Islands with everything from laundry to telegraph poles. A new engine was fitted in 1976. De-commissioned in 1981 and sold in 1986.

Name: GENERAL McHARDY
Dimensions, feet: 76 x 18 x 9
Displacement, tons: 100 tons gross
Machinery: Compound reciprocating
Speed: 9 knots
Passenger certificate: 200 fine, 100 moderate weather

Built by Philip & Son Ltd, Dartmouth in 1928. Handed over by the British in Berehaven on 11 July 1938. Employed as a harbour and coastal auxiliary. Also used for target towing for coast defence batteries. This involved coastal voyages from Haulbowline Island to Fort Dunree in north Donegal. Sold to Haulbowline Industries on 22 January 1971 for scrap.

Name: SIR JOHN WYNDHAM
Dimensions, feet: 84 x 19 x 10
Displacement, tons: 93 gross, 31 net
Machinery: compound reciprocating 200 hp
Speed: 9 knots
Passenger certificate: 200 fine, 120 moderate weather

Built in 1903 by Cox & Co., Falmouth. Handed over by the British at Cobh on 11 July 1938. Employed as a harbour and coastal auxiliary. Also used for target towing for CDA batteries. Passenger certificate withdrawn by Surveyor in April 1967. Sold for scrap to Haulbowline Industries on 6 June 1968.

Passenger transport launches

Name: SIR CECIL ROMER
Dimensions, feet: 38' 10" x 10' 5" x 4'
Displacement, tons: 10
Machinery: Single Lister Marine Diesel
Passenger certificate: 35 fine, 20 moderate weather

Built by Yacht Engineering Co., Swansea in 1929. Handed over by the British at Berehaven on 11 July 1938. The *Sir Cecil Romer* was transferred to An Slua Muiri in 1986 and renamed *Deiseach*. In early 1990, the *Deiseach* was employed as a static training boat in Waterford City.

Name: RAVEN
Dimensions, feet: 37' x 10' 2" x 4' 5"
Displacement, tons: 17.5
Machinery: Single Lister Marine Diesel.
Passenger certificate: 32 fine, 20 moderate weather.

Built by Henry B. Hornby, Wallesley, Cheshire in 1931. Handed over by the British at Cobh on 11 July 1938. The *Raven* was scrapped in 1985.

Name: JACKDAW
Dimensions, feet: 37' x 10' 8" x 3' 9"
Displacement, tons: 7.5
Machinery: Single Lister Marine Diesel.
Speed: Between 7 and 9 knots
Passenger certificate: 24 fine, 12 moderate weather

Built in 1935, handed over in Berehaven on 11 July 1938. The *Jackdaw* was scrapped in 1985.

Oil barge

Name: CHOWL (ex-Crampin No.1)
Dimensions, feet: 76 x 18 x 7' 10"
Displacement, tons: 100
Machinery: 50 HP diesel. Replaced in 1981 with 180 BHP Volvo outboard
Cargo capacity: 25,725 gallons of diesel

The name *Chowl* stood for Cork Harbour Oil Wharf Ltd. This company owned and operated the water and oil barge in the period 1923-32. She was taken over by the DoD in 1938. During her service with the DoD, *Chowl* was used for the refuelling of the old corvettes, as well as transferring fuel from vessels in dry dock. She was sold for scrap in 1988.

Harbour launch

Name: COLLEEN (ex-*Wuzzer*)
A 35-ft launch built in Wales in 1930. Single 30 hp diesel. Sold in 1980.

Yacht

Name: ASGARD
Dimensions, feet: 44 x 13
Displacement, tons: 18.33 gross, 16.63 net.
Built in 1905 in Lerwick, by Colin Archer. Registered in Ireland 1961. Two masted ketch with auxiliary motor. Semi-elliptical stern. Carved built wood.

Acquired by minister of finance on 30 May 1961, from Clifford Hughes, Southampton. Handed over to the Naval Service on 19 March 1962. Transferred to Office of Public Works in September 1967.

DoD auxiliaries currently in service

Harbour transport vessel

Name: DAVID F
Dimensions: 75 feet in length
Displacement, tons: 69 GRT
Machinery: 230 BHP Gardner Engine
Freight/passenger capacity: 315 passengers

The *David F* is the largest auxiliary vessel currently in service. She was built in Zwolle in the Netherlands in 1962. Marine Transport Services Ltd employed her in Bantry Bay, where she served the Whiddy Oil Refinery until 1970. The vessel was then leased by the DoD as a garrison launch in Cork Harbour. In January 1989, she was eventually purchased after the expiry of her lease.

Harbour passenger craft

Name: FAINLEOG (ex-*Gretna*)
Dimensions: 46 feet in length
Displacement, tons: 14.8 GRT
Machinery: Saab Scania V8 Turbo 410 BHP
Speed: 14.5 knots
Capacity: 50 passengers

Built in Den Dever in the Netherlands in 1971. *Fainleog* was acquired from Marine Transport Ltd in November 1982.

Name: FIACH DUBH (ex-*White Point*)
Dimensions: 43 feet in length
Displacement: 18.7 GRT
Machinery: 180 BHP Gardner engine
Speed: 8 knots
Capacity: 51 passengers

Built in 1981 by Arklow Engineers Ltd, *Fiach Dubh* was acquired from Marine Tranport Ltd in December 1985.

Harbour Tug

Name: SEABHAC (ex-*Rafeen*)
Dimensions: 35 feet in length
Displacement, tons: 8.65
Machinery: 180 BHP Gardner engine
Speed: 8 knots

Built in Arklow by Arklow Engineering Ltd in 1979. She was purchased from Marine Transport Ltd in 1982. ML *Seabhac* is the Navy's tug and workboat.

APPENDICES

APPENDIX 1: OFFICER LISTS

A. SENIOR OFFICERS IN THE COASTAL AND MARINE SERVICE, 1923-24

Name	Rank	Appointment
Joseph Vize	Major-General	Commanding Officer CMS
Seamus Fullerton	Colonel	Adjutant, CMS
Michael O'leary	Colonel	Quartermaster, CMS
P. Caldwell	Captain	Asst. Adjutant, CMS
T. Kirkpatrick	2nd Lieutenant	Staff
Eamon O'Connor	Superintendent	I/C Coastal Patrol
Liam O'Connor	Shore Captain	I/C Haulbowline Base
Robert Dillón	Shore Captain	I/C Galway Base
James Brown	Shore Captain	I/C Killybegs Base
Robert Jeffers	Shore Captain	Harbourmaster, Dun Laoghaire
Michael Love	Commandant	O/C Coastal troops, Dun Laoghaire
Peter Murtagh	Captain	Adj., Coastal troops, Dun Laoghaire
Thomas Waters	Commandant	O/C Coastal troops, Haulbowline
Neil Duffy	Captain	I/C Training, Haulbowline Base
George O'Reilly	Superintendent	Coastal and Marine Service

B. OFFICERS COMMANDING THE MARINE AND NAVAL SERVICES, 1939-93

Name	Rank	Dates	
J. O'Higgins	Colonel	September	1939
A. Lawlor	Colonel	January	1940
S. Muiris	Commander	May	1941
H.S. Jerome	Captain (NS)	December	1946
T. McKenna	Captain (NS)	December	1956
P. Kavanagh	Captain (NS)	June	1973
P. Kavanagh	Commodore	November	1979
L.S. Moloney*	Commodore	September	1980
W.J. Brett	Commodore	February	1986

| J. Deasy | Commodore | January | 1990 |
| J.J. Kavanagh | Commodore | April | 1993 |

*Between February 1986 and December 1988 Commodore L.S. Moloney served as Assistant Chief of Staff of the Irish Defence Forces. He was the only naval officer to hold such a post.

C. OFFICERS COMMANDING THE NAVAL BASE AND DOCKYARD

Name	*Rank*	*Years*
N.C. Harrington	Commandant	1939-41
G. Grosby	Commander	1941-4
O.J. Murphy	Lieutenant	1944-6
T. McKenna	Commander (NS)	1946-56
W.J. Reidy	Commander (NS)	1956-8
P.O. Kavanagh	Commander (NS)	1963-73
C.J. Bryne	Commander (NS)	1973-80
L.S. Moloney	Captain (NS)	1980-7
W.J. Brett	Captain (NS)	1987-9
M.R. Murphy	Captain (NS)	1989-93
J.J. Kavanagh	Captain (NS)	1993 (3-month period)
P.J. McElhinney	Captain (NS)	1993-to date

APPENDIX 2: DISTINGUISHED SERVICE MEDAL

NAVAL SERVICE RECIPIENTS OF AN BONN SEIRBHISE DEARSCNA (THE DISTINGUISHED SERVICE MEDAL)

Rank	*Name*	*Class*	*Date of Incident*	*Location*
Petty Officer	Michael McIntyre	2nd Class	November 1981	LE *Aisling*
Lt.-Cdr.	James A. Robinson	with distinction	June 1985	Air India disaster
Petty Officer	Muiris S. Mahon	2nd Class	June 1985	Air India disaster
Leading seaman	John M. McGrath	2nd Class	June 1985	Air India disaster
Able seaman	Terence J. Brown	2nd Class	June 1985	Air India disaster
Chief PO	Patrick Tumulty	3rd Class	November 1981	LE *Aisling*
Leading seaman	Michael Quinn	3rd Class	January 1990	Atlantic Ocean
Able seaman	Paul Kellett	3rd Class	January 1990	Atlantic Ocean

Sources: An Cosantóir and Naval Headquarters, Dublin.

APPENDIX 3: DIRECTORY OF NAVAL SERVICE GRADUATES

EXECUTIVE BRANCH

1st Cadet Class (1946)
H.L. Henry, W.A. Murray
2nd Cadet Class (1946)
J.A. Flanagan, C.J. Blundell,
   L.S. Moloney
3rd Cadet Class (1947)
J. Grannell, W.J. Brett, N.C. Murphy,
   K. St. J. O'Brady
4th Cadet Class (1950)
J.A. Deasy, P.A. O'Mahony,
   J.N. Reville
5th Cadet Class (1952)
J.J. Daly, M.R. Murphy, F.B. Cahill,
   M.O. O'Gallagher
6th Cadet Class (1959)
J.J. Kavanagh, P.J. McElhinney,
   E. McNamara, P.C. O'Donnell
7th Cadet Class (1961)
P.A. Kavanagh
8th Cadet Class (1967/8)
K.R. Costello, F. Lynch
9th Cadet Class (no commission)
10th Cadet Class (1971)
B.M. O'Shea
11th Cadet Class (1972)
E.P. Ryan, M.P. Quinlinan
12th Cadet Class (1973)
C. Lawn, A. Mahony
13th Cadet Class (1973)
J. Lynch, T. Meehan, T. Touhy
14th Cadet Class (1974)
S. Anderson, M.G. Gibbons, C. Grant,
   G. O'Donoghue
15th Cadet Class (1975)
D.J. Barry, D. O'Callaghan, H. Tully
16th Cadet Class (1976)
B. O'Halloran, M. Mellett
17th Cadet Class (1977)
T.M. Doyle, A.N. O'Dwyer, B. Hevers,
   E.A. Barrett, B. O'Sullivan,
   G. O'Flynn
18th Cadet Class (1977)
J.T. Buckley, R. Borough-Counihan, G.K.
   Curley, P. Logan, G.P. McLoughlin,
   P. Gallagher, G. O'Riordan

19th Cadet Class (1978)
Engineering Branch
J.V. Dowding, M.L.M. Minehane,
   R.D. Smyth, E.J. Whelehan
20th Cadet Class (1978)
J.M. O'Halloran, M.J. O'Dwyer, S.M.
   Walsh, A.J. Sheedy, M.G. McGrath
21st Cadet Class (1979)
Engineering Branch
M.A. Boyle, B.M. Cassidy, N.G.M.
   Corbett, A.P. Costello, T.A. Gibney
22nd Cadet Class (1979)
P. Allen, M.S. Counihan, J.F. Leech,
   T.P. O'Donnell, S.F. O'Keefe,
   G. Rooney, E.J. Clonan,
   G.E. Delaney, C.P. Nalty,
   T.P. O'Keefe, C. Reynolds
23rd Cadet Class (1980)
Engineering Branch
N.E. Lowe, Ward
24th Cadet Class (1980)
M.D. Boyle, A. Cleary, J. Gallagher,
   D. Keeley, R.J. Long, D.J. McMyler,
   C. Rynne
25th Cadet Class (1981)
Executive Branch
R. McCarthy, C.J. O'Shea, J. Shaloo
Engineering Branch
A.P. Henry, M.J. Malone,
   D. McLoughlin, P.J. Mitchell,
   W.C. Roberts
26th Cadet Class (1982)
B.W. Fitzgerald, D.F. Kavanagh,
   B.C. Nolan, T.W. Roche,
   P.J.N. Twomey
27th Cadet Class (1983)
D. Brady, L. Brennan, P. O'Giollain,
   T. Ward
28th Cadet Class (1986)
Executive Branch
J.P. Burke
Engineering Branch
A.R. O'Leary

29th Cadet Class (1988)
Executive Branch
K.J. Minehane, D.J. Power,
 T.E. Mulligan
Engineering Branch
N.A. Lacey
30th Cadet Class (1989)
M. Brett, A. Geraghty

31st Cadet Class (1991)
O'Mullowney, B. Boylen, C. Manning,
 P. Harkin, B. Dempsey
Engineering Branch
C. O'Sullivan, I. Travers

Source: Naval Headquarters, Dublin.

APPENDIX 4: IRISH MILITARY MEDALS

At present Irish Defence Forces' personnel may, if they meet the particular requirements of the award, qualify for five different military medals. In addition, IDF personnel who serve overseas with the United Nations are entitled to UN Service Medals. The IDF does not have any designated Naval medals e.g. the Navy Cross in the USA, or the Medals of Naval Merit in Germany, Argentina or Italy.

 The medals which are currently available and in order of seniority are:

AN BONN MILEATA CALMACHTA
(The Military Medal for Gallantry)
Classes: (1) With Honour. (2) With distinction. (3) With Merit.
This medal was instituted on 24 July 1948. It may be awarded in recognition of the performance of any act of exceptional bravery or gallantry (other than one performed on war service) arising out of, or associated with, military service and involving risk to life or limb

 No member of the Naval Service, past or present, has ever been awarded this medal.

AN BONN SEIRBHISE DEARSCNA
(The Distinguished Service Medal)
Classes: (1) With Honour. (2) With distinction. (3) With Merit.
This medal was instituted on 18 February 1964. It may be awarded in recognition of individual or associated acts of bravery, courage, leadership, resource or devotion to duty (other than any such acts or duty performed on war service) arising out of, or associated with service in the Defence Forces and not meriting the award of An Bonn Mileata Calmachta.

 Eight members of the Naval Service have been awarded this medal.

AN BONN DEA IOMPAIR
(The Good Conduct Medal)
This medal was instituted on 16 September 1987. It is confined to non-commissioned officers and privates/ratings, and may only be awarded once to an individual. The minimum qualifying service for the award of the medal is 3650 days continuous service in the Permanent Defence Force. The required conduct rating shall be "exemplary" with a period of ten years free of any convictions or awards of punishment.

The medal is designed to recognise meritorious service characterised by exemplary conduct of an individual non-commissioned officer or private/rating. A maximum of sixty medals may be awarded in any one year.

AN BONN SEIRBHISE
(The Service Medal)

This medal was instituted on 13 June 1961. It is awarded to members of the Defence Forces who possess the qualifying service set down hereunder:
1. Officers, chaplains, and nurses - 5475 days satisfactory and continuous service
2. Other ranks - 3650 days satisfactory and continuous service.
This service can be made up of aggregate service with the Permanent Defence Force and the Reserve Defence Force (First Line). One class only.

Bar

A bar is awarded after a further 5 years' qualifying service.

AN BONN SEIRBHISE (FCA AND SLUA MUIRI)
(The Service Medal - Second Line Reserve)

This medal was instituted on 13 June 1961. It is awarded to members of the Second Line Reserve who have seven years satisfactory service. There is no distinction between officers and other ranks. One class only.

Bar

This may be awarded to members who have 12 years satisfactory service. A second bar may be awarded to members who have completed 21 years' satisfactory service. This Bar will bear the inscription "21".

THE PEACEKEEPER'S MEDAL

This medal was instituted in 1988 in recognition of Irish Defence Forces' personnel who have served overseas with the United Nations. It is awarded to members of the Permanent Defence Force (all ranks) who have served overseas with the United Nations.

Naval Service personnel who have served with the United Nations qualify for this medal.

UNITED NATIONS' SERVICE MEDALS

Irish Defence Forces' personnel who serve overseas with the United Nations are entitled to service medals which are issued by the United Nations Organisation. Naval Service participation in these operations is very limited. To date Irish naval personnel have served in the Congo (Zaire), Cyprus, Lebanon and Central America. All of these individuals have been issued with the appropriate United Nations' Service Medal.

APPENDIX 5: UNIFORM AND INSIGNIA

The uniform of the Irish Naval Service stems from the wartime Marine Service. The uniform is distinctive in its detail, but in the main it conforms to the general pattern which is universal to all navies. The current rank insignia came into effect on 1 February 1973.

Officers and petty officers wear the "fore-and-aft rig" with collar, tie and peaked cap.

Ratings wear the the 'square rig' with the jean collar. The Irish collar has a border of two white tapes—the outer being thicker and with an anchor embroidered in each corner. The seaman's cap is of the universal shape and style—the black tally-band bearing the EIRE in gold and with the band falling down the back to form two tails. On top is a light blue wool bobbin. A brass Irish Defence Forces badge is worn above the tally-band. Up until the late 1970s it was customary to wear a dark blue cap from 1 October to 30 April and a white cap during the summer period, i.e. 1 May to 30 September. The use of blue caps was discontinued and today white caps are worn all year round.

An Slua Muiri

From 1959 Slua Muiri personnel have worn the same uniform as regulars but with black shoulder flashes with the lettering AN SLUA MUIRI

QUALIFICATION BADGES

Parachutist Wings

Although the IDF does not possess any airborne units, suitably qualified candidates may merit Parachutist Wings. In order to qualify, one must complete the prescribed number of parachute jumps. These are conducted by the Air Corps at Gormanston Air Station. Cessna 172 and Casa 235 aircraft are employed for parachute training. Several Naval Service candidates have successfully completed this course and these individuals now proudly wear the metallic parachutist wings.

Diver's Badge

In 1987 recognition was finally given to the INS's trained divers, when a silver Diving Qualification Badge was introduced. In order to qualify, the Naval diver must have either successfully completed the Royal Navy's arduous Long Diving Course at Portsmouth, or the Naval Service's own diving courses. A gold badge is awarded to Naval officers with underwater explosives qualifications.

S.B.A. Badge

Naval Service personnel who have qualified as para-medics, are entitled to wear a distinctive Sick Berth Attendant's cloth badge.

Marksman's Badge

In 1942 recognition was given to the role and importance of marksmen in the IDF, when the Marksman's Badge was introduced. Today this cloth badge is a triangular form; the champion IDF marksman's badge is issued in a circular form and is much more ornate. Naval Service personnel are permitted to compete for these badges.

Commodore

Captain & Commander

Officer, Chaplain & Cadet

Commodore

Captain

Commander

Lieutenant Commander

Lieutenant

Sub Lieutenant

Ensign

Senior Chief Petty Officer
& Chief Petty Officer

Warrant Officer

Senior Petty Officer
& Petty Officer

Chaplain

Officer

Warrant Officer
(With appropriate Branch Insignia)

Non Commissioned
Officer

Cadet

Senior
Chief Petty Officer

Chief Petty Officer

Senior Petty Officer

Petty Officer

Leading Seaman

An Slua Muirí
(Naval Reserve)

Seaman

Working Dress Beret (All Ranks)
With appropriate Badge for Officers
or other ranks

Able Seaman

Blue Jean Collar

Ordinary Seaman

Engineer Branch

Executive Branch

Diver's Specialist
Badge

Communications
Branch

Administrative
Branch

APPENDIX 6: FLAGS OF THE IRISH NAVAL SERVICE

Ensign

Green-white-orange tricolour. It is the national flag of the Republic of Ireland and is the ensign worn by all Irish ships and by Irish-registered merchant shipping.

Jack

The Naval Jack is flown by all Naval Service vessels while alongside in port or at anchor during the hours from sunrise to sunset. It is also flown from the main mast at the naval base while courts martials are sitting. It is a flag of green wool with the yellow harp centrally embroidered.

Commordore's Burgee

A green wool flag with a yellow 5-pointed star centrally embroidered.

Senior Officer Afloat

A green wool triangular flag.

Commissioning Pennant

A blue and white bunting with a white harp in the blue portion.

JACK   COMMODORE'S   SENIOR NAVAL OFFICER
                   BURGEE   AFLOAT

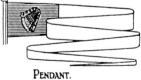

PENDANT.

35 Irish Naval Service flags

NOTES

CHAPTER ONE: IRISH MARITIME TRADITIONS

1. de Courcy Ireland, p. 37.
2. de Courcy Ireland, p. 294. I am indebted to this book for information included in the preceding pages.
3. Cf. *An Cosantóir*, March 1970, p. 98.
4. Quoted in *An Cosantóir*, 1965, p. 263.
5. Ibid.
6. Cf. *An Cosantóir*, April 1947, pp. 289ff for the story of the *Aud*.
7. Cf. Kearsley, "Irish Security and the Sea".
8. Cf. *Jane's Fighting Ships*, 1993-4, p. 474.
9. Ibid., p. 53.
10. Cf. *An Cosantóir*, April 1947, "The Holland Submarine" p. 430.

CHAPTER TWO: EARLY BEGINNINGS, 1921-39

1. Jellicoe, *The Submarine Peril*, p. 79.
2. Jellicoe, *The Crisis of the Naval War*, p. 189.
3. Jellicoe, *The Grand Fleet 1914-16*, p. 172.
4. Fundamental Factors Affecting Saorstát Defence Problem, 1936.
5. Cf. Churchill, volume 1, p. 247.
6. Cf. Harrington, p. 17.
7. Cf. Younger, p. 316.
8. Tormey and Byrne, p. 117
9. Cf. article in *An t-Oglac* on Irish Air Service, 24 February 1923.
10. Younger, p. 232.
11. Cf. Boyce (ed.), p. 287.
12. Younger is a source for this section.
13. Harrington, p. 71
14. *Irish Times*, 10 August 1922.
15. Younger is a source for this section.
16. *Irish Times*, 10 August 1922.
17. Ibid., 11 August 1922.
18. Ibid., 15 August 1922.
19. *An Cosantóir*. April 1973. p. 104.
20. *Irish Times*, 13 June 1923.
21. *An Cosantóir*. April 1973, p. 104.
22. Ibid., p. 104.
23. *An t-Oglac*, 1 September 1923 (Defence Orders no. 27).
24. *An Cosantóir*, April 1973, p. 104.
25. Memorandum by Minister for Defence, undated but received 25 September 1923. Department of the Taoiseach 1980.
26. *An Cosantóir*, April 1973, p. 104.
27. Ibid., p. 105.
28. Ibid.

29. Memorandum on The Naval Problem – Peace, 1964, (Annex A).
30. Cf. *An Cosantóir*, April 1973, p. 107.
31.ʹ *An Cosantóir*, April 1973, p. 107.
32. Cf. *Jane's Fighting Ships*, 1924, pp. 93ff and 142f.
33. *An Cosantóir*. April 1973, p. 107.
34. 'Ireland – Two Treaty ports and the one that never was: Part 1' in *Fortress Journal*, 1993, p. 34.
35. Fundamental Factors Affecting Saorstát Defence Problem, 1936, the source for the following three paragraphs.
36. Cf. Roskill, vol. II, p. 319.
37. Cf. Fisk, p. 36
38. Churchill, vol. I, pp. 215f.
39. Ryle Dwyer, *Eamon de Valera*, p. 107.
40. Quoted in Churchill, vol. I, p. 217.
41. Cf. Fisk, p. 8.
42. Comdt. Dawson, 'Coast Defence Artillery', in *An Cosantóir*, November 1973, p. 393.
43. Cf. Fisk, p. 9.

CHAPTER THREE: THE EMERGENCY, 1939-45

1. Martin Gilbert, *The Second World War*, p. 4.
2. *An Cosantóir*, April 1973, pp. 108ff is the source for this section.
3. Authorised comments made to the author by Capt. John Moore RN dated 11 August 1993.
4. *An Cosantóir*, April 1973, p. 107.
5. World Ship Society Monograph No. 4.
6. *An Cosantóir*, May 1973, p. 162.
7. World Society Monograph No. 4, p. 17.
8. Naval Policy Memorandum, 1961, Part I.
9. *An Cosantóir*, May 1973, p. 166.
10. Naval Policy Memorandum, 1961, Part I.
11. *Sharpe*, p. 97.
12. Naval Policy Memorandum, 1961, Part I.
13. *An Cosantóir*, April 1973, p. 136.
14. Naval Policy Memorandum, 1961, Part I is the main source for these paragraphs.
15. *An Cosantóir*, April 1973, p. 116.
16. Naval Policy Memorandum, 1961, Part I.
17. Tormey and Byrne, p. 120.
18. *Sharpe*, p. 99.
19. Ibid., p. 101.
20. Fisk, p. 252
21. Duggan, *A History*, p. 181.
22. Fisk, pp. 220-6.
23. Foster, p. 516.
24. *The Holocaust – The Jewish Tragedy*, p. 281.
25. Fisk, pp. 263f, 221ff.
26. Monserrat, p. 161.
27. Ibid., p. 160.
28. Fisk, p. 380.
29. D.R. Dwyer, *Eamon de Valera*, p. 114.
30. Fisk, p. 266.
31. Dublin's vulnerability to aerial attack was clearly illustrated in May 1941, when the city was accidentally bombed by German aircraft. Thirty-four people were killed on this occasion. Throughout the war, Irish anti-aircraft gun batteries did fire on foreign intruders, but there is no record of any aircraft being shot down. Similarly, the Irish Air Corps was unable to intercept and force down any intruder aircraft.
32. According to D. Ryle Dwyer (*Eamon de Valera*, p. 112), a possible solution to the Ulster question envisaged by de Valera was an "exchange of populations". This would be along the lines of a provision in the Treaty of Lausanne (1923) between Greece and Turkey. On that occasion the Greek communities which had lived in western Turkey since the days of Alexander the Great were transplanted *en masse* to Greece. Apparently if no other solution could be found, de Valera suggested that the Ulster question could be solved by transferring the Scottish-Irish

Protestants from Northern Ireland to Britain and replacing them with Roman Catholics of Irish extraction from Britain. How this was to be achieved is unclear. However, the objective seems to have been to create a state with a completely homogenous ethno-religious composition. A similar policy of ethnic engineering was pursued with ruthless efficiency by Poland in 1945-6. On that occasion 7 million Germans in western Poland (formerly Silesia and East Prussia) were "relocated" to Germany.

33. According to British military historian Basil Liddell-Hart, "Eire's refusal to allow the Allies use ... of her western and southern coastlines, even though she herself depended largely upon the supplies the convoys brought her, contributed greatly to the Allied losses in the Atlantic" (*History of the Second World War*, London 1970, p. 371).

34. The very negative reaction to de Valera's visit of 2 May 1945 was unfair. De Valera's period as President of the League of Nations and his courageous opposition to Italy's invasion of Abyssinia in 1936 were proof that he was no friend of the Axis Powers. In 1945 Ireland gave £3,000,000 of food aid to the starving of Europe; 500 Jewish children were also given asylum. (See Keesing's *Contemporary Archives*, 1945 p. 722)

CHAPTER FOUR: THE NAVAL SERVICE, 1945-70

1. *An Cosantóir*, April 1973, pp. 111f is the source for the above information.
2. Memorandum on Naval Policy, December 1961, Part 1.
3. Ibid.
4. *Ships Monthly*, June 1993, p. 16.
5. *The Cruel Sea*, p. 13.
6. *The War at Sea*, volume 1, p. 133.
7. *The North Atlantic Run: The RCN and the Battle for the Convoys*, p. 37.
8. *Warship Monthly*, June 1993, pp. 16f is the source for statistics given above.
9. *Business in Great Waters: the U-Boat Wars 1916-45*, p. 620.
10. *Jane's Fighting-Ships* 1970-71, p. 92.
11. Memorandum on Naval Policy, December 1961, Part I.
12. Memorandum on the Defence Forces, July 1949, p. 10.
13. Cf. Memorandum on Naval Policy, December 1961, Part 11.
14. Memorandum on Naval Service, Annex B, 1956.
15. Memorandum on Naval Policy, December 1961, Part 11.
16. Memorandum on Seaward Defence, 26 July 1956, p. 1 and pp. 2-4 is the source.
17. Memorandum on Naval Policy, December 1961, Part 11 is the source above paragraphs.
18. Quoted in Foster, *Modern Ireland 1600-1972*, p. 567.
19. Report on overseas visits by senior IDF personnel, 1 April 1957.
20. Cf. Memorandum to the chief of staff on annual inspection of Naval Base, 1956, pp. 22, 24, 26.
21. Report on overseas visits by Senior IDF personnel (incl. the Admiral Brown centenary ceremony in Argentina, 1 April 1957, p. 2.
22. *An Cosantóir*, April 1973, p. 116.
23. Memorandum on foreign training cruises, 1959.
24. Memorandum on Naval Policy, December 1961.
25. *An Cosantóir*, April 1973, p. 117.
26. Ibid.
27. *An Cosantóir*, May 1963, p. 206f.
28. Cf. Memorandum on the conference held at Haulbowline on 4 October 1962 for above statistics etc.
29. Memorandum on Naval Policy, December 1964, p. 10.
30. Memorandum on Naval Manpower, 28 May 1965.
31. *An Cosantóir*, April 1973, p. 119.
32. Memorandum on Fishery Protection Measures, 9 December 1968.

CHAPTER FIVE: THE NAVAL SERVICE, 1970-90

1. Duggan, *History of the Irish Army*, p. 281 and p. 247.
2. World Ship Society Monograph No. 4, p. 51.
3. Cf. *An Cosantóir* April 1973, pp. 119-22.
4. World Ship Society Monograph No. 4, p. 66.
5. Kearsley, "Irish Security and the Sea", p. 44.

6. *Whitakers Almanack* 1970 & 1978.
7. *Keesings Contemporary Archives*, 1973, p. 25685.
8. *Irish Times*, 2 October 1984 & 30 March 1973.
9. *Keesings Contemporary Archives*, 1973, p. 25685.
10. *Irish Times*, 31 March 1973.
11. World Ship Society Monograph No. 4, p. 56.
12. Interviewed by author on 14 October 1993.
13. Letter from Naval Headquarters, 21 March 1993.
14. *Jane's Fighting Ship* 1979-80, p. 262.
15. *Irish Times*, 13 March 1985, "Catching up with lost centuries", special article on the Naval Service by Colonel E.D. Doyle (Retd.).
16. Letter from Cdr. John Jordan, NS (Retd.), 4 March 1993.
17. Ibid.
18. Barzilay, *The British Army in Ulster*, vol. 1, 1974, p. 45.
19. Morton, *Emergency Tour, 3 Para in South Armagh*, p. 84.
20. Letter from Brigadier Peter Morton (Retd.), 2 September 1993.
21. Letter from Merlyn Rees, September 1993.
22. On the seizure of *Marita Ann*, see *Irish Times*, 1 and 2 October 1984.
23. *Irish Times*, 4 November 1987.
24. Letter from Captain A.E. Slater, RN, Secretary to the First Sea Lord, ministry of defence, London, 9 September 1993.
25. Interviewed on 14 October 1993.
26. Interviewed on 8 October 1993.
27. *Irish Security and the Sea*, p. 44.
28. *Maritime Journal of Ireland*, Winter/Spring 1989, p. 2.
29. *Irish Security and the Sea*, p. 45.

CHAPTER SIX: THE IRISH NAVAL SERVICE TODAY

1. Statistics supplied by department of defence 19 January 1994.
2. Interviewed by author on 15 October 1993.
3. Tormey and Byrne, *A View from the Tower*, 1990, p. 125.
4. Ibid., p. 77.
5. Memorandum on Naval Policy, December 1961.
6. Information provided by Naval Headquarters, 28 October 1993.
7. Information provided by Defence Forces Press Office, 21 January 1993.
8. Interviews with Lt. Cdr. Shane Anderson NS and Lt. P. O'Giollain NS at Naval Headquarters, 6 October 1993.
9. *An Cosantóir* interview with Commodore J. A. Deasy, February 1990, p. 38.
10. *An Cosantóir*, April 1973, p. 110.
11. Interviewed by author, 8 October 1993.
12. Memorandum on the manning of the corvettes, 1967.

CHAPTER SEVEN: THE 1990S AND BEYOND

1. Letter from Capt. Young, Defence Forces press office, 21 January 1993.
2. Letter from Capt. John Moore, RN, 11 August 1993.
3. *An Cosantóir*, February, 1990 (interview with Commodore J. Deasy).
4. "Irish Security and the Sea", pp. 59 and 60.
5. *Irish Times*, 2 October 1993.
6. Interview on 14 October 1993.
7. Interview on 18 August 1993.
8. Letter from Defence Forces press office, 21 January 1993.
9. Interview on 14 October 1993.
10. Letter from Cdr. U. Stickdorn, German naval attache, London, 6 March 1993.
11. DDR Handbook, Ministry of Intra-German Affairs, Bonn, 1985, p. 1466.
12. Taken from my interview with Mr Brian Lenihan TD, 14 October 1993.

BIBLIOGRAPHY

BOOKS

Archibald, E.H.H. *The Fighting Ships in the Royal Navy, 1897-1984*. Blandford Press, Poole, Dorset, 1984.

Barzilay, David. *The British Army in Ulster*. 2 vols. Century Books, Belfast, 1973-81.

Boyce, E.D., ed. *The Revolution in Ireland 1879-1923*. Macmillan Educational, London, New York, 1988.

Carroll, Joseph T. *Ireland in the War Years 1939-45*. David & Charles, Newton Abbot; Crane, Russak & Co., New York, 1975.

Churchill, Winston. *The Second World War*. Cassell, London, 1948.

Collier, Simon, ed. *The Cambridge Encyclopedia of Latin America and the Caribbean*. Cambridge U.P., Cambridge, 1985.

Bird, W.D. *Direction of War: A Study and Illustration of Strategy*. Cambridge U.P., Cambridge, 1925.

de Breffni, Brian, ed. *The Irish World*. Thames & Hudson, London, 1977.

de Courcy Ireland, John, *Ireland and the Irish in Maritime History*. Glendale Press, Dublin, 1986.

Duggan, John. *Neutral Ireland and the Third Reich*. Gill & Macmillan, Dublin, 1985.

Duggan, John. *A History of the Irish Army*. Gill & Macmillan, Dublin, 1987.

Dwyer, T. Ryle. *Strained Relations: Ireland at Peace and the USA at War 1941-45*. Gill & Macmillan, Dublin, 1978.

Dwyer, T. Ryle. *Eamon de Valera*. Gill & Macmillan, Dublin, 1980.

Elley, David, ed. *Variety Movie Guide*. Hamlyn, London 1993.

Fisk, Robert. *In Time of War: Ireland, Ulster and the Price of Neutrality, 1939-45*. Andre Deutsch, London, 1983.

Foster, R.F. *Modern Ireland, 1600-1972*. Allen Lane, London, 1988.

Gilbert, Martin. *The Holocaust: The Jewish Tragedy*. Fontana/Collins, London, 1986.

Gilbert, Martin. *The Second World War*. Fontana/Collins, London, 1989.

Halsey, William, ed. *Collier's Encyclopaedia*. Macmillan Educational, New York, 1985.

Harrington, Niall C. *Kerry Landing, August 1922*. Anvil Book, Dublin, 1992.

Hough, Richard. *The Great War at Sea, 1914-18*. Oxford University Press, London, 1983.

Jellicoe, Earl. *The Submarine Peril – Admiralty Policy in 1917*. Cassell, London, 1934.

Jellicoe, Admiral Viscount of Scapa, *The Crisis of the Naval War*. Cassell, London, 1920.

Jellicoe, Admiral Viscount of Scapa. *The Grand Fleet, 1914-16*. Cassell, London, 1919.

Jones, Maurice. *A History of Coast Artillery in the British Army*. K.W., London 1959.

Kemp, Peter ed. *The Oxford Companion to Ships and the Sea*. Oxford University Press, London, 1976.

Lee, J.J. *Ireland 1912-1985*. Cambridge University Press, Cambridge, 1989.

Liddell-Hart, B.H. *History of the Second World War*. Cassell, London, 1970.

Lord Longford and O'Neill, T.P. *Eamon de Valera*. Hutchinson, London, 1970.

Lyons, F.S.L. *Ireland Since the Famine*. Fontana, London, 1989.

Mansergh, Nicholas. *The Irish Free State: Its Government and Politics*. George Allen & Unwin, London, 1934.

Meally, Victor ed. *Encyclopaedia of Ireland*. Allen Figgis, Dublin, 1968.

Milner, Marc. *The North Atlantic Run: The Royal Canadian Navy and the Battle for the Convoys*. University of Toronto Press, Toronto, 1985.

Monsarrat, Nicholas. *The Cruel Sea*. Penguin Books, London, 1956.

Morton, Brigadier Peter (Retd.). *Emergency Tour – 3 Para in South Armagh*. William Kimber, 1989.

Ready, J. Lee. *Forgotten Allies (The military contribution of the colonies, exiled governments and lesser Powers to the Allied Victory in World War Two)*. MacFarland. North Carolina, 1947.

Roskill, Stephen. *Naval Policy Between the Wars*. 2 vols. Collins, London, 1968 and 1976.

Roskill, Capt. S.W., DSC, RN. *The War at Sea 1939-45*. HMSO, London, 1954.

Shirer, William. *The Rise and Fall of the Third Reich*. Book Club Associates, 1959.

Sharpe, Bernard. *The Emergency (Neutral Ireland, 1939-45)*. Gill & Macmillan, Dublin, 1978.

Terraine, J. *Business in Great Waters, The U-boat Wars, 1916-45*. Octopus, London, 1989.

Tormey, Comdt. Peter and Capt. Byrne. *A View from the Tower (The Irish Air Corps)*. IDF Printing Press, Dublin, 1991.

Younger, Carlton. *Ireland's Civil War*. Frederick Younger, London, 1968.

Young, Brigadier Peter. *The Almanac of WWII*. Bison Books, London, 1981.

Watson, Bruce. *The Changing Face of World Navies – 1945 to the present*. Arms & Armour, London, 1991.

Webb, William. *Coastguard! An offical history of HM Coastguard*. HMSO, London, 1976.

BOOKLETS, PERIODICALS AND OFFICIAL MEMORANDA ETC.

Adams, Thomas. Monograph No. 4 'Irish Naval Service', by World Ship
    Society, 1982.
An Cosantóir. Irish Defence Journal, department of defence, Dublin.
An t-Oglac. Army Headquarters, Dublin.
Brassey's Military Balance, 1993-94. International Institute for Strategic Studies
    (IISS), London.
Connemara, Journal of the Clifden and Connemara heritage group. Vol. 1, No. 1
    August 1993. Article on Commander O'Muiris by Colonel Anthony Morris
    (Retd.)
DDR Handbook. Ministry of Intra-German Affairs, Bonn, 1985.
Department of defence. *Irish Army Handbooks*: 1941, 1968, 1974, 1987.
Fundamental Factors Affecting Saorstat Defence Problem, G2 Branch, Irish Free
    State Army, May 1936 (G2/0057).
Jane's Fighting Ships. Jane's Information Group: 1924, 1935, 1939, 1942, 1946,
    1969, 1977, 1990, 1993.
Kearsley, Harold. "Irish Security and the Sea." An academic paper by Prof.
    Kearsley of the University of Southeastern Louisiana, USA, 1990.
Keesing's Contemporary Archives: 1940, 1945, 1946, 1973, 1976, 1984, 1987.
Memorandum on Naval Policy 1946-61, department of defence, December 1961.
Memorandum on the Naval Problem – Peace, 1964.
Memorandum on Naval Service. department of defence, 1956.
Memorandum on the requirement for seaward defence boats and minesweeping
    craft, 26 July 1956 (Doc: 3/17571/CS.25/19).
Memorandum on manning of the corvettes (CS/25/6) 3/48088.
Memorandum on official visit to Argentina (3/16415). 1 April 1957.
Memorandum on seaward defence training (CS 25/4).
Memorandum on An Slua Muiri (CS/25/79) dated 19 May 1972.
Report on annual inspection of the naval base (Haulbowline). 16 July 1956.
Report on annual inspection of the naval base (Haulbowline), 16 July 1956.
Ships Monthly. (Special section devoted to *Flower* class corvettes by Richard
    Osborne). Waterway Publications, June 1993.
Whitaker's Almanack for 1918, 1937, 1939, 1940, 1969, 1970 and 1977.

GLOSSARY

Corvette
: A flush-decked warship of the 17th-18th centuries with a single tier of guns, smaller than a frigate. The type name was re-adopted during World War II to describe a class of escort vessel of less than 1200 tons.

Hydrography
: The science of marine surveying and of determining the position of points and objects on the surface of the globe, depths of the sea etc.

Naval Dockyard
: An establishment in a strategic position ashore which not only serves as a base for warships but also provides all services they can require, such as repair, refit, replenishment, etc. Most dockyards of any size have building slips for the construction of warships and dry docks for their servicing.

Sloop
: A description used during the two world wars to describe one of the smaller classes of anti-submarine convoy escort vessels.

Sonar
: Formerly known as Asdic, the name is derived from the words SOund, Navigation And Ranging.

Radar
: An abbreviation of RAdio Direction And Range. A method of detecting objects by sending out pulses of radio waves.

Rating
: A term used to describe a seaman in a warship. Men hold rates according to their abilities, the normal chain of lower deck promotion in the Naval Service being ordinary seaman, able seaman, leading seaman, petty officer and chief officer.

INDEX